NONFICTION FILM

RICHARD MERAN BARSAM received his Ph.D. in English from the University of Southern California, where he also studied in the School of Cinema. He has worked on the production units for several documentary films, has supervised student film productions, and taught courses in nonfiction film. Mr. Barsam is an Assistant Professor of English at Richmond College of the City University of New York.

RICHARD DYER MACCANN, professor of film at the University of Iowa, is editor of *Cinema Journal* and author of *Hollywood in Transition* (1962), *Film and Society* (1964), and *Film: A Montage of Theories* (1966). He was Hollywood columnist for *The Christian Science Monitor* from 1951 to 1960 and has taught documentary film and film writing at the University of Southern California, Los Angeles, and the University of Kansas, Lawrence. The National Endowment for the Humanities awarded him a senior fellowship for 1973 to study cinema in Britain.

NONFICTION FILM
A Critical History

by Richard Meran Barsam

Foreword by Richard Dyer MacCann

LONDON   GEORGE ALLEN & UNWIN LTD
Ruskin House   Museum Street

ISBN 0 04 791030 5 hardback
     0 04 791031 3 paperback

This book was originally published in the U.S.A.
and American spelling and usage have been retained.

Printed in the U.S.A.

for
my Mother and my Father

CONTENTS

ILLUSTRATIONS

ACKNOWLEDGMENTS

Fourteen years ago, at the University of Southern California, I first saw *Nanook of the North* and began, although I did not know it then, the study of nonfiction film that reaches a certain stage of completion in this book. Several years later, as an instructor at Glendale College in California, I joined a colleague, Thomas Toohey, in arranging a film program and continued my acquaintance with the major documentaries. In 1968, when I first thought of this study, I re-read Paul Rotha's seminal and still useful *Documentary Film,* but felt that a new study could be written.

In my research I have had generous assistance and advice from many people. However, I am most deeply indebted to Kathleen Endress, who assisted me with her careful research, enthusiastic attention to detail, and genuine interest in the project.

Every film scholar and enthusiast is aware of the Department of Film of The Museum of Modern Art, New York, for this splendid organization puts us in the dark while illuminating it for us with its vast collection of films and printed resource materials. Director Willard Van Dyke treated me with utmost generosity and made helpful suggestions about the scope of my study. Margareta Akermark, Assistant Director, organized screenings and went out of her way to help me. I feel a special gratitude to Charles Silver, of the MOMA Film Study Center, for his many courtesies. Also at MOMA, I wish to thank Barbara Shapiro of the Film Study Center, and the staff of the International Study Center Library, especially Joel

Zuker; Mary Corliss was very helpful in obtaining many of the still photographs reprinted in this book. I must also record my thanks to the staff members of the Donnell, Lincoln Center, and Main Libraries of the New York Public Library, and of the Richmond College Library for their assistance.

In London I was extended every courtesy and cooperation by the British Film Institute, and wish especially to thank Jeremy Boulton for arranging film screenings and Roger Holman for guiding me through the Cataloguing Department. For their help in the BFI Library, I am grateful to Gillian Hartnoll and Betty Leese.

Without the film archives and research facilities of The Museum of Modern Art and the British Film Institute, I would not have been able to begin this study, but without the help of other historians, film makers, and distributors, I would not have been able to complete it. At the outset of my study, Paul Ballard of Los Angeles made many helpful suggestions. I owe a special gratitude to D. A. Pennebaker, Albert and David Maysles, Jonas Mekas of the Anthology Film Archives, New York, and to Contemporary Films, New York. While a student at the University of Southern California, I had the pleasure of listening to Professor Richard Dyer MacCann's lectures on documentary film, and I am indebted to him for his encouragement, his many valuable suggestions, and for his very generous Foreword. I have listened to their wise advice, but hasten to add that the faults here are mine, not theirs. For their comments on the chapter about Robert Flaherty, I thank Mrs. Frances Flaherty and Professor W. Jack Coogan of the School of Theology at Claremont, California. And I am indebted to Mark Berman for his understanding and assistance in the completion of this manuscript.

It is a pleasure to acknowledge the substantial financial support of the Research Foundation of the City University of New York which made possible the many film screenings and the trip to the British Film Institute. Also I wish to acknowledge the assistance I have received from Richmond College of the City University of New York. For their help in locating and supplying the still photographs reprinted here, I thank Gerald Mast, Pare Lorentz, Willard Van Dyke, D. A. Pennebaker, Albert and David Maysles, Frederick Wiseman, and Allan King.

R. M. B.

FOREWORD

In a time of communicative overkill, with multiple commercials at every station break, we are in danger of growing deaf to the persuasions that will help us most.

The documentary film is one such persuasive force. It is an ideal instrument for democratic communication, because it is so often concerned with measuring and valuing a present way of life by what it ought to be. Rational, yet passionate, the documentary is especially suited for cutting through the commotion of noise and vested interests characteristic of the contemporary American scene.

Is it passionate enough? Is its sound too muted, its focus too fairminded, to catch and hold the attention of the public that needs its help?

Two great traditions of documentary have come down to us. Robert Flaherty, explorer and romantic, has given us the gentle observation, the conservative acceptance of human nature, which focuses on a single individual or a ritualized way of life. Even this is a mission of interpretation and understanding, but it does not criticize and does not ask for action. From John Grierson, student of practical politics and the new media, comes the active concern with ideas, the liberal's determination to be an educational instrument, which focuses on social issues and institutions. The mission is both praise and dissatisfaction, always asking for judgment and sometimes for action.

Right-wing and left-wing radicals claim that these traditions are not enough. The conservative impulse, willing to reveal man as he is, the liberal impulse, which insists that man can be educated to be better, are not enough for the extremist who is too pessimistic to act at all or too excited to act in the light of experience. And so it is that, just at the time when population pressure closes in and complexity has come to stay, the cry is to overthrow everything and return to the simple life.

The mission of the documentary film maker is to make complexity understood, to show that complex issues come from conflicting human needs and desires. The documentary producer is always in the middle of some controversy. He has lost his function if he can see only one side; he has lost his passion if he is both-sided all the way to the end. He is conscious of needs for new goals, yet alert to the consequences of change. He is neither naïve nor cynical, but devoted to the practical processes by which society works. In spite of the present excess of communication, which seems to call for stridency and shouting, he knows that his best posture is informative, conscientious, and persistent. His best work is done, as John Grierson said, "not by searchlight but in the quiet light of ordinary humanism." He knows that the documentary film is a crucial medium of self-criticism in a democracy, an expression of faith in man's ability to understand himself and to improve his lot.

The documentary therefore needs its advocates—and its critics—and the textbooks and teachers who can give praise where praise is due. Sponsors and film makers are glad to know that there are people who care whether they have courage, convictions, and a willingness to do the work. The audience, for its part, should know more about the process of communication—how hard it is to reach into the heart of an issue and make it visible. Schoolrooms in the past have struggled with composition, literature, history, society, and science. Surely one challenge of the future is to add the moving image to these concerns, especially when it deals with public affairs.

Those of us who have been teaching about the nonfiction film have long needed a new history that is comprehensive and up to date. Richard Barsam is a teacher and critic of film and literature who has read the earlier books and looked at the films from a contemporary standpoint. His extended descriptions are helpful for those students who cannot see all the films. His thoughtful judgments, more evenhanded than Paul Rotha's, are nevertheless personal, as they must be, and alive with enthusiasm. Together with the anthologies, case studies, and interviews that have recently appeared, we now have a considerable range of valuable commentaries on a vital aspect of the art of the film.

From this book we gain a sense of the historic sweep of events. The record is rich in variety and quality. The student of society finds in the documentary a resource for history, controversy, and insight into the human condition. The student of cinema, too, finds in the documentary a wide range of styles, themes, and techniques. Often his first attempt at film making is in this mode.

Hans Richter, devoted to the magical and experimental potentialities of the screen, has rightly said that documentary is "an original art form" and that "with the documentary approach the film gets back to its fundamentals." Cinema returns periodically to its basic realistic impulse, and the documentary is often the source of such refreshment—a lively contributor to a healthy national film culture, an essential part of effective public communication.

RICHARD DYER MACCANN

INTRODUCTION

In my writing of this critical history of nonfiction film, I have been guided by Lytton Strachey's observation in the preface to *Eminent Victorians* that "ignorance is the first requisite of the historian—ignorance which simplifies and clarifies, which selects and omits, with a placid perfection unattainable by the highest art." With that criterion, and always admitting that I am not a historian, I have simplified and selected with the goal of clarity, and have established the following limitations.

The major emphasis in this book is on nonfiction films produced in Great Britain and the United States. It would have been desirable to include coverage of the many outstanding films produced in languages other than English, but several factors make this difficult. First, many of these films are so closely linked to specific social, economic, and political problems of their respective countries that it would have been impossible, in a study of limited scope, to provide the necessary background for understanding them. Second, the soundtracks would create language problems, not only for translation here, but also, and more important, for readers whose unfamiliarity with the Czechoslovakian, Russian, or Italian languages, for example, would prevent them from seeing these films with maximum enjoyment. Third, foreign nonfiction films are not easily available. American and British film archives catalog only a few of these films, and most distributors neglect them altogether.

For these reasons, I have chosen to discuss only those early European films which had a direct influence on the development of British and American nonfiction film making.

In a similar way, I have omitted discussion of nonfiction films of the United States Information Agency, from the National Film Board of Canada, and from UNESCO, as well as films made for television. These films have been covered in other recent studies; the reader interested in them should consult the Bibliography.

Because most of the films discussed here are "idea" films—films which present solutions to major problems—the thoughtful viewer will understand that there are alternative solutions to the ones they present. For this reason, it is difficult, if not impossible, to view them objectively and one must evaluate the thematic as well as the cinematic aspects of each. It is not the intention of this study to praise or to fault film makers for their ideas, but it is its intention to evaluate those films in the larger social context out of which the problems arose. Because there have been thousands of nonfiction films produced over the past fifty years in response to the world's social problems, it has been necessary here to choose only those that cover the most significant areas. I have neglected many films, but, hopefully, not any important ones.

In discussion and analysis, my concentration has been on what the films say, not on how they say it, because, for the most part, the technique of a nonfiction film is less important than its content. For this reason, I have tried to establish (after Rotha) certain basic traditions in nonfiction film making, and to locate each major film in its tradition (where applicable) and in its time.

The dates quoted are for the year in which the film was released or completed. The reader will find major production credits in Appendix A for each major film discussed.

RICHARD MERAN BARSAM

New York
November 8, 1971

NONFICTION FILM

CHAPTER 1

Defining Nonfiction Film

The most familiar, but most abused and most misunderstood term in the film lexicon, *documentary,* has been applied to everything from newsreels to instructional films to travelogues and television specials. Its meaning has been extended by special film-making movements and special interest groups, by individual directors pursuing a specific goal, and by film historians and critics. Clearly it is time to reexamine the term, to reevaluate those films labeled by it, and to redefine it for purposes of clearer understanding. But, more important, it is necessary to see that *documentary* is a term which signifies only one approach to the making of nonfiction film. All documentaries are nonfiction films, but not all nonfiction films are documentaries.

In 1948, the World Union of Documentary defined documentary film as

> . . . all methods of recording on celluloid any aspect of reality inter-
> preted either by factual shooting or by sincere and justifiable recon-
> struction, so as to appeal either to reason or emotion, for the purpose
> of stimulating the desire for, and the widening of human knowledge
> and understanding, and of truthfully posing problems and their solu-
> tions in the spheres of economics, culture, and human relations.[1]

The word *documentary* was first used to describe Robert Flaherty's *Moana* (1926) by John Grierson, perhaps the single most important theorist and influence on the development of films which deserve that label. Grierson calls documentary film "a creative treatment of actuality,"[2] but he also thinks the word *documentary* is "clumsy."[3] Other film makers and critics have added their own variations to this basic definition. Pare Lorentz, who did much to develop a wholly American approach to nonfiction film making, calls it "a factual film which is dramatic."[4] British film maker Basil Wright insists that "documentary is not this or that type of film, but simply *a method of approach to public information*."[5] In his study of the American documentary film, Richard MacCann leans toward the belief that it is not "authenticity of the materials but the authenticity of the result"[6] that matters in documentary film, while American film maker Willard Van Dyke says that the documentary is

> a film in which *the elements of dramatic conflict represent social or political forces rather than individual ones.* Therefore, it has an epic quality. Also, it cannot be a re-enactment. The social documentary deals with real people and real situations—with reality.[7]

And another American film maker and producer, Philip Dunne, defines documentary this way:

> By its very nature the documentary is experimental and inventive. Contrary to the general impression it may even employ actors. It may deal in fantasy or fact. It may or may not possess a plot. But most documentaries have one thing in common: each springs from a definite need, each is conceived as an idea-weapon to strike a blow for whatever cause the originator has in mind. In the broadest sense, the documentary is almost always, therefore, an instrument of propaganda.[8]

These are but a few of the many attempts to define the documentary film form, for a great deal has been said by film makers, historians, and critics. Recently, Andrew Sarris suggested that *all* films are documentary films in the sense that all films are *documents* of someone, something, some time, some place.[9] Without further contributing to the complexity and confusion, it seems desirable now to adopt a new term—*nonfiction film*—not to replace *documentary film* as a label, but to include it in a larger, more flexible concept, one that recognizes the many different approaches to this exciting form of film making.

To attempt the definition of any art form can often be a hazardous and meaningless task. For in his attempt to be precise in definition, the theorist or critic encounters the clarifying reality of each artist's vision and technique. Definitions are useful, of course, in the establishment of distinctions and categories, and certainly one can make these distinctions as precise as he wishes. However, in the approach to this study, it became increasingly clear that a concept such as "nonfiction film" should be broad enough to include *Nanook of the North* (1922) and *Woodstock* (1970). The former was made on a small budget in the frozen wastes with a crude hand-held camera, while the latter was made with every technical convenience available to the modern film maker, including helicopters and specially built editing equipment. It may be argued that there is a closer relation between these two films than a historical approach would suggest—that they both celebrate life, for instance—but it is apparent that the factors of time, technique, artistic vision, production budget, facilities, and audience are important factors in the defining of the cinematic art form to which they both belong.

The intention of this study will not be to formulate rigid definitions or to classify films with the subsequent precision that such definitions might necessitate. Instead, it will be to identify and, when necessary, to define the broad distinctions within the nonfiction film rubric and to analyze the more representative and significant films to illustrate these distinctions. It is not always possible, for example, to formulate a definition so workable as to include Eisenstein's *Old and New,* Flaherty's *Man of Aran,* Ivens' *The Spanish Earth,* Huston's *Let There Be Light,* Anderson's *Every Day Except Christmas,* and the Maysles brothers' *Salesman;* to try to define such a broad spectrum of film making with some comprehensive and all-inclusive terminology could be self-defeating. Broad lines can be drawn, of course, but even when drawn, they can be crossed without serious penalty.

Nonfiction Film: Some Basic Distinctions

The nonfiction film dramatizes fact instead of fiction. The nonfiction film maker focuses his personal vision and his camera on actual situations—persons, processes, events—and attempts to render a creative interpretation of them. A librarian once remarked to me that the difference between the two sections of the library was simple: the fiction section contains books that are "not true," while the nonfiction section contains the books that are "true." A perplexing distinction, to say the least, when one considers the problems of shelving *War and Peace, Ulysses,* or *Mein Kampf* under such a system. While there are some analogies between nonfiction and fiction books and films designated by the same labels, it is still necessary to distinguish the nonfiction film from its more familiar counterpart.

Generally, the nonfiction film stems from, and is based on, an immediate social situation: sometimes a problem, sometimes a crisis, sometimes an undramatic and seemingly unimportant person or event. It is usually filmed on the actual scene, with the actual people, without sets, costumes, written dialogue, or created sound effects. It tries to recreate the feeling of "being there," with as much fidelity to fact as the situation allows. The typical nonfiction film is structured in two or three parts, with an introduction and conclusion, and tends to follow a pattern from problem to solution. Even more typically, it is in black-and-white, with direct sound recording (or simulated sound), a musical score written expressly for the film and conceived as part of a cinematic whole, and, often as not, a spoken narration. Its typical running time is thirty minutes, but some films run less and some are ninety-minute feature-length films.

The nonfiction film maker can choose from many approaches in making his "creative treatment of actuality," but, from the beginning, two have been most apparent: the documentary approach and the factual approach. The direct cinema approach, a development of the 1960's, will be discussed in the final chapter of this study.

Documentary Film

The documentary is distinguished from the factual film by its sociopolitical purpose. It is the film with a message, and since messages are not necessarily consistent or even compatible with what we generally call art, it then becomes apparent that the documentary film is a very special art form indeed.

Great art is always powerful; in its most intimate way, it can create powerful personal reactions and emotions, while in its most public way, it can create powerful group actions and reactions. It can be an instrument for social influence and change, although it rarely sets out with this intention. However, the documentary film does have this purpose, and the film maker who works in this form wants to use cinema for purposes more important than entertainment or even an effective blend of entertainment and instruction. He wants to persuade, to influence, and to change his audience. His purpose can be an immediate one, such as the justification of his country's invasion of another in time of crisis (*Target for Tonight*) —or a general one, such as the romantic documentation of a primitive people for generations of viewers in the years to come (*Man of Aran*). What becomes apparent, then, is that the content of the film is more important, at first, than the style by which that content is communicated. Here the distinctions between form and content are important ones, and while it is not the intention here to imply that the documentary film maker places politics above aesthetics, it should be emphasized that he has a job to do, a sponsor (usually) to whom he is responsible, and a specific goal to achieve. While these factors do not preclude great art, they do not always encourage it.

Factual Film

The second approach to nonfiction film making is that of the factual film maker. The difference between documentary and factual film is a basic one, but it is important and should not be overlooked. Essentially, the factual film lacks a specific message; however, if it happens to have one—and many factual films do—it does not necessarily take precedence over the other aspects of the film. Once again, the problem of formulating a definition for an artistic form occurs, but perhaps an analogy to another means of expression will help to clarify the matter. Nonfiction films share many characteristics of journalism, and the difference between documentary and factual film is roughly the difference between the editorial and the news pages of the daily newspaper. The editorial page is labeled as such, and the reader generally knows that he is reading opinions based, hopefully, on facts. The news pages, though, are a different thing. Sometimes they contain the homogenized press releases of the wire services, and at other times they contain the signed releases of reporters on the spot. No matter how "objective" they try to be, the reporters often filter the facts through the subjectivity of their own responses. Nonetheless, they are factual.

It should be apparent at this point, then, that to distinguish too precisely between the documentary and the factual approach would be to formulate inflexible concepts which would tend to defeat any fluent analysis. If we can remember that documentary films are concerned with facts *and* opinion, and that factual films are generally concerned with only the facts, then the problem is, if not solved, at least settled for the purposes of this study.

One final distinction should be made, and that is the difference between the fictional (theatrical) film and the nonfictional (nontheatrical) film. Theatrical films, or "story" films, as they are often called, are those generally made by independent producers or major studios for showing in public theaters; they feature actors or stars, real locations or constructed sets, and seek to make a profit. They are, of course, the major source of film entertainment, and one of the most important art forms of the twentieth century. *Theatrical* generally implies *commercial,* and the main purpose of most of these films is to make money, to turn a profit for the studio, at least until the producer or the studio can afford the losses frequently incurred by a film made by an unknown director. Because of the material, the costs, the political problems, and the distribution difficulties, the great nonfiction film makers of the past—Flaherty, Lorentz, Ivens, to name a few—made only a handful of films, in comparison to the great directors of fiction films. That pattern began to change in the 1960's as audiences and distributors developed a new interest in the nonfiction film, but it is too early to tell whether there will be prolific directors of nonfiction films to compare, in quality and quantity of output, with Renoir, Hitchcock, Ford, Bergman, Truffaut, and others.

Nonfiction films are not generally intended to be commercial, and are not distributed by commercial producers or shown in public theaters unless they are unusually broad in their appeal, or, as in the most recent cases, unless they appeal to a sufficiently large and specialized group, such as teen-agers, rock music enthusiasts, or those interested in wild animal conservation. "Nontheatrical" often means simply those films that are shown without admission charge in schools, colleges, churches, unions, industrial, social, and cultural organizations. While there are, of course, many exceptions, they are exceptions rather than the rule. Many great directors began their careers with nonfiction films, and many nonfiction films have been shown in large commercial theaters and have turned a profit, but the distinctions listed above will serve as a useful means by which to separate the two most obvious forms of film making: the theatrical and the nontheatrical. When there are films which successfully straddle the two fields—Sidney Meyers' *The Quiet One* (1949) for example—then one is only reminded of the infinite possibilities of the film art.

Nonfiction film was pioneered and developed by the Americans, the Russians, and the British, in that order. The important founders are the film makers Robert Flaherty and Sergei Eisenstein, the producer John Grierson, and the critic-historian Paul Rotha. The Russians and their approach will be discussed in Chapter Two, and Robert Flaherty's work and influence in Chapter Six. At this point, a brief acquaintance with John Grierson and Paul Rotha, the two most prolific theorists of the nonfiction film, is desirable, although it is necessary to remember that both are British and both tend to favor the "documentary" approach to nonfiction film making.

John Grierson

John Grierson was truly the father of the documentary film. He was the first to apply the term *documentary*—when reviewing Flaherty's *Moana* in 1926—and he was the head of the first documentary film production unit, the Empire Marketing Board Film Unit, sponsored by the British government, and established in

1928.[10] Grierson provided a sound, if not always systematic and consistent, philosophical foundation for the development of documentary film. From the beginning, he sought to develop a sense of community, and always placed his patriotism and his commitment to national goals over and above any personal achievement he might have made with his films. The British documentary movement began not so much in affection for film as art as in affection for national education. Its origins lay in sociological rather than in aesthetic aims.

Grierson was convinced that the documentary approach was basically propagandist rather than aesthetic, and, for him, the film medium happened to be the most convenient and the most dramatic means to implement his ideas of community and world peace. Grierson was deeply affected by the two world wars, although his major theories were formulated before World War II. To make films with a social message was all-important in the context of the world as he knew it. While other artists might have responded to war by analyzing the responses of others, Grierson was determined to prove that the world could be made a better place in which to live through mass education and communication. For him, art and aesthetics were only a means to an end: national education.

Grierson's principles of documentary are fundamental: he believed, first, that documentary was a new and vital art form which observed, selected, and opened up the real world; second, that the documentary film maker had a more imaginative degree of interpretation over his material than the maker of story films; and, third, that the materials and stories taken "from the raw" could be more real than the acted article. This so-called "minor manifesto of beliefs" is not without confusion and contradiction, but it does help to strengthen his essential convictions that documentary film should be a creative treatment of everyday actuality and that the film maker should be committed to crystallizing civic sentiments and to furthering national goals.

His position is not sufficiently consistent and systematic to be called a philosophy, but at its core is the simple belief that "somehow we had to make peace exciting, if we were to prevent wars. Simple notion that it is—that has been my propaganda ever since— to make peace exciting."[11]

John Grierson's writings and films are dedicated to the immediate patriotic goals of his country as well as to the transcendent goal of world peace. While his films are actually more concerned with day-to-day English activities than these lofty goals might suggest, his influence, especially during the 1930's, was extraordinary. Without Grierson, the documentary film might never have been born.[12]

Paul Rotha

Paul Rotha, an Englishman, has both produced and directed many documentary films and written a study of the genre. He is an energetic and crusading spokesman for the production, study, and appreciation of what are essentially documentary films. In the foreword to the first edition of his *Documentary Film* (1935), he speaks of a film with a message for the community of today as well as tomorrow.[13] His concept of the documentary film is often idealistic, but his argument reveals a sound and fundamental belief in the form. He suggests that documentary film makers take greater care in the production of their films, that they are more skillful craftsmen, and that there is "more profound reasoning" behind their choice of theme and approach than that of the theatrical film maker. One must remember that he was writing in the 1930's with a very clear purpose: to convince his countrymen of the value of documentary films and to ask that they continue to support the government's film making unit, of which he was a major member. This should not detract, however, from the integrity of his theories and from his dedication to the art and science of documentary film.

Rotha's emphasis has always been a humanistic one. He favors films which illuminate the past, explain the present, and enrich the future. He is concerned with issues that transcend time and place, and he is also concerned with finding immediate examples in the contemporary world that exemplify these issues. He asks that the documentary film maker be both a sociologist and a cameraman, and, when possible, a poet, too. Rotha is able to make important films as well as to avoid becoming what he has called a "henchman or mercenary" in his relations with his sponsors and critics. It is a difficult achievement to produce films of specific political comment while maintaining one's personal integrity, but that achievement is fundamental to the idea and purpose of documentary film, and it is not a small achievement, on Rotha's part, that he established an example for film makers on both sides of the Atlantic in questions of artistic control *versus* government policy. His contemporaries— Lorentz, Van Dyke, Flaherty, and others—all experienced the pressures which ask artists to bend their vision to the requirements of government propaganda.

Rotha stresses that the documentary film artist is a man of goodwill, a man who, in Grierson's words, can "make peace exciting." Indeed, he sees the role of the film maker much in the same way as Flaherty saw it long before and long after Rotha's influence was greatest—the role of the artist as educator, illuminator, and, finally, of conciliator. Like Shelley, Rotha would have his film makers be "legislators of mankind," but he would also have them be acknowledged, respected, and supported, and it is to this end that his writing and his films carry with them the unmistakable stamp of a man of faith and vision, and of a man whose art, however "political," was ultimately nonpolitical in its attempts to unite mankind. If the social consciousness of the 1930's characterizes Rotha's vision of art and society, it is founded on a belief that is, perhaps, naïve—that art and science can work together to solve the problems of this world. But we have been to the moon and back since then, and many of the same world problems exist still and with increasingly more deadly consequences. If Rotha's vision of the film maker as a true artist is a little tarnished today, that is not his fault, but ours. Grierson and Rotha assure us that nonfiction film, like its fictional counterpart, is an art, and that it can serve, as any art, to illuminate the human condition.

Types of Nonfiction Film

Nonfiction film includes documentary itself; factual films; travel films; educational, training, or classroom films; newsreels, and animated or cartoon films. We have seen above that documentary is as specifically different from factual film as form and technique can make it. Because the concern of this study is the major documentary and factual approaches to nonfiction film making, we shall examine only briefly those minor forms of nonfiction film with which they are generally grouped.

Travel Films

Travel films, or travelogues, as they are more commonly called, are one of the oldest and most popular forms of nonfiction film. People are inveterate armchair travelers, and will seemingly endure the most banal images and the most unctuous narration in return for a few hours on the beaches of Hawaii or in the villages of Ireland. These travel films, the staple of small-town film clubs everywhere, are usually little more than films by amateur travelers with professional camera equipment.

From the earliest date in the history of film, travel films have been popular. In fact, the first important nonfiction films—such as Flaherty's *Nanook of the North* (1922) and *Moana* (1926), Cooper's *Grass* (1925) and *Chang* (1927), and even Ponting's later *Ninety Degrees South* (1933) —were travel films in that they derived much of their essential appeal and interest from their presentation of distinctly different ways of life. These films, and others, demonstrated the power of the camera to bring people together through a visual awareness of one another. Early travel films were so faithful in their visual depiction of other places and people that the French called them *documentaires*. But the meaning of the French term is different from the English term *documentary;* early travel films did create documents, or, to be more precise, factual visual records, but they did not function within the overall scope of documentary film as we have defined it.

Looking at the history of travel films, one sees that their chief purpose is to promote tourist trade and to increase the profits of the airline, railroad, or government tourist board which sponsors them. Sometimes the films are sponsored by industrial or other commercial agencies or businesses, and sometimes they are independently produced, yet they still exist to encourage travel. With tourism as their goal, they make little effort to approach their subject from a creative or dramatic point of view; indeed, they often focus on the most ordinary customs in an attempt to record the life-style of a particular people. Smiling faces, tranquil villages, sunny beaches, towering mountains, rushing waterfalls—every cliché in the travel agent's book is paraded in front of the static cameras in the hope that Mr. and Mrs. Armchair Traveler will feel secure enough to leave the comforts of their own home for a few weeks in a "strange land," a "land of contrasts," but with not so many contrasts—or so say the films—that they will be uncomfortable. To review the history of the travel film is to understand the mediocrity of the mind which would have all people look, act, and behave alike, the mind which would reduce all the beauties and mysteries of differing cultures to one boring film.

Travel films have been successful on many levels, in local travel film society groups, and in commercial theaters. For many years, the travelogue was a standard at the local theater, just after the cartoon and just before the feature. Its format was predictable, its music was, at best, a pastiche of native melodies and familiar stereotypes, and its overall approach—"as our ship leaves this sleepy little island"—tried to convince the viewer that people are pretty much the same the world over. This conclusion may be inescapable, from the standpoint of human nature and behavioral psychology, but it is a disservice to film art when that art could exist both to instruct and to entertain an audience with regard to the distinguishing characteristics of another life-style or culture.

There have been some excellent travel films, of course, but they are few among the many which try to sell everything from the joys of surfing in New Zealand to those of skiing in the Alps. One must not ask too much of these films, though, for they do not pretend to do more than sell. They do demonstrate, on the other hand, the compelling appeal of film; when that colorful, flickering image shows pretty girls on a sunny beach to an audience in a distant town on a cold winter's night, then the strength of film as a commercial tool simply cannot be denied. But since, with few exceptions, travel films have been commercials for promoting tourism, it is enough here to indicate their relatively small position within the development of nonfiction film as we are discussing it here.

Educational, Training, or Classroom Films

The power of the nonfiction film to attract an audience, to engage its attention, and to influence its behavior is demonstrated with equal success in that large and generally undistinguished body of films that teach and train people. These training films are used everywhere, from kindergarten classrooms to battlefield information centers, and within their modest expectations, they are generally successful. Children can be introduced to safety procedures, teenagers to sex education, soldiers to the prevention of intelligence leaks, and farmers to the advantages of crop rotation. These training or information films are used extensively by such agencies as UNESCO in their efforts to inform and educate backward peoples to the benefits of such things as pest control and proper irrigation. They can be used to train salesmen how to sell more, to teach housewives how to spend less, to show Sunday golfers how to drive the ball farther, and to instruct industrial workers in plant safety. In short, they can be used to teach almost anything to almost anyone, and their quality and success are limited only by the seriousness of the effort and the thoroughness of the approach used in making them.

There is, of course, another large use to which these films are put, and that is specific educational films, those directly related to the curriculum of classes in all levels of school from elementary through college. These films are usually well researched and carefully presented, and often they are produced by such organizations as the film-making unit of the *Encyclopaedia Britannica;* when they are, they carry with them the accuracy and the authenticity of these groups. They are offered free to schools, or rented or sold to them, by such organizations as IBM or Shell Oil to introduce such important topics as computer communication and conservation. Frequently, these films are expensively produced, in color, with animation and lively sound tracks. No student resents the replacement of his teacher with a good film, but nobody will complain louder than a student when so-called educational films lack the immediacy and enthusiasm he expects from a good teacher. In that distinction, of course, is the problem and the solution. Educational films for use in the classroom must be good teachers as well as good films.

Newsreels

A once-flourishing but now-vanishing species of nonfiction film is the biweekly or weekly newsreel. These newspapers of the screen were sometimes shown in special newsreel theaters in larger cities, or, more generally, on the same bill as a cartoon, a travel film, and one or two major feature films. Some of them, such as the "March of Time" series, reflected a particular editorial bias, while others—such as those of Paramount or Pathé—presented fairly objective reportage.

Except for rare instances, though, the newsreel is quickly becoming extinct. As with other nonfiction films, the newsreel relied on actual events for its raw material, and usually the more spectacular these events were, the better chance they had for inclusion. Newsreels presented this material in simple, descriptive terms, and within a mimimum amount of time. Usually, they were without bias or viewpoint although they often took a humorous view of such topics as fashion. Frequently, there was a naïve and almost innocent approach to such items as transatlantic ship races or track meets, and, to be sure, the newsreel was part of the vanishing enthusiasm for day-to-day events that characterized America in the earlier decades of this century. The theatrical newsreel has been all-but-replaced by the broadcasting of news reports and editorial documentaries on television.

NOTES

1 Paul Rotha, *Documentary Film* (New York, Hastings House, 1952), pp. 30–31. A very useful collection of essays, reviews, and articles has been gathered in *The Documentary Tradition: From Nanook to Woodstock,* ed. Lewis Jacobs (New York, Hopkinson and Blake, 1971).

2 John Grierson, *Grierson on Documentary*, ed. Forsyth Hardy (London, Faber and Faber, Ltd., 1966) , p. 13.

3 Grierson, p. 145.

4 Robert L. Snyder, *Pare Lorentz and the Documentary Film* (Norman, Oklahoma, Oklahoma University Press, 1968) , p. 3.

5 Basil Wright, "Documentary To-Day," *Penguin Film Review*, No. 2 (Jan. 1947) , p. 38.

6 Richard Dyer MacCann, "Documentary Film and Democratic Government: An Administrative History from Pare Lorentz to John Huston" (unpublished Ph.D. dissertation, Harvard University, 1951) , p. 8.

7 Harrison Engle, "Thirty Years of Social Inquiry: An Interview with Willard Van Dyke," *Film Comment*, 3, No. 2 (Spring 1965) , 26.

8 Philip Dunne, "The Documentary and Hollywood," *Hollywood Quarterly*, 1, No. 2 (Jan. 1946) , 167.

9 In a comment to me, 1971.

10 John Grierson, "Review of *Moana*," *New York Sun*, Feb. 8, 1926.

11 Grierson, *Grierson on Documentary*, p. 25.

12 See Chapters Three and Four for a full discussion of Grierson's work and influence.

13 Rotha, pp. 25–28; the prefaces to the first and second editions are printed in this third edition. My subsequent analysis of the historical evolution of the nonfiction film is partially based on the stylistic distinctions drawn by Rotha in Part II of his study, although I disagree with Rotha on the importance of what he calls the "news-reel tradition" and further feel that his concept of the "naturalist romantic tradition" should be seen in a predominantly American context.

CHAPTER 2

The American, Russian, and Continental Beginnings

In comparison with the other arts, the movies are, of course, a young mode of expression, although they are undoubtedly the most popular art form of the twentieth century. During the relatively short history of film, extraordinary advances and achievements have marked all of its aspects. From the early experiments of such men as Edison and the Lumière brothers, to the experiments of today (when Orson Welles says that "everybody under 30—and his idiot brother—wants to be a film director"),[1] people have been fascinated with the ability of the motion picture to capture both the real world and the world of their imagination. The history of film making is traceable through many factors, not the least of which is the series of technical developments in still and motion picture photography through the late nineteenth and early twentieth centuries.[2]

Movies have come a long way from the early days, when cameras were as big as pianos and film emulsions captured only the most basic images, to the present-day lightweight portability of most equipment and the fastest emulsions and processing techniques. Today, kids experiment with super 8mm cameras in their back-yards. College students major in film courses on a countrywide basis, where only a few years ago serious film study was limited to a few campuses, and, even then, was further limited by a dying indus-try in which few students could expect employment and by equipment which was still not sufficiently advanced to afford the portability so necessary to the amateur film maker. Now the independent film industry is growing in rather unpredictable ways, and some of its products which reach the screens bear about as much resemblance to the early Hollywood features as the Edison Kinetoscope bears to today's portable 16mm camera with sound-on-film recording equipment small enough to carry on the camera operator's back.

The history of the movies is changing with every frame of every film that comes out of the processing laboratories, but several factors seem indicative of the direction of that development. First, movies are quite obviously here to stay. Second, technical developments are making it possible for almost anyone to try film making, although such ease of production is hardly compatible with quality. As everyone thinks of himself as a young genius, audiences will suffer some of the same pains that the early audiences must have experienced watching the first efforts of the first film makers, although this pain will be caused more by their relative sophistication than by their inexperience with the medium. Third, film is being studied as an art, and students are not only interested in production, but are also taking courses in film appreciation and film history to understand the place of this art in the cultural development of the twentieth century.[3]

The beginnings of the nonfiction film span the decade of the 1920's. While the earliest fiction films—such as George Méliès' *A Trip to the Moon* (1902), Edwin S. Porter's *The Great Train Robbery* (1903), and D. W. Griffith's *The Birth of a Nation* (1915) —were made in the first twenty years of the twentieth century, the first important nonfiction films were made a few years later: Robert Flaherty's *Nanook of the North* (U.S., 1922), Sergei Eisenstein's *Ten Days That Shook the World* (Russia, 1928), Dziga Vertov's Kino Eye experiments (Russia, c. 1923), Alberto Cavalcanti's *Rien que les Heures* (France, 1926), Walther Ruttmann's *Berlin: The Symphony of a Great City* (Germany, 1927), and John Grierson's *Drifters* (England, 1929). These films represent the major nonfiction film achievements in the 1920's, and form the foundations for the three major traditions in which the nonfiction film was to develop:

the American romantic tradition; the Russian (and English) propagandist tradition; and the continental realist tradition. Each of these traditions began with an approach that found its full development in the 1930's and 1940's, and, to some extent, each continues to develop, although not necessarily with the national distinctions which categorize its beginnings.

The American Romantic Tradition

The American romantic tradition forms one of the earliest and strongest strains in nonfiction film making, and also one of the most popular. It is romantic in its essential idealization of nature, and in its dominant preoccupation with man's proper relationship to the world around him. Many of the films are concerned with conservation and show an early awareness of the need for ecological balance in a world which grows more industrialized and urbanized with each passing year. These films use natural scenery and surroundings for their own sake, and generally allow the narrative to emerge from the situation rather than impose a story upon the material.[4]

Except for the early work of D. W. Griffith (the snow scenes in *Way Down East*, 1920, for example), little had been done with the realistic use of scenery in early American films. American ingenuity has always found artificial sets more practical, especially in major Hollywood productions where all the elements—including those usually controlled by supernatural forces—could be monitored and altered when necessary. Before it became commonplace for the American western film to glorify the sweep and stretch of the frontier plains, the Swedes began to make imaginative use of the exterior in fiction films; later, the nonfiction films of Arne Sucksdorff continued that Swedish interest in some of the loveliest nature footage ever photographed in any country. The first American films to establish the epic grandeur of the American environment were *The Covered Wagon* (1923) and *The Iron Horse* (1924). Admittedly, these films are in the fiction class, but they represent an early recognition of the possibilities of nature photography, as well as a commercial recognition of the public's desire to see its own country.

To a larger extent, these first westerns established what is probably the most durable story line in American film history, and, in so doing, not only recreated a substantial aspect of the American dream, but also a continuing series of profit-making films.

This should not suggest, though, that the American romantic approach limited itself to an investigation and a glorification of only the American west, for the American nonfiction film movement has been extremely active in capturing all phases of nature, both in America and around the world. Early travel and exploration films include H. A. Snow's *Hunting Big Game in Africa* (1923), Henry McRae's *Wild Beauty* (1927), and Rear-Admiral Byrd's *With Byrd at the South Pole* (1930). An early silent by Charles Sheeler and Paul Strand, *Manhatta* (1921), is not exactly a travel film, for it juxtaposes impressionistic shots of New York City with lines from Walt Whitman's poetry; nonetheless, it is a forerunner of the "city symphony" film so popular in Europe in the 1930's. The first important American travel films brought back from expeditions are Merian C. Cooper's *Grass* and *Chang*.

Grass (1925) is a strangely incoherent, but fascinating film about the "forgotten people" of Asia Minor who make epic trips across desert and mountains to find grassy pastures for their livestock. This lengthy silent film records their battle with nature, but there is no focus (as in *Nanook of the North*) on an individual, and the viewer is never clearly told why they endure unmapped trails, treacherous rapids, glacier passes, and frozen, bleeding feet. Awkward title cards ("B-r-r-r. The water's cold!") do little to enhance the action of the film, or to explain the meaning of the journey. Cooper's second film, *Chang* (1927), is an altogether different achievement. The subject of *Chang* is Siam, and Cooper avoids accentuating the exotic aspects of this then-unfamiliar country; instead, he shows the interesting and the unusual spirit of the jungle in such a way that the tedious, Kiplingesque captions are totally unnecessary.

Today Cooper's experiments are of historical interest only, and we recognize that the true father of the romantic tradition in American nonfiction film is Robert Flaherty. His interests took him from the Arctic Ocean to the South Seas, from the coast of Ireland to the swamps of Louisiana, from the cliff dwellings of New Mexico to a final around-the-world project for the producers of Cinerama. Flaherty insisted that his films be shot on location and that the story evolve from the day-to-day activity that he filmed; he never worked with a prepared script, but instead shaped his films as shooting proceeded and, finally, in the cutting room. He was most concerned with the fundamental natural activity of man in his relationship with nature, and his greatest films (*Nanook* and *Man of Aran*) are classics in showing the struggle of man to prevail over the most hostile elements of his environment.

The romantic tradition is strong in nonfiction film, although it has been broadened to include many visions of natural life other than Flaherty's essentially idyllic and affirmative approach. The films of Arne Sucksdorff, Thor Heyerdahl, the Walt Disney studios, and Jacques-Yves Cousteau continue to record human and animal life, as well as man's ability to appreciate, to live with, and, when necessary, to conquer nature. Many of these films not only affirm man's strength of spirit, but also teach valuable lessons in conservation of vital resources. And while the focus has widened considerably since *Nanook* first appeared on the screen fifty years ago, film makers continue to be fascinated with the beauties, dangers, and wonders of the natural world in such films as *Kon-Tiki* (1951), *The Sea Around Us* (1953), *Silent World* (1956), *Blue Water, White Death* (1971), and *African Elephant* (1971).

The Russian Propagandist Tradition

The American romantic tradition in nonfiction film making grew slowly in response to commercial factors, but the Russian propagandist tradition—whose ideology is quite different from that underlying either European or American films—found its principal reason for existence in politics, and its principal product in propaganda. The Soviet film industry was born in and developed by the social and political events that took place after the 1917 Revolution; the Marxist-Leninist society demanded that the aesthetics of film reflect the values of the new society. For Sergei Eisenstein,

Soviet film making began primarily to educate the new masses, to give them both a general and a political education; film was just "one of many instruments used on the battlefronts of the class struggle for socialist construction,"[5] but it has come to be one of the most highly regarded achievements in the Russian culture of the 1920's and 1930's. Like the American film, however, the early Russian nonfiction film stressed the greatness of its vast country and showed the beauty of its land and the strength of its people. Setting political considerations aside for a moment, one sees that film makers in both countries were interested in documenting the immediate world around them, in introducing the people of the country to each other, and in stimulating an awareness and a consciousness—through visual means—of culture and personality.

The beginnings of the Russian propagandist tradition in nonfiction film making can be seen most clearly in the work of three directors: Sergei Eisenstein, Dziga Vertov, and Alexander Dovzhenko. Of course, other names are of importance here: Grigori Alexandrov, V. I. Pudovkin, Lev Kuleshov, Victor Turin, and Yakov Blyokh.[6] The achievements made by these men and others in film, the art which Lenin called "the most important for us," are important to all aspects of cinematic development, from scenario to editing and photography, but often their work avoids the neat categorization implied by such terms as *fiction* and *nonfiction*.

The formal attributes of Soviet "expressive realism" are represented in the distinctive theories and the finished films of such diverse men as Eisenstein and Vertov. But, for the most part, these early Russian films are most notably characterized by their dynamic editing, or montage, and by their strong visual sense. The rhythm and excitement of an Eisenstein montage, for example, is almost indescribable in words, while the strength of a Dovzhenko close-up, framed against the sky, carries yet another kind of power that is reserved only for the visual arts. And for a different reason, one never forgets a Vertov film. Often characters are represented not so much as individuals as they are as representatives of the group; thus the epic style of Eisenstein and the collective hero. On the other hand, with Pudovkin, for example, the character is more individual, and the development and revelation of character are specific, not general. His characters are always social beings, of course, but they are, first of all, human beings. Russian films of this early period are distinguished by a kind of impressionistic photography emphasizing low-key lighting and the use of a soft-focus lens to create slightly blurred and shimmering images. Finally, since the film was used to foster and encourage a collective spirit, there is great emphasis on epic composition in these films; the group effort is the good effort.[7] While man is often photographed against the sky, he is rarely, with the notable exception of Dovzhenko's films, seen as an isolated figure. That the films of this period can be characterized as having such distinctive and unified traits is, of course, a direct product of the nationalization of the film industry in 1919 and the determination of the government to link this vital new art with politics. The inferior physical facilities of the studios and the lack of sufficient raw film stock may have been an obstacle, but a minor one, considering the output.

Sergei Eisenstein

The most important of all Russian film makers is Sergei Eisenstein; his influence extends beyond his films through his prolific theories regarding all aspects of the film art from artistic vision to the ratio between playing time on the screen and elapsed time in real life. If he had done nothing else, the Odessa Steps sequence in *Potemkin* (1925) would be enough to ensure his immortality among film makers, for it is a handbook of the basic principles of editing and montage.[8] Eisenstein sought to bring the highest aesthetic considerations to his films of social realism, though their theatricality often gains more attention than the underlying principles on which his effects are based. Trained as an engineer and a theater director, Eisenstein's early experience proved invaluable to the creation of his own cinematic style, and can be seen both in his sense of cinematic time and the dramatic moment. In a climate of artistic experimentation, Eisenstein produced his first film, *Strike* (1924), and though he conceded that it exhibited elements of "rank theatricality," he also saw it, more importantly, as his revolt against the theater. He said,

I did away with a very vital element of theater—the subject-story. At that time this seemed natural. We brought collective and mass action onto the screen, in contrast to individualism and the "triangle" drama of the bourgeois cinema. Discarding the individualist conception of the bourgeois hero, our films of this period made an abrupt deviation— insisting on an understanding of the masses as hero. No screen had ever before reflected an image of collective action.[9]

Eisenstein's second important film, and one of the masterworks of world cinema, is his collaboration with Grigori Alexandrov, *Ten Days That Shook the World* (1928, also titled *October*). It was commissioned to depict, to commemorate, and to celebrate the tenth anniversary of the 1917 Bolshevik Revolution. Like *Potemkin*, it is, of course, a reenactment of history, not a factual film. *Ten Days* is remarkably powerful, re-creating the dramatic nature of one of the most crucial incidents in modern history. Although the film was criticized as representing a viewpoint that was too personal,[10] the technical virtuosity of the film's reenactment gives it the air of objectivity. Because his theories and his films were often in disagreement with the prevailing official notions of what Russian films should be, Eisenstein's career was not as fruitful as it might have been. Nonetheless, he directed four more major films: *Old and New* [*The General Line*] (1929), *Alexander Nevsky* (1938), *Ivan the Terrible* (1944), and the unfinished *Que Viva Mexico* (c. 1930).

Eisenstein's films have a documentary and historical foundation, even though they are historical reenactments. Closer to the spirit of the documentary nonfiction film, as it was developing in America, England, and on the continent was the work of Dziga Vertov.

Dziga Vertov

During and after the 1917 Revolution, Russian film makers were very much involved in documenting the fighting, the wars, and the governmental changes. In Moscow, Vertov, a young poet and film editor, was charged with shaping and editing a mass of film into a finished product; his achievement was the three-hour *The Anniversary of the October Revolution* (1918). While this is a monument of revolutionary film making, and Russia's first feature-length film as well, it suffers by comparison to Eisenstein's *Ten Days*, a film which proves, among other things, that art can be better than reality. Almost ten years later, another Russian film maker, Esther Shub, made some notable compilations of newsreel footage: *Fall of the Romanov Dynasty* and *The Russia of Nicolai II and Lev Tolstoy.*

Vertov's fame is not as an editor, but as a theorist and developer of the approach to film making that is similar in many ways to today's *cinéma vérité,* or direct cinema. Vertov called his theory Kino Eye, and began working on it alone from 1918 to 1922; between 1923 and 1925, he worked with others, making films and issuing manifestos about the politics of perception. Externally, the Kino Eye method has much in common with the newsreel, but it is a purer form of factual film, for its aesthetic intent is to separate and to preserve the more permanent aspects of everyday life from the transient stuff that makes up newsreels. Arguing against theater and fiction film, Vertov wrote, "Kinodrama is an opium for the people. Kinodrama and religion are deadly weapons in the hands of the capitalists. The scenario is a tale thought up for us by literary people. . . . Down with the bourgeois tale scenario! Hurrah for life as it is!"[11] Vertov's films celebrate the function of the eye as much as they celebrate life, and his masterpiece, *The Man with the Movie Camera* (1929), is a lively demonstration of the flexibility of the camera eye. The camera has the power and flexibility of the human eye; it is not fixed, and may roam in and out, up and down, around and about, substituting actuality for the rehearsed necessities of the so-called fiction film. The Kino Eye approach uses all the grammar of cinema, including slow motion, rapid motion, reversed movement, still photography, divided screen, microscopic images, and all forms of montage. Of Vertov's approach, Leyda writes,

> While most films produced at that time approached revolutionary subject matter of the past with attitudes strongly influenced by the cheapest theatrical and adventure-film traditions, both in selection and method, Vertov's films dared to treat the present and, through the present, the future with an approach as revolutionary as the material he treated.[12]

In short, the Kino Eye was a lively cinema which called the viewer's attention not only to the camera and the cameraman, but also to his own eye and to his own sense of visual perception. Following the Kino Eye success, Vertov was commissioned to make two films: *Stride, Soviet* (1926) and *A Sixth of the World* (1926). Commenting on these films, Leyda writes,

> *Stride, Soviet* employed a simple structure of parallelism: this is the way things are now, this is how they were then, or this is the way things are with us, and this is how they are in capitalist countries. *A Sixth* was the first Vertov film to be generally well received by the Russian press. Its publicity purpose was lost sight of in the grandest and most complicated system of travelling cameramen that Vertov yet had at his disposal.[13]

Alexander Dovzhenko

Alexander Dovzhenko represents yet a third Russian approach to film making, and stands between Eisenstein and Vertov, not so concerned with the mass epic as the first, and not so fascinated with the camera as the second. Dovzhenko is the poet of the three, and his films are, perhaps, best remembered for their remarkable, but often isolated images. While his films do not easily fit the nonfiction traditions established by his contemporaries, his symbolic vision transcends the immediacy of the politics which characterizes the others' work. His most important achievement is *Earth* (1930), a slowly paced but rhythmical and dramatic film about the Russian soil. Specifically, the subject matter is the Soviet collectivization of farms, but generally, and more successfully, the film's overall concern is nature. While the film advocates conservation, though not in the direct manner of films such as Lorentz' *The Plow That Broke the Plains* and Flaherty's *The Land,* it also reflects an intense feeling for the cycle of life and death. Here, as in the work of Flaherty, the lives of people cannot be separated from the nature around them. The film's poignant acceptance and understanding of death were misunderstood when the film was released, and it was attacked in *Izvestia* as "defeatist."[14] Since, however, it has become one of the few acknowledged classics of Russian film making, and like many artistic statements founded on politics, survives, fortunately, not as politics, but as art.

Dovzhenko's vision is a symbolic one, in the sense that the

subject matter of his films—the arsenal in *Arsenal* (1929) and the dam in *Ivan* (1932) —is always a central symbol meant to represent something in the evolution of Soviet economy and culture. But it is in his elaboration and expansion of these central symbols that Dovzhenko's art takes its shape and achieves its distinction. As his films slowly expand, the symbols begin to take on new shades of meaning and to provide new insights for understanding. As a true symbolist, Dovzhenko sees each thing with such an intensity that its poetic suggestiveness is both captured and released. In his quest to observe and to document contemporary Russia, Dovzhenko succeeded in serving both propaganda and art, and while he and others were criticized for their intellectual approach, he is remembered now for the poetic and stimulating value of that approach.

The Russian propagandist film forms a unique chapter in the beginning pages of Soviet film history. For the purposes of this study, its major importance is its influence on the origin and development of the British documentary movement in the early 1930's. Films such as *Potemkin, Ten Days That Shook the World, Old and New, Man with the Movie Camera,* and *Earth* had a profound influence on the development of film as a specific instrument of political propaganda. But even more important as a direct influence on the British documentary method was Victor Turin's *Turksib* (1928), a film which both pictured the building of the Turkestan-Siberian railway and argued for its acceptance as an economic necessity. *Turksib* was important to the British, not only because Grierson's editing of the English version helped to articulate its sociopolitical theme, but because precise statement of theme is one of the hallmarks of 1930's British documentaries. It might be argued that the British concept of the documentary film could have developed without the Russian influence, but it cannot be denied that the Russians showed the rest of the world that political ideology and film aesthetics could be compatibly fused. Their memorable films demonstrate that the spontaneity and flexibility of the film art was the best possible means to capture the dynamic, changing political and social reality of the twentieth century. In long-range influence on the development of nonfiction film, their imaginative, didactic films have proved to be more significant than the approaches of the American romantics or the continental realists. Their pioneering in the area of the political film gave birth to the extensive experimentation and development of the nonfiction documentary film in England and in America during the 1930's, and the film masterpieces of World War II owe much to the examples set by the Russians in the late 1920's.

The Continental Realist Tradition

During the 1920's, the cultural avant-garde in Europe experimented with film as they were experimenting with, and revolutionizing, the directions that poetry, prose fiction, and painting would take. In the major cities, Berlin and Paris especially, young artists developed startling theories of aesthetics based on the flexibility of the camera eye, and they investigated the dramatic possibilities to be obtained from cinematic manipulation of time. These experiments were similar to those in fiction. Where James Joyce and Virginia Woolf were recording the importance of the immediate moment, the depth of the individual consciousness, and the cyclical and yet free-flowing nature of time, film makers were attempting to capture these same aspects by showing patterns of repetition, recurring images, and the texture of everyday life.

While the Americans were shaping a film approach that would become a tradition based on a romantic vision of life, and the Russians were busy adapting the dynamics of film making to the necessities of politics, the experimental film makers of France, Germany, and Holland were working in an area unbounded by sentiment or politics. Not as idyllic as Flaherty, nor as progressive as the Russians, these film makers had, nonetheless, a distinct vision of life. Occasionally, they produced immature films that were strident in ironic emphasis and banal in structure. For the most part, however, their films represent an important step in the experimental approach to film making, and create a tradition of their own.

The Americans and the Russians focused most often on the power and beauty of their respective countrysides, on the strength of their people, and on the magnificence of their natural resources.

But the film makers in the large European cities were not interested in pastoral or romantic hymns to nature; long before our present-day concern, they were involved with the rushed, dehumanizing atmosphere of the city. There seems to be an agreement in their attitude toward the city: it is cramped, dirty, brutalizing, and almost unlivable, but, at the same time, it has its eccentricities, its charms, its beauties. Where others saw man in a romantic conflict with nature, these film makers saw man in a realistic conflict with the city streets. One can sing as loudly and as critically about the city as one sings about the countryside; the theme and the style of the hymn may be different, yet the praise is there all the same.

These continental realists developed a film genre generally called the *city symphony*. These rhythmic and kaleidoscopic films are realistic, nonfiction views of brief episodes of city life, united within a larger structure—a symphony—by the recurrence of images, motifs, and themes that provide continuity and progression of ideas. The least successful of these films are little more than a cross-section of life, good exercises for beginning film makers. At their best, however, they are poetic records of the camera's ability to capture the rhythm and pattern of ever-changing city life; at the same time, they transcend that subject matter by discovering significant human themes beneath the surface of mechanization and industrialization. The mere juxtaposition of the rich and the poor or the office worker and the factory worker was not enough; to see why there are rich people as well as poor people, and to understand why the city can be both ugly and beautiful is the achievement of those film makers who emerged from this early period as the founders of a minor but very contemporary approach: the city symphony. It appears in films as diverse as *Gamla Stan* (1931), Steiner's and Van Dyke's *The City* (1939), and Francis Thompson's *N.Y., N.Y.* (1957); even Chaplin's *Modern Times* (1936) opens with a sequence that intercuts the crowds in the New York subway with herds of sheep. And few beginning film makers overlook the opportunity to film the cities around them, seeing recurring patterns, forming ironic contrasts, and developing sociological insights. The city *is* alive, and if it reveals an aspect of the human condition less triumphant than that revealed in the cycle of nature in the countryside, it is nonetheless important and very much a part of the film maker's concern. It was only natural then that Cavalcanti in France, Ruttmann in Germany, and Ivens in Holland would turn their cameras toward the city with the hope that, in documenting it, they and their audience might understand it better.

France

Time and space are the interrelated themes of Alberto Cavalcanti's *Rien que les Heures* (1926), the first and still one of the most influential of the films which depict a day in the life of a city. A printed title at the end of the film only confirms the paradoxical fact that the camera can record the flow of time while, at the same time, stopping it in space: "We can fix a moment in space or immobilize a moment in time." *Rien que les Heures* appeared several months before Ruttmann's *Berlin;* while both films attempt to express the life of a city on film, they are different. In contrast to Ruttmann's film, the rhythm of Cavalcanti's film is paced, rather than orchestrated; his vision is episodic, rather than symphonic; and he relies on the cumulative impression of a series of images, rather than on a unified thematic approach. Nevertheless, the film reveals a definite vision of Paris.

Rien que les Heures begins with images of morning: people awaken; a poor, old beggar woman staggers along a passageway; and a window dresser begins to clothe a mannequin. At midday, a surrealistic clock announces the time. People stop their labors to take the midday meal; working men sit on the curb eating out of hand, while more prosperous office workers enjoy a restaurant. Some rather heavy-handed ironies (shots of men eating intercut with a cow being butchered) are less effective than intended, and the continual reminder of the food-to-garbage cycle is overdone. The day becomes evening, and people turn their attention to leisure activities; we see an elegant card game, a street fortune teller, and the old woman (from the first part) sleeping in an upright sitting position (later, we will see her staggering along a passageway again). Shots of two kissing couples are intercut and juxtaposed against shots of food and a Rodin statue of lovers, again in a heavy and unsuccessful attempt at irony. A running news vendor is seen against the ever-increasing speed of newspaper headlines. The lights and whirling pattern of the rides at an amusement park are recorded with some very conscious use of the camera. Shots are superimposed, speeded up, and sometimes out of focus. Night falls and there is mystery and suspense everywhere. A lady news vendor is robbed, and a sailor seduces a girl, but the shots of the lip-smacking lovers and of the bed are, again, overdone and unnecessarily heavy for the weight of the irony intended.

When the film is over, we are left with the impression that life goes on, that the next day will again bring work and play, love and hate, food and garbage. Young people will play, artists will create, old people will wander unregarded, and lovers will kiss. Some of the images are linked through contrast, others through irony, and still others are unrelated, but the overall impression is that of a mosaic. The images relate only when they are considered in their relation to the whole picture. In addition to establishing one approach to the city symphony, Cavalcanti's film is important to students of film technique, for it is the first nonfiction film to use the "wipe" in place of the cut or dissolve (the wipe is a form of transition from one shot to another in which a line appears to travel across the screen, removing, as it travels, one shot and introducing the next). A Brazilian, Cavalcanti later became one of the leaders of the British documentary film movement, where his impressionistic visual sense and sociological insight characterized some of the finest British films of the 1930's.

Germany

Walther Ruttmann's *Berlin: The Symphony of a Great City* (1927) reflects Eisenstein's influence more clearly than Cavalcanti's. Its rhythmic effect relies heavily on editing, and while it presents a day in the life of Berlin—as Cavalcanti's *Rien* shows us a day in Paris—it is less episodic and less thematic than its French counterpart. It criticizes city life with a caustic tone, and it exaggerates the pace of workers and of industrial processes; spinning images, optical effects, and a suicide contribute to its vision of mechanized city life. Like *Rien, Berlin* moves from morning to night, but its episodes are shaped by larger thematic concerns—movements—which give order to the many incidents depicted. In the lunchtime sequence, for example, we not only see workers eating, but also horses, elephants, businessmen in pubs, ladies in restaurants, a lion, a baby, a camel, an outdoor café, the elegant banquet preparations in a hotel kitchen, a monkey, and, only then, the dishwashing machines of a large restaurant and the final end-product, garbage. All of these vignettes are rhythmically linked by the editing, as well as by the chronological continuity and overall structure of the whole film. This lunchtime sequence is a complete sequence, opening with the workers and animals eating, and closing with them all resting.

Ruttmann seems concerned with presenting as many facets of each experience as possible, but there are times when this attempt at cross-sectional representation is overdone. *Berlin* opens with a fast train entering Berlin; as the train slows to enter the station, the film cuts to quiet city streets. Now the pace is slow, the windows are shuttered, the streets are empty, the stores closed; the few visible people include a poster hanger and a group returning from a party. The film cuts to a railroad roundhouse, and the pace slowly begins to increase. Now the day's activity begins, as men go to work, on foot, on bikes, in cars, on trains; as crowds slowly form, the pace increases correspondingly, and gates and doors seem to open by themselves in response to the activity. Now it is the rush hour in the crowded railway station, and the pace of the film quickens. Men arrive at work, machines begin the industrial processes of milk bottling, steel rolling; stores open, shutters open, pushcarts fill the street, children leave for school, shopping begins, trash is collected, and the postman begins his rounds. By mid-morning, we see the leisure class riding in the park, the working class scrubbing or pitching hay, and businessmen going to their offices. The pace is now rapid and the images are those of hurrying feet, elevators, and movement everywhere. Offices are opened in much the same way stores were; Ruttmann is fascinated with opening blinds, opening shutters, opening doors. As agitated businessmen argue on the phone, the film cuts to two fighting dogs, and then to two screaming monkeys. The pace and tone are set: movement becomes madness, hurrying becomes hysteria, men become machines.

Later in the day, as work stops, this procedure reverses itself, and we see machines slowing and stopping, people leaving their desks, and gates and doors closing for the night. The evening is devoted to leisure activity, and again Ruttmann presents a wide range of contrasts. There is Chaplin at the movies, ballet dancers, an orchestra, a vaudeville show, hockey, ice skating, an ice show, outdoor skiing, tobogganing, a bicycle race, a boxing match, dancing, a jazz band, a beerhall with singing, champagne cocktails, a smart nightclub with a floorshow, a card game, roulette, and, finally, a piercing searchlight and a bang-up ending of fireworks and spinning images. Such a cross-section could be incoherent and tedious, but the film's visual rhythm unites the kaleidoscope into an exciting vision of reality.

Ruttmann's reality is a vision of madness, a composite metaphor of revolving doors and roller coasters, of scattering leaves, hurrying feet, and suicide. Without sound, without musical score, without any narrative comment, *Berlin* creates the illusion of sound rhythm through purely visual images.[15] Through its comprehensiveness, its contrasts, its transitions, and its thematic unity, it exceeds Cavalcanti's achievement by adding intensely unified criticism to factual observation.

Holland

In Holland, experimentation with the nonfiction film form was not as ambitious as that in France and Germany, but it was, nonetheless, impressive and influential. The early films of Joris Ivens are careful, intense studies of the kinds of local phenomena that are of such characteristic interest to the nonfiction film maker. His later work in the 1930's and 1940's was more ambitious, and more political, but his early films, shot in Holland, are short, sharp impressions of everyday life.

The Bridge (1927–28) is a detailed visual analysis of a simple

Berlin: The Symphony of a Great City: Motor traffic in constant motion around a traffic circle symbolizes the visual rhythm of this city symphony. Photograph courtesy The Museum of Modern Art Film Stills Archive.

process, the workings of a railroad bridge near Rotterdam. The bridge is raised to allow river traffic to pass underneath, and lowered to connect with the railbed on the banks. This process is a basic one, but it must be handled with precision and efficiency so that the maximum amount of traffic can pass over and under the bridge. Without giving the process any undue dramatic emphasis, Ivens locates the event as a vital part of the region's transportation system. As the film opens, we see the bridge in the distance, followed by a few shots of the cameraman with his equipment. To provide a sense of the full function of the bridge, we see a train crossing it, and then Ivens begins a documentation of various aspects of the bridge's operation, a sequence which seems heavily influenced by Eisenstein. Under the bridge, we see the large engines, turbines, and pulleys which raise and lower the roadbed, and, from above, we follow a workman at the top of the bridge as he checks its operation. The pace of the film is brisk and makes the mechanical process seem much more interesting than it probably is; we observe an entire cycle of raising and lowering, with ships passing beneath on the river, and a train steaming across. Some whimsical contrast is provided by shots of a horse and buggy and one of an airplane.

The Bridge records the complete cycle of the operation of the bridge before, during, and after the process of raising and lowering its central section. Ivens must have been fascinated with this convenient and effective means of giving artistic shape to ordinary experiences, for he used it shortly after in *Rain* (1929), a film he made with Mannus Franken. Ivens' *Rain* is to Ruttmann's *Berlin* what a sonata is to a symphony. Subtitled a "cine poem," it is a lyrical, impressionistic picture of city life before, during, and after a rainstorm. The changeability of nature is contrasted to the relative constancy of human behavior; the weather may change, but the patterns of life in Amsterdam go on. The rhythm of the film is brisk, providing a pleasant contrast to the high-contrast black-and-white images. The shots of the clouds forming, the wind rising, and people scurrying about opening umbrellas and closing windows are particularly evocative. Rain fills gutters and streaks across windows, but traffic continues in the canals and on the streets. A brief and charming film, *Rain* still seems fresh, forty years after its release; admittedly, it is a "finger exercise," but the sort of display that only a master can handle.

Cavalcanti, Ruttmann, and Ivens formed the vanguard of European nonfiction film production and experimentation in the late 1920's, but other film makers, all over Europe, were also developing approaches. Among these were Henri Storck (*Idylle à la Plage* and *Images d'Ostende*), Wilfried Basse (*Abbruch und Aufbau, Markt in Berlin,* and *Deutschland von Gestern und Heute*), and Alexander Hammid (*Prague Castle*).[16] Cavalcanti joined Grierson as a leader of the British documentary movement in the 1930's; Ruttmann continued to make industrial and city symphonies; and Ivens created a tough, political approach to nonfiction film making that was to have a great influence on the Americans in the late 1930's and early 1940's.

NOTES

[1] Orson Welles, "But Where Are We Going?", *Look,* 34, No. 22 (Nov. 3, 1970) , p. 34.

[2] For an account of these technical developments, see Gerald Mast, *A Short History of the Movies* (New York, Pegasus, 1971) , especially Chapters 2, 3, and 9.

[3] In 1970, the American Film Institute reported that more than three hundred colleges and universities in the United States were offering some courses in film production and/or film history and appreciation, and many of these were offering whole programs leading to degrees, on both the undergraduate and the graduate levels.

[4] In the 1950's Walt Disney's nature films offered a charming exception to this precedent.

[5] Sergei Eisenstein, *Film Essays and a Lecture,* ed. Jay Leyda (New York, Praeger Publishers, 1970) , p. 25.

[6] Nikolai Lebedev, *History of the Soviet Silent Cinema* (Moscow, 1965) , writes that the best Soviet documentary films in the 1920's were Vertov's *Strike, Soviet* and *One Sixth of the World;* Turin's *Turksib;* and Yakov Blyokh's *A Shanghai Document,* especially notable for its length and use of comparative montage. I am grateful to Vladimir Petrić for introducing me to Lebedev's study and for translating pertinent sections of it for me.

[7] George Huaco, *The Sociology of Film Art* (New York, Basic Books, 1965) , p. 15.

8 *Potemkin*'s influence on motion picture art is primary, but its importance often overshadows the work in France of the Russian Dmitri Kirsanov. His *Menilmontant* (1924–25) opens with a sequence of terror, accentuated and heightened by editing and psychological use of the camera, that is worthy of study with *Potemkin*.

9 Jay Leyda, *Kino* (London, Allen and Unwin, 1960) , p. 181.

10 Leyda, pp. 240–41.

11 Leyda, p. 200.

12 Leyda, p. 179. Two recent studies reflect the variety of criticism of Vertov's work: Annette Michelson, *"The Man with the Movie Camera:* From Magician to Epistemologist," *Artforum,* 10, No. 7 (March 1972) , 60–82; and the section on Vertov in *Film Comment,* 8, No. 1 (Spring 1972) , 38–51.

13 Leyda, p. 200.

14 Leyda, p. 275.

15 J. Kolaja and A. W. Foster, "Berlin: The Symphony of a City as a Theme of Visual Rhythm," *Journal of Aesthetics and Art Criticism,* 23, No. 3 (Spring 1965) , 353–58. It may originally have been shown with sound accompaniment.

16 Alexander Hammid was formerly Alexander Hackenschmied.

CHAPTER 3

John Grierson and the Early British Documentary

The "documentary film"—as it was called and as we know it today—had its simple beginnings in a program established by the British government to promote trade and a sense of economic co-operation among members of the British commonwealth of nations. The one man most responsible for the documentary film, and the one whose name was inextricably linked with its development during the 1930's and 1940's, was John Grierson. With his colleagues at the film units of the Empire Marketing Board and, later, at the General Post Office, he created, pioneered, and spurred the rapid development of the new film form. Between 1928 and 1939, the documentary film units in England—E.M.B., G.P.O., commercial, institutional, and individual production units—produced about three hundred films, all of them, in one degree or another, owing their existence to Grierson's leadership.

In 1924, John Grierson visited the United States to study factors influencing public opinion, including the press and the motion pictures. Grierson's insight into the power of motion pictures was considerable; he was among the first to recognize the extent to which the popular arts were replacing the more traditional sources of information, such as the church and the school, as shapers of public opinion. In Hollywood, Grierson met the pioneers of the film industry, but he was apparently unimpressed, for his own theory of film aesthetics bears little resemblance to the com-

mercial approach of the early days of film history. But in Flaherty's
Nanook and Eisenstein's *Potemkin*—the two most important seminal influences on the documentary film—Grierson saw the possibilities for a new form of film making.

Though Grierson and Flaherty were friends, Grierson did not
altogether accept Flaherty's personal approach to film making; he
saw Flaherty as an innocent naturalist too concerned with observation to care about making a social statement.[1] Grierson underesti-
mated Flaherty, of course, for he equated Flaherty's gentleness and
subtlety with social irresponsibility. And as much as Grierson
admired Eisenstein's *Potemkin* (he helped to prepare the English
version of it), he referred to the film as a "glorified newsreel."[2]

When Grierson returned to England, he was convinced that
film was a serious medium capable of shaping public opinion, and
he reached this conclusion:

> I have no great interest in films as such. . . . Art is one matter, and
> the wise, as I suggest, had better seek it where there is elbow room for
> its creation; entertainment is another matter; education, in so far as
> it concerns the classroom pedagogue, another; propaganda, another;
> and cinema is to be conceived as a medium like writing, capable of
> many forms and many functions.[3]

Grierson took a course different from Flaherty's, but his goal was
equally important: to make film a great social force. He was fortunate in having before him, in the 1930's especially, a great social
laboratory in which to work. The times were depressed and would
end in war; in between were the myriad social problems of education, housing, pollution, trade, and communications. Film was new,
dynamic, and the right medium for educating the public, and Grierson was the right man to lay the foundation for the British documentary film movement. Looking back, in 1939, over a decade of
production, he observed that the documentary film movement

> was from the beginning an adventure in public observation. It might,
> in principle, have been a movement in documentary writing, or docu-
> mentary radio, or documentary painting. The basic force behind it was
> social, not aesthetic. It was a desire to make drama from the ordinary;
> a desire to bring the citizen's mind in from the ends of the earth to the
> story, his own story, of what was happening under his nose. From this

came our insistence on the drama of the doorstep. We were, I confess, sociologists, a little worried about the way the world was going. . . . We were interested in *all* instruments which would crystallize sentiments in a muddled world and create a will towards civic participation.[4]

If Grierson was a self-admitted sociologist, he was also a self-professed evangelist. Convinced that film was a medium of education and persuasion, Grierson devoted his unflagging persistence, not to say missionary zeal, to the task of convincing others that film could and should be used to further social progress.

E.M.B. Film Unit

With its establishment of the Empire Marketing Board in 1928, the British government also began, unknowingly, what would become an almost unprecedented program of state support for film making (there were, of course, nationalized film industries in Russia and Germany). This large organization of forty-five departments, including the Film Unit, was charged with promoting "all the major researches across the world which affect the production or preservation or transport of the British Empire's food supplies."[5] The Film Unit was, admittedly, only one part of this effort, but in time it grew in production capacity and influence to become, without question, the founding source of the "documentary film" as we know it today. *Documentary* is Grierson's own term (he first used it in a review of Flaherty's *Moana* in 1926),[6] and the association of this particular approach to film making with the British is due largely to the efforts of Grierson and the E.M.B. Film Unit.

Concerned that England had long been indifferent to the world's opinion, Sir Stephen Tallents, of the Empire Marketing Board, was impressed when Grierson first came to him in 1927 with his ideas for putting cinema to work in the national interest. Tallents recognized such Russian films as *Potemkin, Storm over Asia, Turksib,* and *Earth* as working examples of what one country could do with film as an "incomparable instrument of national expression."[7] He was dedicated to the "projection" of England's

life and the work of its people, and he listed those characteristics in
which he felt the world would be most interested. It is a predictable
list of English achievements, and it was to become Grierson's task to
supervise the "projection" of these achievements around the world.
Tallents' list includes such national institutions and virtues as

> The monarchy (with its growing scarcity value)
> Parliamentary institutions (with all the values of a first edition)
> The British Navy
> The English Bible, Shakespeare, and Dickens
> In international affairs—a reputation for disinterestedness
> In national affairs—a tradition of justice, law, and order
> In national character—a reputation for coolness
> In commerce—a reputation for fair dealing
> In manufacture—a reputation for quality
> In sport—a reputation for fair play.[8]

Certainly this listing is one in which any Englishman would take
justifiable pride, but it is more than a chauvinistic stock-taking.
The need for projecting England's "image" stemmed from economic and political factors: a need for international cooperation
and communication and a concern with her status in the world
market. Tallents must be credited as one of the first to realize the
vital role which film can and does play in the modern science of
public relations. He showed further foresight in his suggestion that
a program of such film making should not rely solely on financial
support from the government or from private enterprise, but,
rather, should be supported jointly. This was to occur later, of
course, as the E.M.B. Film Unit was dissolved and replaced by the
Film Unit of the General Post Office and by the increase of films
from private and institutional producers.

The E.M.B. Film Unit was a group effort, and, outside of the
Soviet Union, it was the only such group effort in the beginning
years of nonfiction film making; later, in 1937, the private Frontier
Film Group was formed in the United States for the production of
politically oriented documentaries. Grierson believed strongly that
film had the power to change men's minds, but his aesthetic approach was a practical one, and he insisted that the personnel of his
unit have a freedom to experiment in a way that would be denied

them in the commercial studios.[9] Even though motion picture production is, by necessity, almost always a group effort, such effort is always open to question in matters of artistic quality, and while the E.M.B. Film Unit was criticized by members of the British film industry and by those unfamiliar with or convinced by the relatively new art form, this particular group was particularly successful. In his evaluation of the group's effort to bring certain aspects of modern Britain to life on the screen, Paul Rotha wrote that they possessed "a sincerity and skill unapproached by any commercially operating company, at the same time bringing into existence a co-operative method of working and a spirit of loyalty which is notably absent in most other centres of film manufacture."[10]

In contrast to the novels, plays, and poetry of the late 1920's, the efforts of the E.M.B. were distinctive in presenting the lives and problems of the British working class as a vital and important aspect of the contemporary scene; later, of course, W. H. Auden, Stephen Spender, C. Day Lewis, and others would make the working-class man into a hero, but documentary film led the way in a culture still very much oriented to the artistic representation of the upper-class way of life. In comparison with the other approaches to nonfiction film making already in existence—the Russian propagandist, the American romantic, and the continental realist—the British approach, under Grierson's influence, was nearest to that established by the Russians, but with some obvious differences. Not the least of these differences is that while the British unit was government sponsored, it was not so tightly controlled by the government that its creativity and freedom of expression were regulated. Grierson realized, though, that this artistic freedom was relative and that state propaganda had its own ideological limits. While his mission was relatively clear, his emphasis was more on presenting a cross-sectional view of British life than it was on the Russian concerns of awakening and strengthening the viewer's sense of state, history, or political destiny. In Grierson's view,

> *Cinema is neither an art nor an entertainment;* it is a form of publication, and may publish in a hundred different ways for a hundred different audiences. There is education to serve; there is new civic education which is emerging from the world of publicity and propa-

ganda; there is the new critical audience of the film circles, the film societies and the specialized theatres. All these fields are outside the commercial cinema.

Of these the most important field by far is propaganda. The circles devoted to the art of cinema mean well and they will help to articulate the development of technique, *but the conscious pursuit of art carries with it, in periods of public difficulty, a certain shallowness of outlook* [author's italics].[11]

From this statement, it is clear that Grierson saw the film maker first as a patriot, and second as an artist. Nothing is more important than the common good, and, drawing a rather terse distinction between commercial and propaganda film making, Grierson says, "To command, and cumulatively command, the mind of a generation is more important than by novelty or sensation to knock a Saturday night audience cold; and the 'hang-over' effect of a film is everything."[12] By "hang-over effect" Grierson meant, of course, the lingering ideological impression that a film makes on a viewer, the effect that, hopefully, channels his mind and his reactions in the direction pointed by the film. One has only to look at the long list of titles produced under Grierson's supervision to know that he was not always successful in his propaganda approach to film making, but films such as *Night Mail* and *The Song of Ceylon* are impressive testimony to the validity of his theory and approach at this particular time in British film history.

The first films produced in the E.M.B. Film Unit in 1929 were Grierson's *Drifters* and Walter Creighton's *One Family*. *One Family* is an ambitious feature-length film which attempts to illustrate the economic interdependence of the nations of the British Empire. Despite its lack of success,[13] it was an important first step. *Drifters* is important for several reasons. First, remarkably enough, it is the only film which Grierson ever directed personally. Second, it concerns a routine and supposedly insignificant activity—herring fishing—yet brings it alive, not only in terms of the physical process, but, more important, in terms of the human drama involved in this vital part of the British economy. Third, it demonstrates to the British—as Flaherty had demonstrated several years before—that artistic vision can transform existing everyday material, through photography and editing, into a film of interest, quality, and drama. To Grierson, however, the film was more than a gesture in tribute to Flaherty; he said, "Its subject belonged in part to Flaherty's world, for it had something of the noble savage and certainly a great deal of nature to play with. It did, however, use steam and smoke and did, in a sense, marshal the effects of modern industry."[14] Fourth, it is closer to Eisenstein than to Cavalcanti or to Ruttmann.

Drifters (1929) is a simple, beautifully photographed, well-paced film, considerably more mature than its early place in the development of the British documentary would suggest. Its underlying theme is the shift in the herring fishing industry from small, independent operations to a large, industrial effort. But its overall focus is on the men who brave the rough seas, do the hard work, and bring home the catch; their wonderful faces alone are enough to preserve the film's interest. In this sense, *Drifters* established Grierson's primary concern with the dignity of labor, the worth of the individual working man; the student even remotely familiar with the British documentary movement will understand its influence. To the student of film editing, *Drifters* shows Grierson's fine understanding of Eisenstein's editing principles, especially in a sequence which brings alive the boat's engines through a rapid montage of gears, levers, and pumps. The film is uneven, and some sequences are more interesting than others; however, Grierson recorded the complete process from the time the men prepared to board their ship, through their waiting for the fish to appear, the catch itself, and the auction, cleaning, icing, and distribution of the fish in barrels. A certain tension underscores these scenes as we are reminded of the economic necessity of making a quick catch and of an early return to port. In this way, Grierson related the work of one small boat to a national fishing industry. With only printed titles to complement the first-rate photography, Grierson told the story of one of Britain's most important industries; rarely seen, *Drifters* is an impressive beginning and compares favorably with *Granton Trawler* and *North Sea,* later films on the same subject.

After the success of *Drifters,* Grierson convinced Tallents that the Film Unit should be expanded. It began to grow with the purpose of creating good documentaries, "not on the basis of one

director, one location and one film at a time, but on the basis of
half-a-dozen directors with complementary talents and a hundred
and one subjects all along the line."[15] The film makers who formed
the unit included Basil Wright, Arthur Elton, Stuart Legg, Paul
Rotha, John Taylor, Harry Watt, and Edgar Anstey. Between
January 1930, and July 1933, the Film Unit grew from two people
to over thirty, and acquired substantial technical facilities for
production. Before the government disbanded the E.M.B. in 1933,
the Film Unit produced over one hundred films; these were distinguished as a collective effort, rather than by the particular style or
vision of one director, although Flaherty's work on *Industrial
Britain* (1933, completed by Grierson) constituted an important
"outside" influence. Grierson said,

> The documentary idea, after all, demands no more than that the affairs
> of our time shall be brought to the screen in any fashion which strikes
> the imagination and makes observation a little richer than it was. At
> one level, the vision may be journalistic; at another, it may rise to
> poetry and drama. At another level again, its aesthetic quality may lie
> in the mere lucidity of its exposition.[16]

Some of the notable early experiments and achievements in-
clude Arthur Elton's *Upstream* on salmon fishing in Scotland, *The
Voice of the World, Shadow on the Mountain* about pasture experiments in Wales, and *Aero-Engine;* Basil Wright's *O'er Hill and
Dale, Country Comes to Town* about London's market services,
Cargo from Jamaica, and *Windmill in Barbados;* Stuart Legg's *New
Generation;* and Donald Taylor's *Lancashire: Home of Industry.*
Elton's *Aero-Engine* (1933, silent) is a well-photographed and
highly detailed observation of every step in the manufacture of an
airplane engine; its value lies more in its completeness of detail
than in its brief, straightforward narrative. Wright's *O'er Hill and
Dale* (1932) is a brisk account of sheep farming in the border hills
of England and Scotland. Typical of the E.M.B. films, this is an
unpretentious and delightful picture of a small, but valuable part
of one of the major elements of the British economy. Wright's
Cargo from Jamaica (1933, silent) records the harvesting and
shipping of bananas. This seemingly prosaic business is enhanced
by beautiful photography and a rhythmic sense of editing that fore-

Drifters: In 1929, John Grierson's pioneering silent documentary set a remarkably high standard for photography and editing as it presented the importance of the fishing industry to the overall British economy.

shadows Wright's later lyricism in *Song of Ceylon* (1935). Another silent film, Donald Taylor's *Lancashire: Home of Industry* (1935), shows the diversity of a particular region's industrial production, and although it is briskly edited, it is a routine and often dull account that would have been saved either by a spoken narrative or by the particular feeling for industrial craftsmanship evident in Flaherty's *Industrial Britain*.

The most important among these early films, even though it is an "outside" film, is Robert Flaherty's *Industrial Britain* (1933), a work that has little to identify it with the master except its beautiful photography and concern with craftsmanship in various areas of British industry. Completed and edited by Grierson, it is more Grierson than Flaherty, and provides a rare opportunity to study the work of the two men on a single film. From Grierson, there is narration and explanation, a rather insistent pace, and a heavy musical score. The film was obviously patched together from Flaherty's footage, and the two sections (Part I, "Steam," and Part II, "Steel") are not as effectively related as the narration insists. Nonetheless, it works as a collection of beautiful images paying tribute to the tradition of British skill.

The theme of the film—"the old changes, giving place to the new"—is meant to underscore the shift in industrial production from the steam age to the steel age. Linking these two periods is Flaherty's attention to the human factor, the spirit of craftsmanship and care which distinguishes all British products from coal to pottery making to glass blowing. Needless to say, such a transition strains credibility, but by keeping a fairly consistent focus on the idea that quality relies on an individual's work, the film is able to make its points. *Industrial Britain* is a simple film, obviously meant to explain and to inspire pride in the country's work. It is the sort of documentary film that Grierson would learn to master; left to his own, Flaherty might well have completed a film of similar impact, but it would probably have been one in which the concern for a single worker's skill and quality output would have said it all. And yet it was a successful film to which workers responded, one that nudged a viewing audience into a continuing respect for its nation's traditions and resources. It is not a bad film, by any means, but it is an example of what can happen when two different approaches to film making are brought together with the eventual dominance of one over the other. The subordinated approach comes through, almost in counterpoint to the dominant one, and points the way not to fusion, but confusion.

Grierson objected to Flaherty's extravagance in shooting and feared that this, in addition to his lack of script, would deplete the meager budget before the project was finished.[17] He was right, of course, and this financial factor, as much as any other, contributed to Grierson's assumption of control over the final film. Yet the completed product established a fundamental distinction between the cinematic approaches of the two men, a distinction much more important than money. Of their work together, Grierson wrote,

> When he made *Industrial Britain* with me, his flair for the old crafts and the old craftsmen was superb, and there will never be shooting of that kind to compare with it; but he simply could not bend to the conception of those other species of craftsmanship which go with modern industry and modern organization.[18]

What Grierson was saying here is, ironically, what the film was also saying: the old ways change, giving way to the new, but the old ways are good ways, careful ways, and must be preserved and respected if the new approaches are to continue their tradition. What Grierson could not know was that Flaherty's "old" way with films would outlive his own approach.

Note should be taken of Herbert G. Ponting's *Ninety Degrees South* (1933), a record of Captain Robert Falcon Scott's second expedition to the South Pole between 1910 and 1912. In 1933, Ponting edited his footage into the present film, and while it exhibits a few of the clichés of the travel film, it is also an old-timer's sea yarn that is intimate and interesting. The narration has a certain men's club joviality, friendliness, and humor. The music is a whimsical complement to the scenes of penguins running about like slapstick comedians. But the film is not all description of Scott's travels with his ship, the *Terra Nova;* its final scenes record the bitter disappointment and despair that came when his group reached the South Pole to find that a Norwegian expedition led by Roald

Industrial Britain: This early E.M.B. film concentrates on the British craftsman and on the individual pride he places in his work. Filmed in part by Flaherty, it was completed and edited by Grierson.

Amundsen had reached the South Pole one month ahead of them. Ponting gives the harrowing details of their retreat, and using actual entries from Scott's diary, he recounts the events and finally the deaths of all members of the heroic party. *Ninety Degrees South* is an engaging prototype for the exploration film; although it benefits substantially from modern editing, sound, and music, the completeness of its excellent photography attests to its original power. And the epic drama of this British exploration film makes the events recorded in *Conquest of Everest* (1953) seem easy and uninteresting by comparison.

G.P.O. Film Unit

The development of the British documentary film movement was slowed down momentarily when the government disbanded the Empire Marketing Board. Commercial organizations and other institutions continued to produce films, and the successful union of the documentary approach and sponsorship can be seen, for example, in the beautiful *Song of Ceylon* (1934). While the government withdrew its support from the E.M.B., it also realized the necessity for continued support of film production; as a result, the General Post Office was designated to support the work of the Film Unit as an aspect of its own public relations program. The G.P.O. Film Unit continued under the supervision of Tallents and Grierson. Now at the Post Office—in what might appear to have been an unlikely and unimaginative atmosphere for creative film production—the British tradition continued and prospered. Grierson and his associates saw and accepted the continuing challenge to "bring the Empire alive"[19] by translating the complexities and magic of modern communications, industry, and technology into creative and compelling films. Along with their new support, they had the satisfaction of continuing their experiments with sound, the involvement of ranking artists from fields such as literature and music, and the opportunity to develop the techniques of color, graphics, and animation. It was at this time, with solid financial and organizational support and with a viable creative atmosphere, that the

British began to produce the memorable series of films that represent the most characteristic achievements of the early British nonfiction film.

Among the early films designed to present and explain the myriad communications activities of the General Post Office were *Cable Ship, Six-Thirty Collection, Weather Forecast, Under the City,* and *Droitwich.* They are all brief, succinct, and effective in their unpretentious attempt to demonstrate the importance of simple tasks, and they are professional in their handling of the subject matter. In addition, they represent some significant developments in the use of direct sound recording and narration by actual men who perform the work that is seen on the screen. Alexander Shaw's and A. E. Jeakins' *Cable Ship* (1933) presents the work of the G.P.O. vessel which repairs cables lying at the bottom of the English Channel. Its technique is similar to Shaw's later *Under the City* (1934), in which the voices of a narrator and the working men recount the work involved in maintaining the water, gas, telephone, and telegraph cables which run beneath London's streets. Edgar Anstey's and R. H. Watt's *Six-Thirty Collection* (1934) is a commonplace explanation of the collection, sorting, and routing of mail, and it fails to find the human focus in this activity which distinguishes the later G.P.O. masterpiece *Night Mail. Weather Forecast* (1934) is the most sophisticated of these early films, for here director Evelyn Spice has presented not only the general aspects of the forecasting methods, but also the dramatic effect of such broadcasts on a specific group of ships, aircraft pilots, and farmers. The film's use of direct sound effects is distinctive, and it makes its major points through these and through visual images, rather than through straight narrative. Less effective, but nonetheless interesting, is R. H. Watt's *Droitwich* (1934), a clear, well-organized explanation of the function of what was then the most modern long-wave transmitter in the world.

While it is not a G.P.O. film, Alberto Cavalcanti's *Coal Face* (1935) is important as the source of the technical experiments that reached successful fruition in *Night Mail.* As an explanation film about the processing and distribution of coal, it is strident. The verse is by W. H. Auden and the music by Benjamin Britten, but their attempts to integrate choral singing, chanting, narration, and music do not reach the successful symphonic fusion that they achieved in *Night Mail*. Important, however, and unique among these early British films is the strong voice of social protest that comprises the film's message. The chorus of oppressed miners relates its submission to the pits with a tone of bitterness and futility that is surpassed in intensity and effectiveness only by Henri Storck's brilliant *Les Maisons de la Misère* (1937).

The most successful and certainly the most memorable of these early G.P.O. film productions was *Night Mail* (1936), produced by Grierson, written and directed by Basil Wright and Harry Watt, with music by Benjamin Britten, and verse narrative by W. H. Auden. Predictably, the film concerns a humble subject, the "Postal Special," a crack express train that transports the mail from London to Glasgow. The overall structure of the film follows the progress of the train, but within this structure is presented the actual internal operation of this post office on wheels. The process is shown and explained from loading and sorting to routing and final delivery. But it is in the dramatization of this ordinary process that the film achieves its distinction, for there is mystery in the priority of the train's run on the English right-of-way; there is excitement in the mechanized method of picking up the mail pouches at high speed; and there is a certain sense of power, strength, and even inevitability as the mail goes through. The film stresses the importance of the train to people along the route, some of whom even set their watches by its appearance: "All Scotland waits for her." That all of this should come through in a film devoted to a post office train is simply an expression of how good a documentary film can be.

Unlike Anstey's *Granton Trawler*, *Night Mail* endows ordinary activity with drama. *Granton Trawler* (1934) pays too much attention to the ocean and not enough to people. Its achievements include an integrated sound track, using fishermen's voices, and an almost textbook approach to photography, but the final effect is static, not dramatic. In *Night Mail*, the constant focus is on the men working in the train, on their dedication and efficiency; even the sequence which shows a new man learning how to handle the mail pouches is beautifully done with a sense of urgency and humor.

Night Mail: A new employee learns how to prepare mail bags in a humorous sequence that balances the rhythmic poetry of the Wright–Watt study of the British postal service.

The film derives its power from several sources. First, it handles ordinary people in ordinary situations in such a way that they appear to be special. Second, it keeps the speed and the sound of the train as an important part of the sound track; underscored with a mix of Britten's music and Auden's staccatolike poem, the film moves with an almost breathtaking rhythm. Third, it emphasizes the importance and dignity of a job well done, as well as the emotional importance of mail to the lives of everyday citizens. Indeed, it makes the postal service seem the most important thing in the world, not only because it is efficient, but also because it brings communication between human beings: "None will hear the postman's knock without a quickening of the heart, for who can bear to feel himself forgotten."[20]

There is power in *Night Mail*, the power of sight and sound, and there is also charm, and a particularly British feeling for detail, for efficiency, and, finally, for the working man, that gives this film a very special quality. The overall impression is of workers who are dedicated to precision efficiency, yet the importance of each simple operation is occasionally broken by characteristic British humor. For instance, when a sorter on a routine assignment handles a letter with an unfamiliar Scottish address, his supervisor shows him that it is actually addressed to a place in Wales, and wryly comments, "Makes a nice change for you." The film is a pleasure to watch, it is instructive, and it is a technical landmark in its use of sound and integration of image, music, and narrative. The influence of *Night Mail*'s use of direct sound can be seen in Alexander Shaw's *Cover to Cover,* in Cavalcanti's *We Live in Two Worlds* and *Line to the Tschierva Hut,* and in Cavalcanti's and Watt's *The Saving of Bill Blewitt* and *North Sea.*

Night Mail represents the British documentary school in the early 1930's at its best, for it combines social purpose with cinematic experimentation. The job of the documentary film maker was, as Grierson put it, to render a "creative treatment of actuality," but then the creative aspects of that treatment became more sophisticated and more professional. He was, however, still making films with a didactic purpose, and he was still obligated to enlighten, not just to entertain. The titles of many of these films show Grierson's belief that drama can be found in what would ordinarily appear to be unlikely subjects: *Weather Forecast, Under the City, Six-Thirty Collection, Cable Ship,* and the full-length documentary feature *B.B.C.: The Voice of Britain.*

Stuart Legg's *B.B.C.: The Voice of Britain* (1935) provides a beautifully integrated picture of the complexities of the British Broadcasting Corporation, from preparation to programming. The visual unity between the sequences in the film is excellent, as is the variety, from children's story-telling programs to sports to drama to the famous Dancing Daughters tap-dancing team. This film is direct and vital, as some of the "explanation" films are not—perhaps owing to the variety of the B.B.C. itself—but the style of the film is fresh and not without its own gentle humor. A full-length feature documentary, this is an ambitious and successful attempt to capture the sounds and sights of the vast radio enterprise.

As the documentary movement developed, its direction underwent certain changes as its dependence on government support increased, its relation to the commercial film industry became more involved, and its appeal to the public broadened. The earlier films are objective records of fairly simple, often humble activities, such as fishing, pottery making, and weaving; but the later films are more complex in their concerns, and it often became necessary to reenact certain activities for the camera or to introduce actors and artificial settings. These changes were particularly evident in *The Saving of Bill Blewitt* and *North Sea,* and in *We Live in Two Worlds* and *Line to the Tschierva Hut.* Outside the G.P.O. Film Unit, in commercial and institutional production, some of these changes were evident in *Workers and Jobs, Housing Problems,* and *Enough to Eat?* The subjects now became immediate social problems: education, housing, social services, public health, air pollution, and unemployment; and the documentary film makers showed the flexibility and the immediacy of their approach as they realistically brought these problems, and suggestions for their solution, to the general public.

During their formative years in the early 1930's, the British documentary film makers were financed by the government. But as the film audience grew and as commercial organizations and other institutions began to learn the value and power of film, the financial basis for production broadened to include these new sponsors. Since advertisers could not reach the public by radio (until 1971, the B.B.C. was free of advertising), they had to look to other media, and film seemed just the thing to reach the masses quickly, dramatically, and at relatively reasonable cost. Once again, Grierson took the lead, encouraging sponsors to finance films which had broad cultural appeal, rather than those which simply sold products. The approach was not new, however, since Flaherty had done much the same thing earlier with *Nanook of the North* and would do it later with *Louisiana Story*.

One of the acknowledged classics of film reportage in the commercially sponsored field is Basil Wright's *Song of Ceylon* (1934). Produced by Grierson for the Ceylon Tea Propaganda Board, the film was specifically concerned with creating a favorable impression for Ceylon and for one of its major exports. However, the film does not sell tea, and, in fact, handles the subject so delicately that one often thinks its real concern is to picture changing customs, not to dramatize the flagging tea market. While the intention behind this film seems commercial, the overall comment is sociological and, ultimately, philosophical. With its juxtaposition of traditional customs against modern methods, the film builds an intelligent and sensitive impression of a changing culture.

Song of Ceylon is structured of four parts, each revealing a different aspect of the Singhalese culture. In a slow, careful manner, the film's beautiful images are presented in counterpoint to the sound, rather than in complement, so that the resulting development is one of contrast. Part 1, "Buddha," explains and shows the natives' religion and their spiritual resources. Part 2, "Virgin Island," documents the island's natural and human resources, its manual labor force, the activity of harvest, and the art of dance as a means of developing poise and muscular control. Part 3, "Voices of Commerce," presents the commercial focus of the film, the harvesting and shipping of tea, and it is in this sequence that the counterpoint sound is most apparent and most effective. Part 4, "Apparel of a God," returns to the subject of the spiritual life, and depicts prayers, the offerings of food, and ceremonial dancing.

Song of Ceylon: With director Basil Wright at the camera, the production unit prepares to film a scene in a street market place in Colombo, Ceylon. Photograph courtesy The Museum of Modern Art Film Stills Archive.

Song of Ceylon is more clearly a factual film than a documentary, although its commercial sponsorship influences, however subtly, its point of view. As a factual film, it shows the land, the people, and their customs, and, most important of all, it integrates all aspects of life into the film, so that one is left with a delicate, impressionistic, but accurate picture of a foreign land and culture. Moreover, it avoids the clichés and predictable juxtapositions of the travel film. Technically, it makes significant advances in the use of combined dissolves, superimposition of visual images, and counterpoint sound. Altogether, it is a film of refined composition, rare power, and restrained impact. Films such as *Night Mail* and *Song of Ceylon* provide a valuable insight into history and tradition, as well as an example of documentary film makers' responses to a dynamic, changing world.

From 1928 to 1937, John Grierson's leadership was undoubtedly the single most important influence on the development of the British documentary film. His insistence on propaganda in the public interest, his interest in cinematic experimentation, and his production supervision of dozens of major documentary films are factors which brought the movement to its high point of maturity in a relatively short period of time.

During the course of Grierson's stewardship, many changes affected the British approach to nonfiction film making. The most important technical change—although unrelated to Grierson—was the shift from silent to sound production; in the latter part of Grierson's tenure, as we have seen, there was much experimentation with sound in such films as *Song of Ceylon, Coal Face,* and *Night Mail.* But the most relevant broad change came in the subject matter, as the rather narrow focus of the early films widened to include a more comprehensive vision of British society. The first films (*Drifters* and *One Family*) were concerned with dramatizing the common laborer; they were limited in scope, and, therefore, in appeal, but they served to acquaint the viewing audience with isolated and relatively unfamiliar patterns of life and industry. The second wave of films (*Industrial Britain* and *Lancashire: Home of Industry,* for example) was concerned with the worker and his immediate industrial or agricultural environment; less impressionistic and poetic than the first films, these productions emphasized technique in film making, especially sound, and mark the turning point toward more sophisticated films. The third stage of development (*Night Mail,* for example) focused on the person first and the job second, so that the process of dramatizing the individual worker reached its high point with films (such as *Men of the Lightship,* 1940, or *Spring Offensive,* 1940) depicting the importance of all kinds of work, from that done at the desk to that performed in the field or on the seas. In these early films, it is possible to observe three distinct approaches to documentary film making. These approaches, or stylistic variations on the documentary, are the lyrical (*Song of Ceylon* and *O'er Hill and Dale*), the analytical (*Aero-Engine* and *Cargo from Jamaica*), and the impressionistic (*Shipyard* and *Night Mail*).

In 1936 and early 1937, Grierson began to phase out his leadership at the G.P.O. Film Unit. During this time there was much important experimentation with narrative, sound, and music, and, both in and out of the Unit, film makers were producing films that were both more intimate in their approach to people and more technically mature. Recognizing that more films were being produced by private industry than by the government, Grierson resigned as producer of the G.P.O. Film Unit in June 1937, to form the London Film Centre in association with Arthur Elton, Stuart Legg, and J. P. R. Golightly. The Film Centre did not produce films, as such, but instead served as a clearinghouse for ideas on planning and producing films, as well as a focal point for the whole documentary movement. Grierson formulated the theories, established the production process, and laid the foundation for the British documentary film. After his departure from the G.P.O. Film Unit, production came under the supervision of Alberto Cavalcanti, who continued in the Grierson tradition, and, in addition, brought a freshly imaginative and experimental approach to his work.

Grierson's career continued for many years, and his influence is still felt in all areas of documentary film production. Besides his direct involvement in the production of many dozens of films, he stimulated his own colleagues and a whole movement in England; he created interest in the social documentary in the United States,

Australia, Canada, and New Zealand, as well as in other countries; and he encouraged much interest in the nontheatrical use of motion pictures. His reviews and his essays (notably those reprinted in *Grierson on Documentary*) are still widely read by film students. In 1939, he was appointed Canada's Film Commissioner, a post he held until 1945; resigning this position, he summarized his career to that point, saying: "I hope I have done something to make of documentary not only an international force but a force for internationalism."[21] The viewpoint of documentary film has not always been international, for most production has been done with a national focus and with a national sponsorship; the films from the United Nations are an exception, of course. However, Grierson knew the power of film to communicate ideas which transcend national and linguistic boundaries, and his work has been second to none in developing the art and use of the documentary film.[22]

NOTES

[1] John Grierson, *Grierson on Documentary*, ed. Forsyth Hardy (London, Faber and Faber, Ltd., 1966), pp. 139–44.

[2] Grierson, *Grierson on Documentary*, ed. Forsyth Hardy (New York, Harcourt, Brace and Company, 1947), p. 5; this remark, in the 1947 edition, is deleted from the 1966 edition; all subsequent references are to the 1966 edition.

[3] Grierson, pp. 15–16.

[4] Grierson, p. 18.

[5] John Grierson, "E.M.B. Film Unit," *Cinema Quarterly*, 1, No. 4 (Summer 1933), p. 203.

[6] *New York Sun*, February 8, 1926.

[7] Sir Stephen Tallents, *The Projection of England* (London, Faber and Faber, Ltd., 1932), p. 31. For a further, more intimate discussion, see Tallents, "The Documentary Film," *Journal of the Royal Society of Arts* (20 December 1946), pp. 68–85. See also: *Journal of the University Film Association*, 22, Nos. 1, 2, 3.

[8] Tallents, pp. 31–32.

[9] *Grierson on Documentary*, p. 18.

[10] Paul Rotha, *Documentary Film* (New York, Hastings House, 1952), p. 97.

[11] *Grierson on Documentary*, p. 185.

[12] *Grierson on Documentary*, p. 165.

13 *The Factual Film: An Arts Enquiry Report* (London, Oxford University Press, 1947) , p. 46.

14 *Grierson on Documentary,* p. 152.

15 *Grierson on Documentary,* p. 167.

16 *Grierson on Documentary,* p. 22.

17 For a full discussion of this matter, see Arthur Calder-Marshall, *The Innocent Eye: The Life of Robert Flaherty* (New York, Harcourt, Brace and World, 1963) .

18 John Grierson, "Robert Flaherty," a copy of which is in files of the Film Study Center of the Museum of Modern Art. Forsyth Hardy writes me that it was probably prepared for U.S. publication, but it has not been possible to document it further.

19 *Grierson on Documentary,* p. 166.

20 In existing prints, the final word of this narration seems to be "forgot," but W. H. Auden (in a letter to me, March 17, 1972) says that "forgotten" is correct.

21 *Grierson on Documentary,* p. 29.

22 Belgian film maker Henri Storck finds Grierson's "creative treatment of actuality" a limiting term, and says,

Grierson always, how shall I say it, saw documentary films as a weapon, as a tool for creating a society. He thought film should deal with problems of information, and even of propaganda, in the service of the general public. That is, he didn't see documentary film as a form in itself, a category of film. For him the documentarist is a man who is above all not preoccupied with expressing his own sensibility but with expressing ideas for the purpose of analysis, and disseminating information about problems with a social character. It was only after his sensitivity as a spectator was touched by a number of documentaries that had greater ambitions than simply this service to the community that he returned—no, he came to; he never returned to because he never came from—he came to a conception of documentary as an artistic form of film. Deep down he didn't see films of a lyric or poetic character as documentary. In G. Roy Levin, *Documentary Explorations* (New York, Doubleday & Company, Inc., 1971) , p. 156.

CHAPTER 4

British Documentary
in the Later 1930's

When the General Post Office assumed sponsorship of the British documentary film movement in 1933, there was both a change in financial support and a shift in emphasis from films dealing with Britain's trade and economic life to those concerned with communications of all kinds. At the same time that the G.P.O. Film Unit widened its focus on Britain, it expanded its facilities to serve as a training school for young film makers, many of whom went beyond the nonfiction film into theatrical film production. Those who remained with the nonfiction approach found important work to be done for the government, for industrial and commercial sponsors, and for private business. A notable change, of course, came in 1937 in the shift of production supervision from John Grierson to Alberto Cavalcanti.

G.P.O. Film Unit After Grierson

The precise distinctions between the film production at the G.P.O. Film Unit during and after Grierson's tenure are less apparent than two general changes. First, the technical experimentation increased; and, second, the films took a wider and livelier look at British society. Alberto Cavalcanti introduced many innovative techniques to documentary film production during the later 1930's. Years later, he summed up his experience in a set of principles for young film makers, and it seems appropriate to reprint that list here for the relevance of its advice. While it does not always apply, the list forms a standard by which to measure and evaluate some of the films by Cavalcanti and his associates. Cavalcanti's fourteen points are

Don't treat generalized subjects; you can write an article about the mail service, but you must make a film about one single letter.

Don't depart from the principle which states that three fundamental elements exist: the social, the poetic, and the technical.

Don't neglect your script or count on luck while shooting. When your script is ready, your film is made; then, when you start to shoot, you begin again.

Don't trust in the commentary to tell your story; the visuals and the sound accompaniment must do it. Commentary irritates, and gratuitous commentary irritates even more.

Don't forget that when you are shooting, each shot is part of a sequence and part of a whole; the most beautiful shot, out of place, is worse than the most trivial.

Don't invent camera angles when they are not necessary; unwarranted angles are disturbing and destroy emotion.

Don't abuse a rapid rate of cutting; an accelerated rhythm can be as pompous as the most pompous largo.

Don't use music excessively; if you do, the audience will cease to hear it.

Don't supercharge the film with synchronized sound; sound is never better than when it is suggestively employed. Complementary sound constitutes the best sound track.

Don't recommend too many optical effects, or make them too complicated. Dissolves and fades form part of the film's punctuation; they are your commas and periods.

Don't shoot too many close-ups; save them for the climax. In a well-balanced film, they occur naturally; when there are too many, they tend to suffocate and lose their significance.

Don't hesitate to treat human elements and human relations; human beings can be as beautiful as the other animals, as beautiful as the machines in a landscape.

Don't be vague in your story; a true subject must be told clearly and simply. Nevertheless, clearness and simplicity do not necessarily exclude dramatization.

Don't lose the opportunity to experiment; the prestige of the documentary film has been acquired solely by experimentation. Without experimentation, the documentary loses its value; without experimentation, the documentary ceases to exist.[1]

This is a workable set of principles and a remarkably concise guide for any film maker. Perhaps most relevant to this discussion are those principles which differ from Grierson's or which take Grierson's approach in more experimental directions. Grierson wrote,

The G.P.O. Film Unit, which succeeded the E.M.B. Film Unit, is the only experimental center in Europe. Where the artist is not pursuing entertainment but purpose, not art but theme, the technique is energized inevitably by the size and scope of the occasion. How much further it reaches and will reach than the studio leapfrog of impotent and self-conscious art![2]

While it seems that the two producers are in agreement about the matter of experimentation, they differ in practice. Cavalcanti is more interested in the visual and literary aspects of nonfiction film, for his emphasis is on shooting, scripts, and story. He deemphasizes sound effects (although he was one of the first to use fully mixed sound tracks), optical effects, and commentary, reasoning that too many nonvisual elements can detract from the primary visual qualities of the film medium. Perhaps the most important difference is Cavalcanti's emphasis on the interrelationship among the three fundamental elements of documentary film: the social, the poetic, and the technical. Grierson would probably insist that the social was more important, and Flaherty that the poetic was more important; it is the measure of Cavalcanti's place in the development of nonfiction film that he emphasizes all three elements as being important.[3]

Films of the British school are generally high in technical quality, but often insistent in narration, or music, or overall message. The photography is almost always first rate, but the sound is frequently unimaginative, although natural, and therefore important to the factual nature of the films. In many of the films, there is a characteristic British seriousness of purpose coupled with a delightful sense of understatement and quiet humor. The lasting value of these films lies not in their technical achievements, but rather in their importance as models for what could be done in the use of films to analyze, inform, and educate.

A good example of such a film is Harry Watt's *The Saving of Bill Blewitt* (1936), a delightfully unpretentious piece of propaganda for two national savings plans. Ironically titled, the film concerns the efforts of Bill Blewitt to purchase a fishing vessel to replace the one he lost in a storm. He is "saved" by his own savings and those of a friend kept in a G.P.O. savings account, but the film's interest in the villagers and their happiness is far more important than any sales campaign for a savings bank. Despite somewhat awkward acting by the residents of a fishing village, this Cavalcanti production (with music by Benjamin Britten) is a charming reminder of the documentary film's power to translate the everyday into the memorable.

Two early films directed by Cavalcanti show the G.P.O. Film Unit in documentary experimentation: *We Live in Two Worlds* and *Line to the Tschierva Hut*. Produced in collaboration with Pro-Telephon-Zürich, both films are concerned with communications. *Line to the Tschierva Hut* (1937) deals with the bringing of telephone lines and service to a mountaineering post in the Swiss Alps, and it exemplifies the achievement that is possible when sight and sound are used with resource and ingenuity. The film explains the need for phone service at the isolated post, and shows the rough tasks of surveying the terrain and the installation of poles and lines. The photography is excellent, especially the angle shots and the contrast between the bright snow and the darkly clad workmen. The music by Britten is very simple, but it augments and contributes to an imaginative film that is a model of subtle conception, shooting, and editing. *We Live in Two Worlds* (1937), subtitled "A Film Talk by J. B. Priestley," is an ambitious but generally unsuccessful statement about the beneficial political implications of communications between the so-called national world and the international world. The film focuses on Switzerland, a country that is both national and international, but it is unclear whether it is a

The Saving of Bill Blewitt: Bill Blewitt and a friend realize the importance of savings accounts as they withdraw funds to purchase a fishing vessel to replace the one he lost in a storm.

tribute to Switzerland or to internationalism. Based on the rather naïve assumption that the power of electronic communications is stronger than the power of guns—a concept which predates Marshall McLuhan by many years—this film loses in its general attempt to tackle an idea what *Line* gains in its fidelity to a specific incident. These two Cavalcanti films neatly demonstrate what can happen when the documentary film maker loses focus on the immediate world around him and attempts to translate larger, abstract concepts into film. Ironically, *We Live in Two Worlds* fails to communicate its points about communication. Much less effective with subject matter that was intrinsically and socially more important is *Men in Danger* (1939), a Cavalcanti production directed by Patrick Thompson. The film concerns dangerous working conditions in England's mines and factories and suggests corrective measures and devices, yet it fails to dramatize the situation in any meaningful way, for it lacks the focus, clarity, and precision of *Line to the Tschierva Hut*.

Successful as a vehicle for informing the public and for generating pride in the British armed services was *Squadron 992* (1939), produced by Cavalcanti and directed by Harry Watt. This film details the work of a Royal Air Force balloon squadron, but it is much less concerned with explaining the function of the balloons (which is hurriedly done) than it is with urging public cooperation with the work. This is a strong effort to show the courteous way in which the RAF commandeers farm fields and buildings; the cooperative good nature of all concerned is obviously intended to build morale at a time when England was preparing for war and the eventual bombing against which the balloons were a defense. *Squadron 992* is especially successful in its patriotic sequences and in its use of familiar songs associated with military camaraderie. An early and influential example of the use of documentary film for war purposes, *Squadron 992* is less clear in its intentions than in its overall effectiveness, but it serves as a transitional point in the development of documentaries made between peacetime and the war effort.

Humphrey Jennings' *Spare Time* (1939) concerns the leisure time activities of British industrial workers, and in spite of its

Squadron 992: One of the earliest examples of prewar British domestic propaganda, this film shows the strategic necessity of launching antiaircraft balloon traps.

structural weakness, it reflects the gentle observation of ordinary people doing ordinary things that is perhaps better reflected in Jennings' later films.

An "obvious" post office film, but a successful one, is *The Islanders* (1939). In the words of the narration, the film is a tribute to the power of communications to unite islands and people. We are shown the different islands off the English coast, ranging from the remote to the agricultural and industrial. The self-contained, isolated characteristics of island life are balanced by the contact-and-communication lifeline provided by mail, telegraph, shortwave radio, steamer, and ferryboat service. With its beautiful black-and-white photography, *The Islanders* is similar to Flaherty's *Man of Aran,* though its musical score by Darius Milhaud is soft and complementary to the images and not as strident as the score of Flaherty's tribute to the Aran islanders. In contrast to *Night Mail,* another film stressing the importance of mail as a lifeline between people, *The Islanders* lacks focus, intensity, and drama because it chooses a general approach to the subject of communications. Of course, this film is concerned with more than the postal service, and to make a film about Cavalcanti's theoretical "single letter" would, in this instance, have limited the scope of its coverage. However, the film succeeds as a factual anthropological sketch and as a poetic record that air and water form bridges that span geographical isolation when they are used to carry radio messages, letters, parcels, and merchandise. Constant contrasts between images of rock and earth, air and water, reinforce this theme.

A major weakness of the 1930's British documentary film was its disappointing treatment of people. Aside from such films as *Night Mail,* the British failed to observe humans as intimately and as wisely as Flaherty did, and while they were familiar with his approach, they did not seem particularly influenced by it. Part of this failure stems from the overall British concern with themes rather than faces, politics rather than people. But they began to remedy this fault by first learning to use actual speech or written dialogue on the sound track. When their nonactors could not lend the necessary credibility, they did not hesitate to use professionals in certain roles. A distinctive landmark in the British attempt to come

The Islanders: By showing the physical remoteness and isolation of off-shore British islands, this G.P.O. film emphasizes the importance of modern postal and telegraphic communications.

closer to the person in his actual job is Harry Watt's *North Sea* (1938). A reconstruction which uses some studio settings, this film seems "real" for the most part, although it balances on the border-line between the fiction and nonfiction film and does not success-fully resolve the contradiction inherent in the combination of these two approaches. The narrative, written by Watt and Cavalcanti, depicts the crew members of the fishing trawler *John Gillman;* we see the men at work and hear their actual voices. The dramatic conflict comes quickly as a storm at sea knocks out the wireless; the ensuing battle between the men and the waves reaches such propor-tions that they must be rescued by another ship. In showing this simple conflict, the film depicts the frightened crew, the calm, reassuring skipper, and the efficient land-based radio service which monitors ship movements and directs rescue operations. An inti-mate portrait of lives of men at sea under pressure, it is superseded by the tight, dramatic wartime documentary *Men of the Lightship* (1940).

Production Outside the G.P.O. Film Unit

Production in the G.P.O. Film Unit flourished under Caval-canti's supervision, but outside the unit, there were interesting developments in films sponsored by commercial and institutional organizations; many of these were influenced by Grierson and his associates at the London Film Centre. Perhaps most characteristic of these films was their immediate response to particular social prob-lems. Some of these films were instructional, and some were closer to newsreels, but most were authentic and realistic and helped to move nonfiction film production to a new level of achievement.

The early films of Paul Rotha, Arthur Elton, John Taylor, and Edgar Anstey, among others, do not resemble those produced in the Grierson-Cavalcanti-G.P.O. tradition, nor do they seem to have had much immediate influence on that mainstream development. In their attempt at realism, many of these film makers used direct interviews and came closer to the journalistic school of the Ameri-can "March of Time" approach than to the carefully scripted approach of the G.P.O. film makers. Among Rotha's early work are three conventional films: *Contact* (1932–33), *Shipyard* (1935), and *The Face of Britain* (1935). *The Face of Britain* presents a challenge to the future growth of English cities, but its unclear focus and emphasis on contemporary social conditions result in a superficial film. Like Rotha's later *Land of Promise* (1945), this film relies too closely on a sequential development of four separate parts ("Heritage of the Past," "The Smoke Age," "New Power," and "The New Age") and on a narration which is much less emphatic than it should be. In its concern for urban planning in the rebuilding of English cities, *The Face of Britain* pioneers the way for Rotha's later and more successful *Land of Promise* and *A City Speaks*. More immediate and more interesting, although thoroughly dated, is Rotha's *Peace of Britain* (1936), in the so-called poster approach that Len Lye developed so imaginatively between 1935 and 1940. This brief film takes the alarming stand that there is no defense against air attack; it features a cross-section of Englishmen who are bewildered that World War I—the "war to end all wars"— is apparently going to be repeated. Hastily assembled to support Anthony Eden's plea that Britain support the League of Nations, this film is overtly political in its bold, poster-type messages: "Demand Peace by Reason" and "Write to Your M.P." One of the few British documentaries that deals strictly with politics, it is as unsubtle as a banner headline, and bears no resemblance to Lye's later development of poster films into what is almost subliminal propaganda. Rotha's *New Worlds for Old* (1938), produced for the British gas industry, is, with the Grierson-Taylor *The Londoners* (1938), notable for its use of studio sets and period costumes. These reconstructions are used to demonstrate the progress which the gas industry made from the Victorian period to the time in which the film was made. The narrator is challenged by another voice, representing the skeptical audience, a technique which Rotha used again in *World of Plenty* (1943). The comic effects, incorporated no doubt to help sell an unpopular commodity, often backfire and seem ridiculous.

Early in 1935, the combined forces of American journalism and film making introduced a new form of screen journalism, the monthly "March of Time" series.[4] Unlike the newsreel, and unlike the documentary and factual films developing then in England and America, the "March of Time" films were based on actual current events, but these events were treated with such heightened drama and editorial opinion that they truly represent a new and different nonfiction film approach. Among the distinctive characteristics of these films are extensive use of actual newsreel footage coupled with reenactment footage, and a thoroughly researched and apparently factual commentary, which so-called voice-of-god narration does much to make persuasive, if not convincing. This series exerted considerable influence on the course of documentary film production; and its possible influence in England can be seen in such films as *Housing Problems, The Smoke Menace, Today We Live,* and *Children at School.*

Housing Problems (1935), directed by Arthur Elton and Edgar Anstey, was produced by the Realist Film Unit for the British Gas Association, and marks the first use of journalistic reporting in the British documentary. Made at the beginning of a slum clearance operation in London, the film presents what is still a remarkably contemporary picture of the human problems of massive urban renewal. The apparently unrehearsed interviews with tenants relate conditions of crowding, vermin, rats, lack of sanitation, and unsafe architectural elements. To balance the despair of unrelocated slum dwellers, there are interviews with two women who have moved to a new building of flats and who emphasize the cleanliness of the new quarters. These interviews underscore dramatically that changes should be made, and convince people living both in and out of slums that change is possible and worth the effort. The interviews are direct and honest, and the immediacy of the problems has not been dimmed by time; *Housing Problems* has been imitated, and film makers will continue to do so as long as they recognize the power of film to assist social reconstruction. Yet, despite its effectiveness, *Housing Problems* lacks a certain immediacy in its picture of the unpleasantness of slum life. The dirt is real and there for us to see, but the gas industry relied on characteristic British good cheer and positive optimism to foreshadow the conclusion. Like the continental realists, the British should have let us feel the dirt, let

Housing Problems: A common theme in films devoted to urban planning is evidenced in this shot depicting crowded housing and inadequate recreation facilities.

us see the misery that these slum dwellers were experiencing. Both Joris Ivens' *Borinage* (1933) and Henri Storck's *Les Maisons de la Misère* (1937) accomplish this and succeed in arousing the viewer's social consciousness through devastating pictures of the injustice of slum life. In *Housing Problems,* the viewer's response is mitigated by the sponsor's facile solutions to major problems. Later, in another commercially sponsored British film, *When We Build Again* (1945), a similar approach was taken, but with greater success.

The Smoke Menace (1937), directed by John Taylor and produced by John Grierson for the gas industry of Great Britain, is an information film with a subtle message. A good example of a sponsored public relations film, it explains how the gas industry helps to combat the menace of air pollution by improving its processing of coal. It suggests that gas is a better, cleaner, and more efficient fuel in its use of natural resources and in its overall effect on the environment. A straightforward film, with little to distinguish it cinematically, it does its job with conviction and authority, not with the unfortunate comic attack on the problem made by Paul Rotha in *New Worlds for Old*. Like *Housing Problems,* it is a model example of a commentary film in which photography, sound, and script are less important than the narrative message. The restraint with which the producers deliver this message is, perhaps, its only distinguishing, if dulling, feature.

Basil Wright's *Children at School* (1937), produced by Grierson for the gas industry, provides a consummate example of the developments that characterized British documentary during the 1930's. While it is apparent that Wright would not allow a commercial message to spoil his films, it is still difficult to recognize that the beautiful *Song of Ceylon* (1934) and the forceful *Children at School* were made by the same director. The subject matter of the two films is totally different, for one film concerns a land of traditional patterns, while the other concerns the need for rapid change to avoid decay. The techniques, too, are different, although there are moments of tenderness, if not lyricism, in *Children at School*. In this film, there is no apparent link between the sponsorship by the gas industry and the problems to be solved; here, the problems and

The Smoke Menace: Although it was produced in 1937, John Taylor's film is still a relevant attack on the dangers of air pollution to the health and safety of people in large cities.

progress in England's best and worst schools are reviewed, with the emphasis on updating and upgrading the entire educational system. With the theme that a "nation depends on its children," the narration suggests that education is more than a national resource; it is a national and even international priority, as references to Hitler and Mussolini demonstrate. Aside from this rather heavy-handed propaganda, *Children at School* represents the concern of an enlightened institutional sponsor and the influence of the "March of Time" style on British documentary film making.

Closer to the "March of Time" approach in spirit, but surpassing it in photography, John Taylor's *Dawn of Iran* (1938, produced by Arthur Elton for the Anglo-Iranian Oil Company) documents and celebrates the growth of the independent, industrial nation. Better as a photographer and editor than as a writer or director, Taylor was unable to give narrative and thematic focus to this film. Though he worked with Flaherty in Aran, with Wright in Ceylon, and with Cavalcanti in Switzerland, Taylor seems less sure of his British experience than of his obvious fascination with the new American style of photojournalism.

Not all documentary film production reflected this new journalistic emphasis, for the British approach was too well founded and too successful to be diverted entirely, as can be seen in two representative films *Eastern Valley* and *Today We Live*. Donald Alexander's *Eastern Valley* (1937), a typical problem-solution film, is concerned with the unemployed miners in a Welsh valley. Produced for the Order of Friends in London, the film suggests that the establishment of farming cooperatives would be a partial aid in getting the men back to work; the film honestly admits that this pragmatic solution to the problem may not be the best one. Like *Housing Problems,* it uses the actual voices of those involved in the situation to create a warm, convincing account of people working together to reverse decay in favor of progress. *Today We Live* (1937) continues the development of the documentary form using strong narrative and actual dialogue. All the actors are nonprofessionals, but the focus of the first half of the film is not altogether clear; by the time the viewer realizes that the film's purpose is to show how people can come together and build community centers,

Children at School: Basil Wright's film, sponsored by the British gas industry, emphasizes the importance of upgrading the British school system in the late 1930's.

he might have become more interested in the ironic use of hymns on the sound track than in the message. Nonetheless, *Today We Live* (produced by Paul Rotha for the National Council of Social Service, and codirected by Ruby Grierson and Ralph Bond) is a true documentary in its searching concern for the quality of English social life in the 1930's.

Most British nonfiction films of the 1930's are pure documentaries concerned with social reconstruction, but other lines of development can be traced in the factual or informational film. Julian Huxley's *Private Life of the Gannets* (1935) is an information film with slight travel film overtones, and Edgar Anstey's *Enough to Eat?* (1936), narrated by Huxley, is a film intended to shock people into the realization that their diets are inadequate. Subtitled "The Nutrition Film," it explains the early development of vitamins and nutrition theory, but it is dreary, despite its reported influence on Britain's official nutrition policies. Also in this information category, but more effective for children, is Mary Field's *Catch of the Season* (1937), which explains, in restrained matter-of-fact narration, the reproductive cycle of trout. Marion Grierson's *For All Eternity* (1935), essentially a travel film, is an attractive record of many English cathedrals, as well as a sensitive account of the role that religion plays in English life. *Transfer of Power* (1939), produced by Shell Oil, provides an interesting, fast-paced, and informative history of the evolution of the lever to the toothed wheel to gears to windmills and finally to lathes and other machines. Using diagrams, simple examples, and very lively narration, this film leaves a lasting impression of a subject that is not usually treated with such imagination; in so doing, it predates the work of Charles and Ray Eames in *A Communications Primer* (1954).[5]

In a totally different area of creativity and expression, Len Lye made his imaginative poster films. Among the first to use color in nonfiction film, he created subtle ads for cheaper parcel post rates (*Colour Box,* 1935), and almost subliminal warnings against enemy spies (*Musical Poster #1,* 1939). His *Swinging the Lambeth Walk* (1940) is an abstract piece of nonsensical fun with no message at all,[6] while *Trade Tattoo* (1937) provides a good contrast to

Flaherty's *Industrial Britain* in its depiction of the workaday world. Not incidentally, it stresses the "power of correspondence" (it was produced by and for the G.P.O.) and seems remarkably ahead of its time with its reverse color images, syncopated rhythms, and fresh, lively appeal. *Rainbow Dance* (1936), also produced for the G.P.O., may be a partial influence on Ed Emshwiller's brilliant experimental film *Relativity* (1966). In each of his films, Lye fuses brilliant graphics, bold colors, and inventive music and sounds to create whimsical but informative "posters" which are as fresh today as they were thirty years ago.

It is ironic and perhaps unfortunate for the development of the art of film making that British film makers began to perfect the documentary approach at precisely the same time—the beginning of World War II—that they were obliged to begin the production of factual, informational, and strictly propaganda films. Just as the directors inside and outside the G.P.O. Film Unit had developed a clearer understanding of the relationship of film aesthetics and utilitarian goals, they confronted the ugly realities of planning for civilian and military communications in war. Just as government sponsorship of films was being phased out in favor of commercial and institutional sponsorship, the government was forced back into a full program of film making for military purposes. And just as experimentation in sound, sight, and color had reached its full peak, newer and different techniques had to be developed for such different aspects as training films and combat photography.

Signaling this change in emphasis was *London Can Take It* (1940), jointly directed by Humphrey Jennings and Harry Watt. A record of one night during the first German blitz bombing of London, it records, through a narration from American journalist Quentin Reynolds, the strength of the British people. This was to be the theme of dozens of films to come, as Britain helped to advocate democracy and the war effort at home and abroad.

Within the relatively limited span of ten years, the British documentary movement in the 1930's created a wholly new film form and established Britain's most permanent contribution to the development of world cinema. It is significant as a movement for the breadth of its achievement and for the consistent dedication of its participants to the improvement of public information and the awakening of social consciousness. The British tradition in nonfiction film making has continued to develop in many different directions, but its foundations—on the principles and productions of Grierson, Cavalcanti, and others—still continue to influence young film makers. The success of these pioneers is only partially represented in the film archives; their real achievement lies in their stimulation of British thought and communication.

NOTES

1 "Alberto Cavalcanti: His Advice to Young Producers of Documentary," *Film Quarterly*, 9 (Summer 1955) , pp. 354–55·

2 John Grierson, *Grierson on Documentary*, ed. Forsyth Hardy (London, Faber and Faber, Ltd., 1966) , p. 181.

3 For an introductory account of Cavalcanti's career, see Emir Rodrigues Monegal, "Alberto Cavalcanti: His Career," *The Quarterly of Film, Radio, and Television*, 9, No. 4 (Summer 1955) , pp. 341–54·

4 For additional comment on "The March of Time" series, see Chapter Five.

5 The Shell Film Unit has been especially active in the production of non-fiction films; for an appraisal, see Stuart Legg, "Shell Film Unit: Twenty-One Years," *Sight & Sound*, 23, No. 4 (Apr.–June 1954) , pp. 209–11.

6 *Swinging the Lambeth Walk* has been confused with *Germany Calling* (1941) , an ironic piece of camp editing of German soldiers marching to the tune of "Swinging the Lambeth Walk."

CHAPTER 5

European and American Nonfiction Film: 1930–1940

While the most important developments in nonfiction film making in the 1930's took place in English-speaking countries, significant experimentation and measurable development and improvement characterized the work of the film makers in major European countries. The avant-garde spirit flourished in France and Belgium; the Russian propagandist tradition influenced the films of Dutchman Joris Ivens, and, later, the films of the American Frontier Film group; and the romantic tradition continued notably in Robert Flaherty's *Man of Aran* and John Ferno's *Easter Island*. When the British were developing the documentary film to fuse aesthetic and political concerns, the European film makers were working within the already established realist and impressionist traditions. In the mid-1930's, Pare Lorentz created a wholly new form of documentary in America, one that reached poetic heights without losing political impact. Near the end of the decade, Willard Van Dyke began the work that was to form the continuing link between the earlier poetic approach of Flaherty and Lorentz and the later realist approach of most American nonfiction film making between 1940 and 1960.

European Developments

In the later 1930's, the events leading up to World War II created a new moral and political climate for film makers. With the exception of the early Nazi propaganda films and the handful of British and American films at the very end of the decade, most of the films related to war in this period were antiwar in sentiment. An early example is Henri Storck's *L'Histoire du Soldat Inconnu* (1930). This "montage d'actualité," as Storck called it, is a silent film relying on the Eisenstein montage and editing techniques for its primary effect.[1] An ironic, repetitive film, it is more important for its influence on subsequent compilation films than for its own statement. But because that statement is silent, the film is a powerful example of how dramatic reedited newsreel footage can become.[2]

The continental "city symphony" tradition, begun with Cavalcanti's *Rien que les Heures* (1926) and Ruttmann's *Berlin: The Symphony of a Great City* (1927), influenced the Swedish film *Gamla Stan* (1931).[3] Directed and photographed by Stig Almqvist, Erik Asklund, Eyvind Johnson, and Arthur Lundqvist, this day in the life of Stockholm seems, much like *Rien que les Heures,* to be a chronicle of despair. Beginning with an image of a doll floating face down in water, and continuing with the lonely, depressed, and seemingly suicidal figure of a woman wandering the streets to her hotel, the film concludes with a fade-out of her being picked up by a man. Perhaps a happy ending, perhaps not, but the recurrent images of water and women at least contribute to the continuity of the film's construction. Its overall ambiguity is underscored with an ironic but delightful musical score, and its psychological use of the camera—attempting to see things as the lonely girl sees them—is an important element. But music, photography, and recurrent images do not form any vision of the city's life, and we are left with a detached and strangely unfulfilling impression. Unlike its French and German predecessors, this short film is more a sonata than a symphony. In Denmark, Poul Henningsen's *The Film of Denmark* (1935) broke even more from the continental city symphony tradition by presenting a lyrical view of everyday life.

In Spain, Luis Buñuel departed from his surrealist experiments to make the angry *Las Hurdes* (*Land Without Bread*, 1932). Unlike his later *Los Olvidados* (*The Lost Ones*, 1950), this early film lacks the control that tempers outrage into convincing argument. A study of the wretched conditions in the Las Hurdes region near the Portuguese border of Spain, this "study of human geography," as Buñuel calls it, observes the lack of hygiene, nutrition, and education in the area, but it does little to suggest solutions to these problems. Unlike Grierson, who would have made the point through narration, Buñuel relies on the ironic use of themes from Brahms' Fourth Symphony. One touch characteristic of the later Buñuel is the luxurious church rising in the middle of squalor. As an information film, even a travel film (but hardly one designed to promote tourism), *Las Hurdes* is an effective and disturbing record of poverty and neglect; but as a social document, it is awkward and as mute as a faded poster despite its tragic theme.

Easter Island (1934) begins as an objective, reportorial record of a Franco-Belgian expedition to Easter Island, but this film provides more than a factual account of the island's geography and the lives of its inhabitants. Underscoring the informational focus of the film is a sense of sadness for the passing of the island's past into the hands of foreigners. In a memorable pattern of rise and fall, the rhythm of the film continually returns us to the past, to the great stone statues, to the grandeur of a culture that is now more represented by a leper colony than by stone guardians. *Easter Island* is the remarkable achievement of director and photographer John Ferno (who was sixteen years old at the time) and editor Henri Storck. The feeling for people, the insight into hopelessness and decay, and the mysterious background music all combine to create, in the Flaherty tradition, an anthropological record and a moving document of human life; not incidentally, these same qualities appear in Ferno's *And So They Live* (1940).

Bad housing conditions and the need for slum clearance and urban planning have been persistent themes for nonfiction film makers. In the tradition begun by Joris Ivens' *Borinage* (1933) and the Anstey-Elton *Housing Problems* (1935), Henri Storck's *Les Maisons de la Misère* (1937) is a distinguished representative. Filmed in a Belgian slum, and sponsored by a society dedicated to slum clearance, this film, unlike its two predecessors, is notable for its consistently dramatic irony, its brilliant sound track and musical score, and its unflinching treatment of human despair. Unlike

Borinage, it controls its outrage in spoken chants and protest songs; unlike *Housing Problems,* it makes the dirt and vermin seem real, not just elements about which people complain in front of an interviewer's camera. Its heavy ironies are memorable: the worn hands of a poor woman doling out coins for rent juxtaposed with a cut to the fat hands of a rich woman entering figures in her ledger; the agent placidly eating a banana as he watches the hungry family he has just evicted, and then slipping on the peel he drops while attempting to catch a boy rescuing his bicycle from the truck carrying the confiscated belongings of the evicted family. The embitterment of these people is written in their faces and echoed in their songs; as the promise of new housing appears, those embittered songs become a happy choral ode at the end of the film. A model social protest film, *Les Maisons de la Misère* achieves what Ivens attempted in *Borinage.*

Not all the European films of the early 1930's were concerned with the ugly themes of war, poverty, and disease. The beautiful French film *Vocation* (1935) depicts the solemn grace in the lives of Benedictine monks as they go about a typical day. Director Jean-Yves de la Cour has mixed narration (in French) and chants as a background for the stark beauty of the photography. Although *Vocation* portrays the ritual dignity of the monks' lives, it has to go behind cloistered walls, into a world where time stands still, to capture beauty. Film makers such as Storck, Buñuel, and Ferno kept their cameras focused on the harsh realities of the contemporary world, realities of poverty, disease, and Nazi aggression. While the wretched of the world looked to death as their only revenge against life, the Germans were coolly planning their total conquest; their hideous precision is recorded in their propaganda films.

Nazi Propaganda Films

Unlike the propaganda films produced in democratic countries, the Nazi propaganda films do not appeal to the reason and understanding of their audience; like their democratic counterparts, they are marked by an emotional-nationalistic fervor, but they go much further in suppressing rational discourse in favor of an outright appeal to the aroused nationalism of Nazi Germany. Like the Americans, they used factual footage, some of it captured from their enemies, and promulgated their themes in a series of psychologically masterful, technically brilliant films.[4] Like the Russians before them, the Nazis emphasized the state as the primary force; individuals were always secondary, always subordinate to the will and good of the state. But unlike the Russians, they were not concerned with the reality of the world, only with the distorted reality of their program for world conquest.

Among the early films advocating the Nazi Party line are *Blutendes Deutschland* (1933), *Hans Westmar, Einer von Vielen* (1934), *Bilddokumente* (1935), and *Für Uns* (1937).[5] But the most revealing of these films, and the greatest propaganda film of all, is Leni Riefenstahl's *Triumph of the Will* (*Triumph des Willens*, 1936). The film records the actual spectacle of the 1934 Nazi Party congress in Nuremberg, but its real purpose is the deification of Hitler as the spiritual leader of the Germans.[6] It is a solemn, symbolic film, beautifully photographed and edited with a sense of structure and rhythm that make it the rival of its Russian masters. It should be studied not as propaganda only, but also as art of the highest order; no film has been more vilified for its subject matter, yet no film has been more misunderstood.[7] *Triumph of the Will* and Riefenstahl's *Olympia* are among the greatest nonfiction films of all time.[8]

The Riefenstahl approach resulted in grandiose, mythic propaganda, but the more conventional approach is continued in Martin Rikli's *Wir Erobern Land* (*We Conquer the Soil*, 1936), a formal film of praise to the young men and women in the Nazi labor camps. Praising their discipline, the film shows the machinelike efficiency of corps of lean and muscular men at work in projects in agriculture, construction, and conservation. The photography here is soft focus and misty at times, and in sharp focus at others, but the musical score recalls the travel film and does not create the intended mystical mood. And at one exercise session, the unlikely presence of Busby Berkeley is reflected in the unintentionally humorous sequence where workers whistle as they perform their calisthenics in the ditches. Like *Triumph of the Will*, this is a film for which history has created a viewing audience more likely to respond to its

Triumph of the Will: In one of the most awesome scenes of this staged spectacle, Hitler marches in review of thousands of massed soldiers. Photograph courtesy The Museum of Modern Art Film Stills Archive.

shape, form, and technique, than to its content; but like the early Riefenstahl effort, it provides an incomparable insight into the regimentation, dedication, and energy of the members of the Nazi party, and like her *Olympia,* it is fascinated with the muscular beauty of the male figure.

Riefenstahl's masterpiece, and one of the greatest of all nonfiction films, is *Olympia* (Parts I and II, 1938). The ultimate sports film, it presents sports as poetry, not politics; it was not a German government film, and Goebbels opposed it.[9] With this film, as with *Triumph of the Will,* careful planning assured that every possible camera position and angle would be available.[10] There are cameras mounted on cars, boats, planes; cameras in ditches and under water; and cameras on traveling cranes, electrically propelled tracks, and balloons. The film is a triumph, not of nihilistic will, but of photography and editing. Every kind of photographic device is used, from still cameras, to slow motion, to telescopic lenses. It documents, it studies, it records that peculiar blend of national pride and individual skill which underscores the patriotic and athletic competition of the Olympic Games. In its appreciation of the sensual beauty of the muscular male body, it is unequaled. Aside from the theatrical opening, picturing the flame carrier leaving the ruins of Greece, the film is a straightforward account, with especially beautiful introductory passages preceding each section. As film essay, *Olympia* is superb; whether it was the subject matter that resisted manipulation for propaganda, or whether it was the director's decision to record the beauty of physical motion, the film transcends propaganda politics. In the sublime sequences portraying the diving events, it transcends earth, providing a poetic experience of flight unparalleled in motion picture history. If Leni Riefenstahl had made no other film, *Olympia* would have secured for her a place in motion picture history.[11]

Joris Ivens and the Political Documentary

At the same time the British developed the documentary with its clear but subordinate political message, the Nazis perfected the propaganda film with its dominant political voice and predetermined reaction. Working, too, with politics and film was the Dutch film maker Joris Ivens. For Ivens, whose first films (*The Bridge,* 1928; *Pile Driving,* 1928; *Rain,* 1929; and *The Breakers,* 1929) were silent impressionist experiments, film could not be separated from politics. It was the film maker's duty and responsibility to participate "directly in the world's most fundamental issues,"[12] not only to document these issues, but to record his own political feelings and impressions about them. Defending this position, Ivens writes,

> My only answer was that a documentary film maker has to have an opinion on such vital issues as fascism or anti-fascism—he *has* to have feelings about these issues, if his work is to have any dramatic or emotional or art value. . . . I was surprised to find that many people automatically assume that any *documentary* film would *inevitably* be objective. Perhaps the term is unsatisfactory, but for me the distinction between the words *document* and *documentary* is quite clear.[13]

In his distinctions about nonfiction film, Ivens seems to be in agreement with Grierson. For both, a documentary film records a fact, an event, a life, but, more important, it takes a point of view, and registers an opinion. In short, it makes politics out of photography. The difference between Grierson and Ivens is one of degree; Grierson never allows politics to dominate his art, while Ivens almost always does. At times his politics becomes art (*The Spanish Earth*), and at other times his art becomes politics (*The 400 Million*). At his best, in a film such as *Power and the Land,* he combines poetry, politics, and photography into a statement of uncommon beauty and strength. On most of these early films, he had the benefit of working with cameramen John Ferno and Robert Capa and with editor Helen van Dongen.

Ivens' first films are silent, lyrical impressions of rhythmic processes: the operation of a railroad bridge, the pile driving that helps to build dikes, the pattern of rain on city streets, and the fluctuation of waves as they break upon the shore. With *Philips-Radio* (also known as *Industrial Symphony*) in 1931, he experimented notably with sound.[14] Traveling to Russia, he realized an empathy with the Russian people's cause and made *Song of Heroes* (1932). But it is not until *Borinage* that Ivens' distinctive approach and style can be seen.

Borinage (1933) reflects Ivens' outrage at the conditions in which miners lived and worked in the Borinage coal region of Southwest Belgium. Writing of his concern for the same district that earlier attracted Vincent Van Gogh, Ivens said, "That is where I went to make my next film, not as a missionary to soften or treat wounds, but as a film maker to reveal the wounds to the rest of the world because I thought that my best way to help in their healing."[15] This often puzzling and unsatisfactory film recreates real events— workers' parades and strikes—using the people of the region in contrast to those in the Domblas coal-mining region of Russia. These Russian sequences appear to be studio made, and are awkward and lifeless in contrast to the footage made in Belgium, almost under combat circumstances.[16] The frequently poor quality and the directness of the photography indicate the adverse conditions under which it was filmed, but also infuse the film with a vitality and an immediateness that more than compensate for the technical weaknesses.

Among the memorable sequences and scenes in *Borinage* are those which show an underfed miner and his hungry family cramped into a tiny sleeping room; miners forced to grub for bits of coal in a slagheap while piles of coal are kept behind barbed wire because the price is too low; and a spontaneous, clenched-fist political march led by a man carrying a portrait of Karl Marx. *Borinage* reflects the sense of outrage of its maker, and it also suggests comparison with the British *Housing Problems* (1935), Storck's *Les Maisons de la Misère* (1937), and Flaherty's *The Land* (1942), but the conditions under which Ivens filmed were considerably different:

> The urgency in which this film was made kept our camera angles severe and orthodox. Or one might say, unorthodox, because super-slickness and photographic affectation were becoming the orthodoxy of the European documentary film. This return to simplicity was actually a stylistic revolution for me. . . . The style of *Borinage* was chosen deliberately and was determined by the decency and the unrelieved plight of the people around us.[17]

Arguing that *Housing Problems* does not make maximum political use of the disagreeable living conditions it pictures, Ivens continues,

> Our aim [in *Borinage*] was to prevent agreeable photographic effects distracting the audience from the unpleasant truths we were showing.

Borinage: Barbed wire separates striking miners from the stockpiles of coal they helped to mine but which, ironically, they are unable to use to warm their own homes. Photograph courtesy The Museum of Modern Art Film Stills Archive.

. . . The film maker must be indignant and angry about the fate of
people before he can find the right camera angle on the dirt and on
the truth. . . . Although all of Flaherty's work had a gentle humanitarian approach, when he came to make *The Land* for the AAA in the
United States he became so indignant and angry about the waste of
people that he found, and the bad conditions that he saw in agriculture, that he made a forceful, accusing film.[18]

These are the words of a film maker committed to redressing social
grievances and to effecting social change. While flawed in photography and in its juxtaposition of Belgian and Russian subjects,
Borinage carries the Marxist conviction that marks all of Ivens'
political documentaries.

Ivens' first important film, *New Earth* (1934), is an angry,
ironic outcry against the progress that it set out to record: the
reclamation of the Zuider Zee in the late 1920's and early 1930's.
The straightforward buildup documents the massive engineering
problems and accomplishments, but the continuity of the film
becomes ironic as we see that the reclaimed land and dams brought
depression, not prosperity.[19] The wheat, planted on the land reclaimed from the sea, is returned to the sea when the bottom drops
out of the world wheat market in the early 1930's. As the wheat is
dumped, we see hungry children and strikers, and we hear a bitter
song, reminiscent of the agitated, ironic music of Kurt Weill. As
with *Borinage,* there are flaws in the technical aspects of this film.
The photography and use of direct sound record the back-breaking
labor involved in reclaiming the land, but only a brief aerial shot
can reveal the scope of the massive project. As with *The Bridge,* this
is a process film, and its final form is a tribute to Helen van
Dongen's editing as much as it is to the work of the laborers, for the
reclamation of film footage seems to have been almost as much work
as the reclamation of land from the sea. The first two parts of the
film, recording the construction of the dams and the planting and
harvesting of wheat, are heroic, but it is not until the third part,
when we see the results of that harvest, that the film's force and interest are evident. The greatest irony of the film is not the destruction
of the harvest for which so many gave their energies, but the fact that
the completed film could not be screened in Paris because the censors
objected to it as being "too realistic."[20]

Over the years, Ivens' political sympathies have taken him to many countries in which political ferment or revolution was occurring: China, Russia, Indonesia, Cuba, Vietnam. His first film of revolution was half-fiction, half-documentary, *The Spanish Earth*. Produced by a group of Americans who favored the Loyalist cause in the Spanish Civil War, *The Spanish Earth* (1937) is a moving film which suffers, not from a lack of patriotic fervor, but from a lack of political focus. One of the major factors in the Spaniards' defense of their country was agriculture; if the Fascist aggression increased, it would cut off the irrigation and, therefore, the supplies necessary to feed soldiers and citizens alike. For lack of water, they would lose title to their land. Unfortunately, the emphasis of the film is on the war and not on how it affected the irrigation problem. The background of the Civil War is not explained, a fault which is all the more apparent when the film is contrasted, for example, to Frank Capra's "Why We Fight" series, a group of films that had an equally hard task of explaining the background of war. The moral assumptions behind the Spanish resistance are taken for granted, and it is likewise assumed that the viewer knows the facts about the Fascist threat. Perhaps it is not fair to evaluate political propaganda outside the immediate historical context in which it was made. The intrusion of warfare into the quiet landscape seems almost unreal, and that, of course, is the point, but the photography does not capture the combat excitement which Ivens felt was present in the footage.[21]

Some of the photography, especially that taken away from the combat, is beautifully evocative of the bare, dry landscape and the hard life of the Spanish peasants. There is a feeling for place and for the nuances of life that infuses every image. The narration was written and spoken by Ernest Hemingway, and his earnest prose matches the visual images with the same direct, ironic force that Capra was later to achieve in his war films. This is essential Hemingway, calm without outrage, moral without righteousness. He begins, "This Spanish earth is dry and hard and the faces of the men who work on that earth are hard and dry from the sun." And when the fighting begins, he says, "This is the moment that all the rest of war prepares for, when six men go forward into death to

The Spanish Earth: Spanish women flee through the streets as civil-war fighting breaks out in their village. Photograph courtesy The Museum of Modern Art Film Stills Archive.

walk across a stretch of land and by their presence on it prove—this earth is ours."[22]

While the political focus is not clear, the narration and the music are. An arrangement of Spanish folk tunes by Marc Blitzstein, the musical score is a quiet and lilting reminder of prewar happiness. Made under difficult circumstances, with little money, *The Spanish Earth* is a pioneering revolutionary film. In this category, it joins the great Eisenstein films, but unlike them, it seems unfair to judge it as art now that the revolution is over. Ivens participated in a monumental battle against fascist aggression, and aided that cause with his film; if he did not raise that film to art, he raised social consciousness and funds for ambulances, and under the circumstances, those were his intentions.

The Spanish Earth was not successful with the critics;[23] nevertheless, Ivens immediately turned his attention to China, an area of conflict which would later be an important battleground in World War II. *The 400 Million* (1939) is pro-China in the Japanese-Chinese conflict; in its attack on the Japanese brutalities against innocent Chinese civilians, the film resembles the American wartime documentary *The Battle of China*. It shows the efforts of the Chinese resistance, but it does not evoke the same picture of Chinese peasant strength that another "Why We Fight" film, *The Battle of Russia,* does for the people of Leningrad. As a political documentary, it is too reserved, too dull, and too long.

Ivens' work with the Spanish and Chinese themes did more than raise funds in the United States; it helped to arouse American film makers to the potentialities of the politically oriented documentary. In 1935, the New Film Alliance in New York sponsored showings of *Borinage* and *New Earth,* and in 1937, the Frontier Film Group produced two films in the Ivens tradition: *Heart of Spain* and *China Strikes Back*. Ivens was well known, and well respected, when he came to the United States, at Pare Lorentz' invitation, to make a film for the Department of Agriculture about rural electrification and its effect on the prosperity of the American farmer.[24] *Power and the Land* (1940) is a wonderfully evocative piece of Americana, in the tradition of Lorentz' *The River*. Soft and sentimental, rather than challenging, it makes its points with easy

Power and the Land: The need for electrification and refrigeration is dramatically brought home to farmer Bill Parkinson (left) as cans of sour milk are returned to his dairy. Photograph courtesy The Museum of Modern Art Film Stills Archive.

emphasis, occasional irony, and, not incidentally, a beautiful musical score by Douglas Moore. The film was shot on the farm of the Parkinsons in Ohio; by showing their predawn to after-dark routine, it presents the discomfort and tediousness of labor on a nonelectrified farm. The structure follows a parallel pattern, so that every problem presented in the first part of the film is followed by a solution in the second part. In the first half, all the tasks are difficult, but, in the second, with the aid of electricity, they are easier to perform and, more important, bring satisfaction and profits. The theme is presented in a direct and factual manner; the film criticizes the private electric utilities for their reluctance to electrify outlying farms and encourages farmers to form cooperatives financed by the government: "It wouldn't be so hard with power, but one man can't change that alone." The narration, written by Stephen Vincent Benét, resembles that in the latter part of *The River,* but it is less forceful with its soft ironies and effective use of understatement. An emotional film that leaves a lasting impression of the very heartland of America, *Power and the Land,* like *The River,* continues to affect audiences. American documentary films such as these fuse Flaherty's poetic approach with their own particular combination of hard political realism and sentimental values, and are remarkable achievements in the power of art to transcend mere politics. Long after the political questions of rural electrification, soil conservation, and dam building are answered, these films remain forceful— as, for example, Ivens' *The 400 Million* does not—because they are ultimately concerned, not with politics, but with lasting human values, with love of the soil, with love of hard work, and with the love that people share with each other. That *Power and the Land* could have been made by a foreigner, new to the United States, and emerge as wholly American as a painting by Edward Hopper is both a tribute to the subject and to the sensibility and vision of the director. Ivens' affinity for the struggles of peoples everywhere, whether Spain, or China, or America, is nowhere better represented than in this lovely film. It is not a militant film, nor a particularly revolutionary one, since the forming of cooperatives is pictured as a fairly simple process. But with the visual sensibility of master cameramen—Floyd Crosby and Arthur Ornitz—with Van Dongen's in-

Power and the Land: Director Joris Ivens prepares a scene with Mrs. Parkinson. Photograph courtesy The Museum of Modern Art Film Stills Archive.

cisive editing rhythm, and with the integrated commentary and musical score, Ivens has left Americans a classic film document that is too often overlooked.[25]

Pare Lorentz and the U.S. Film Service

The spirit behind Joris Ivens' achievements with *Power and the Land* came from Pare Lorentz, the one man most responsible for the growth and development of nonfiction film making in the United States during the 1930's.[26] Lorentz directed three distinguished films (*The Plow That Broke the Plains, The River,* and *The Fight for Life*) and produced two others (Ivens' *Power and the Land* and Flaherty's *The Land*). He influenced President Franklin D. Roosevelt to create the U.S. Film Service in 1938.

Lorentz' enthusiasm for America, for American problems, and for film were perfect for New Deal America. The country was plagued by the after-effects of the Depression, including the great problems of water and soil conservation and unemployment. People looked to the government for massive financial support programs, but Lorentz felt that they should also ask the government for explanation, information, and direction to help solve these problems. Although various agencies of the government had made informational, training, and propaganda films since the beginning of the century, there was no official, organized production effort until the short-lived USFS was established. Lorentz was convinced that the government should accept the responsibility of producing films which dealt with major contemporary problems, problems in which Hollywood had shown no interest. As a student of film, Lorentz believed that a government-produced film could be both aesthetically pleasing and politically productive. In this sense, Lorentz would seem to be in agreement with Grierson, but the similarities between the two men existed only in their theories. Lorentz' films consistently achieve the highest artistic distinction, blending sight, sound, and theme in a way that no Grierson production (with the possible exception of *Night Mail*) was ever to match. Lorentz was an idealist, and a poet, much like Flaherty, but he was also an accomplished film maker, a sensitive student of film music, and a practical politician; his films are always as beautiful as they are relevant.

The critical success of *The Plow That Broke The Plains* (1936) made it possible for Lorentz to film *The River,* which, despite the political controversy that was to accompany each step of Lorentz' career until 1940, led to the establishment of the USFS in August, 1938.[27] Lorentz became the first director of the USFS, guiding its operations to conform to its two basic purposes: (1) to educate government employees, and (2) to inform the public about contemporary problems. The first year was impeded by Congressional discussion over the propriety and politics of the project and by a general lack of funds for production.[28] Although *The Plow That Broke the Plains* and *The River* were not produced by the USFS,[29] they are best seen as part of the group of films produced by the unit, including *The Fight for Life* (1940), *Power and the Land* (1940), and *The Land* (1941, directed by Robert Flaherty, produced initially by the USFS but completed under the Agricultural Adjustment Administration). Each of these films, in part or in whole, bears the stamp of Lorentz' vision and technique.

The reasons behind Lorentz' success are evident in the films themselves. First, they are notable for their unity of sight, sound (music and narration), and overall sociopolitical vision. Perhaps it was because he wrote and directed his own films, or because he had distinguished collaborators, but whatever the reason, Lorentz was consistently able to produce dramatic nonfiction films that have seldom been surpassed. Second, his films are unmistakably "American." They resound with a naturalist's love of land, with a poet's love of place names, and with a patriot's love of the traditions and heritage out of which the country was built. Often, like Flaherty's films, they seem rational to the point of innocence, enthusiastic to the point of naïveté, but they are as native as Walt Whitman's poetry in their feeling for American values. Third, while they generally conform to the documentary problem-solution structure, these films rely on varying combinations of repetition, rhythm, and parallel structure, so that problems presented in the first part of the films are solved in the second part, but solved through such an artistic juxtaposition of image, sound, and motif that their unity and coherence of development set them distinctly apart from such films, for example, as the British *Housing Problems* or Ivens' *New Earth*. Finally, Lorentz' films brought to the United States, but in a different way, the documentary principles of the British school. They were intended to appeal to patriotic emotion, and to move audiences to realize that the problems of one region were the problems of the whole country. By bluntly showing the erosion and destruction of human and natural resources, they called for social change. But they called for this social change, not with the bluntness of Ivens or the urbanity of Grierson, but with the metaphor, music, and mastery of a poet. Like Flaherty or Ivens, Lorentz was a school unto himself, but an influence on nonfiction film making that provided challenges for the whole generation of film makers that followed.

Lorentz' first film, *The Plow That Broke the Plains* (1936), handles the social and economic effects of the Depression and the Dust Bowl crisis with the same sensitivity and distinction evident in John Steinbeck's *The Grapes of Wrath* and in *Let Us Now Praise Famous Men,* the photo-text collaboration of Walker Evans and James Agee.[30] Sketching the history of the Great Plains, from the westward movement and the settlement of the prairies by cattlemen and farmers, to the agricultural boom created by World War I, to the chaos and despair caused by technological progress, the stock market crash, drought, dust storms, and Depression, the film combines factual footage within a problem-solution structure to make a persuasive statement for the conservation of human and natural resources.[31] In its visual images, the film is as striking and as memorable as the bare, shocking still photographs of Walker Evans and Dorothea Lange, and in its use of sound, it fulfills the experimentation with integrated music, sound, and narration begun the same year in *Night Mail*. Like *Night Mail,* it praises men, not for their efficiency, but for their endurance in the face of inefficiency, carelessness, and greed—their own and others'; unlike *Night Mail,* it has a political and social axe to grind.

The documentary argument of the film is presented in a titled prologue, rather than in continuous narration; however, the irony of the images, the comment, the music, and the sound accomplish

The Plow That Broke the Plains: The plow that broke the plains and destroyed a nation's agricultural economy also caused widespread human
suffering and displacement of families. Photograph courtesy The Museum
of Modern Art Film Stills Archive.

what a more continuous narration was to do in *The River*. The film's strength lies in its use of image and sound, and in its often ironic juxtaposition of images (such as the counterpoint image of tractors and tanks against the sound of threshing machines and bullets). The rhythm of the film's progression is keyed to the laze of the wheat fields and the whirl of the dust storms; it lacks the operatic buildup and excitement of *The River*. *The Plow That Broke the Plains* was made in the cutting room, not from a worked-out shooting script, and only the music remains as a truly distinguished part of this flawed whole. Virgil Thomson's score is magnificent Americana, sprightly and lively when the film depicts good times, and sonorous and ironic in its use of religious anthems and hymns when it pictures the bad times brought by the dust storms. With insight and honesty, Lorentz reviewed his own film:

> Thus, with some outstanding photography and music, *The Plow That Broke the Plains* is an unusual motion picture which might have been a really great one had the story and construction been up to the rest of the workmanship. As it is, it tells the story of the Plains and it tells it with some emotional value—an emotion that springs out of the soil itself. Our heroine is the grass, our villain the sun and the wind, our players the actual farmers living in the Plains country. It is a melodrama of nature, the tragedy of turning grass into dust, a melodrama that only Carl Sandburg or Willa Cather perhaps could tell as it should be told.[32]

Aware that he had found his vision, but not his voice, Lorentz was encouraged by the critical success which greeted the film as it was released commercially in major bookings across the country. Despite the legal and constitutional complications involving the nature of the film (was it information or propaganda, or both?) and the overtones from the presidential election campaign that marred its reception in some areas, *The Plow That Broke the Plains* broke the fertile ground of American documentary development. A year later, in *The River*, Lorentz was to find a voice to match his vision.

For Lorentz, a sense of history was a sense of destiny. As he traced the history of the Great Plains, he traced the history of the Mississippi River and its tributaries to begin *The River* (1937), a film that is both a haunting, memorable document of misuse and an uplifting tribute to conservation.[33] It is a sentimental, liberal film echoing the 1930's: " 'ill clad, ill housed, ill fed'—and in the greatest river valley in the world!" But it speaks with the transcendent power of Walt Whitman (to whose free verse influence Lorentz' narration owes so much) .

By telling the story of the river, Lorentz tells the story of the precarious ecological balance of people, land, water, and crops that depend upon it. The prologue begins,

> From as far West as Idaho,
> Down from the glacier peaks of the Rockies—
> From as far East as New York,
> Down from the turkey ridges of the Alleghenies
> Down from Minnesota, twenty five hundred miles,
> The Mississippi River runs to the Gulf.
> Carrying every drop of water, that flows down two-thirds of the continent,
> Carrying every brook and rill, rivulet and creek,
> Carrying all the rivers that run down two-thirds the continent
> The Mississippi runs to the Gulf of Mexico.
> Down the Yellowstone, the Milk, the White and Cheyenne;
> The Cannonball, the Musselshell, the James and the Sioux;
> Down the Judith, the Grand, the Osage, and the Platte,
> The Skunk, the Salt, the Black, and Minnesota;
> Down the Rock, the Illinois, and the Kankakee
> The Allegheny, the Monongahela, Kanawha, and Muskingum;
> Down the Miami, the Wabash, the Licking and the Green
> The Cumberland, the Kentucky, and the Tennessee;
> Down the Ouchita, the Wichita, the Red, and Yazoo—
> Down the Missouri three thousand miles from the Rockies;
> Down the Ohio a thousand miles from the Alleghenies;
> Down the Arkansas fifteen hundred miles from the Great Divide;
> Down the Red, a thousand miles from Texas;
> Down the great Valley, twenty-five hundred miles from Minnesota,
> Carrying every rivulet and brook, creek and rill,
> Carrying all the rivers that run down two-thirds the continent—
> The Mississippi runs to the Gulf.[34]

The theme of this film is a simple one: improper planting, forestry, and harvesting deplete the land; depleted land cannot hold the top soil, and erosion results; erosion leads to floods; and floods cripple agriculture, industry, and people. The structure of the film's narrative is chronological, but also somewhat circular. *The River* begins with the growth of the Mississippi River from its tributaries all over the central part of the United States. It shows the devastating effect of forestry and cotton farming on the overused land; it depicts the growth of the heavy industries which exploited the river valleys; and, finally, it records the floods, reaching the inevitable conclusion that poor land makes poor people. The epilogue recounts the work of the Tennessee Valley Authority in helping to restore the Mississippi River and its tributary system to something approximating its earlier balance. The story, then, is a simple one, but the treatment is not.

The River is a masterpiece of operatic unity of sight and sound, drama and fact. The three major sequences of the film—water, lumber, flood—open with stirring roll calls of the names of American rivers, trees, and flooded towns; these catalogs are repeated for emphasis and elaboration at other times. Virgil Thomson's score establishes basic themes and motifs for each sequence, and mixes hymnlike sonorities with ragtime syncopation to show not only the richness of American music, but also the ambiguity and unpredictability of the great river valley. The photography by Willard Van Dyke, Floyd Crosby, and Stacey Woodward is superb. The predominant visual movement in the film is from left to right, and from top to bottom. Shot after shot is memorable long after one has seen the film.[35] While most of the footage was shot directly on location, without the benefit of a shooting script, and assembled later in New York by Lorentz, there is some footage from two Hollywood films, *Come and Get It* and *Showboat,* as well as considerable newsreel footage in the film. A great montage depicts the history of erosion and floods from 1902 to 1937. A dripping icicle begins the flow; as the years pass, this trickle becomes a stream, and the streams become rivers as they tear across the land and become floods. The movement of the images of water carries a sense of destiny that is as exciting as any Eisenstein montage. As the flood expands, the shots expand in scope; to increase the tension and to prepare for the climax, shots of turbulent water are intercut with those showing the downward flow of water. The narrator once again calls the roll of rivers and cities; large sections of the previous

The River: Improper planting, poor irrigation, and general neglect led to the erosion that all but destroyed the Mississippi River valley. Photograph courtesy The Museum of Modern Art Film Stills Archive.

narration are reused as the flood and the film build to a dramatic climax. But *The River* defies synopsis, for its values are only partly literary. There is no equivalent way to capture the poetic prose of the narration or the cumulative effect of the music.[36] One does not soon forget the drum rolls which underscore the growth of the cotton and lumber industries, or the ominous sound of dripping water that is soon to become a raging torrent. And one remembers the shots of denuded forests in the dim light: "We cut the top off Pennsylvania and sent it down the river." Repeatedly, continuously, the narration makes its ironic point about progress: "But at what a cost!"

The overall mood of *The River* comes from its skillful use of Americana: names, maps, songs, musical themes. The viewer is reminded, both with image and sound, that the Mississippi River problem is an American problem, one that transcends state boundaries and historical periods, and, ultimately, one that depletes everyone economically and spiritually. Unfortunately, the last one-third of the film (approximately ten minutes) does not have the imagination of the first two-thirds, for Lorentz was obligated to show what the government was doing to solve the problem; it is devoted to a straightforward account of the progress made by the TVA and the Farm Security Administration, and while it records substantial improvement and projects great hope, it does not seem a wholly integrated element of the film.

President Roosevelt encouraged the general release of *The Plow That Broke the Plains,* and when he saw *The River* he was equally, if not more, enthusiastic; but there were political implications inherent in the commercial release of a government film and these created obstacles similar to those that frustrated the release of the earlier film. When it was considered as a possible nomination for the Academy Award for a short film, Walt Disney, among other Hollywood leaders, objected on the grounds that it would create an unhealthy precedent for competition between government and private enterprise.[37] But *The River* was warmly received in London by Grierson and Flaherty, and won the "Best Documentary" award at the Venice Film Festival in 1938 in competition with Riefenstahl's *Olympia.*

This international recognition of Lorentz and the American documentary film had immediate and far-reaching effects in the United States. The public responded favorably to the popular "March of Time" films, and now they began to show interest in original, imaginative American documentary films. On a scholarly level, serious film students and critics began to study the nonfiction film. And in a commercial move similar to the establishment of Grierson's Film Centre in London, Ralph Steiner and Willard Van Dyke formed American Documentary Films, Inc., and later produced *The City* (1939). But none of these factors was sufficient to meet the demand for documentary films dealing with contemporary problems. Since Hollywood was concerned with fictional films and had little or no interest in the nonfiction film before the war, there was no other alternative to these early commercial production units but for the United States government to continue and increase its support for the production of films through the establishment of the U.S. Film Service in 1938.

After devoting several years to the problems of soil and water conservation, Lorentz turned his attention to an equally important national problem: public health. Lorentz was disturbed by the interrelationship of the problems of infant and maternal mortality, unemployed workers, and malnutrition. To deal with the solutions to these problems, he planned a feature-length film, using professional actors, real and constructed sets, with a fully integrated script of dialogue and a dramatic musical score. The result was *The Fight for Life* (1940). In many ways, of course, this is a borderline film, for it combines the documentary and the theatrical approaches in a new form; yet its overriding concern with informing the public with the facts about a grave national health problem makes it one of the landmarks in the history of nonfiction film.[38]

The film does not attempt to present solutions for all health problems, but it does take an especially strong stand against what it calls the "tragic accidents" that occur in the nation's general hospitals. The main argument favors better training for obstetricians and other doctors who handle childbirth cases, but it also emphasizes pre- and post-natal care, proper diet for expectant mothers and their children, and encourages the idea of the tough, dedicated doctor, concerned with his patients' health, the condition of his city, and the hospital with which he is affiliated. Furthermore, it takes the controversial stand that doctors should be prepared to serve the nation's poor so that they, too, can benefit from the medical care that cost and ignorance so often prohibit them from enjoying. Like Lorentz' earlier films, it deals with an explosive public issue, and also like them, it is far ahead of its time in its hard-hitting, honest approach.

The Fight for Life finds drama in a young doctor's disillusionment at the loss of a mother in childbirth. The film opens in a hospital operating room; an operation is in progress, but it is not identified. We see the faces of tense nurses and doctors, and hear the sound of the heartbeat on the sound track. This suspense is relieved only with the camera's revelation that a child has been born. Everything appears to be normal, but the mother's heart fails; a fight for her life begins, but she dies. The doctor decides to resume his education at a maternity clinic in the slums to learn the causes of death in childbirth. To this point, the film is taut, professional, and gripping. The second part of the film is a straightforward but wooden exposition of the training of the doctor and his internship at an actual delivery in a filthy tenement. The film spares none of the dirt in making its points about the dangers inherent in childbirth at home. In the two most dramatic sequences of the film, we follow each step in a difficult childbirth. Here the photography is superbly theatrical: characters are presented almost as if in portrait, spotlighted in dark rooms and laboratories. In a home where the husband has left to look for work in another city, the grandmother tells of the economic problems that have caused changes since she was young. Then, underscoring the generation gap, we see her in soft distance focus in the next room as her grandchild is born in the foreground of the frame. Almost immediately the mother hemorrhages, and emergency surgery is performed. But in contrast to the situation depicted at the opening of the film, this patient lives, even though the childbirth and surgery take place in squalid conditions. The importance of proper planning and well-trained doctors is now self-evident.

The semifictional documentary has its faults, not the least of which, in this case, is that the film is too theatrical and professional. When we see the real farmers in *Power and the Land* or the postal workers in *Night Mail* or the fishermen in *North Sea,* there is a sense of spontaneity and believability in their "performances" before the camera that is lacking in this film using actors speaking lines from a prepared script. Nonetheless, the photography is brilliant, especially in the interior sequences, and the narration is convincing. Under all, Louis Gruenberg's musical score exploits the heartbeat with drums and strings to create at times a haunting rhythm and at times a symphony of life.[39]

Pare Lorentz' films have made a remarkable contribution to the development of the American nonfiction film. Rooted in the different traditions established by Flaherty and Grierson, and carrying some of the passionate social consciousness of Ivens, they take a penetrating look at the necessity for social change without compromising poetic strength, technical brilliance, and convincing realism. With Flaherty, he approaches problems with humanitarian concern; with Grierson, he approaches them with sociological realism; and with Ivens, he approaches them with compassion. But to his own vision of man's condition, he adds a sense of the integral relationship of sight and sound that is the equal of any film maker, fiction or nonfiction.[40]

The "March of Time" Series

In 1935, producer Louis de Rochemont combined his talents with the editorial and reportorial resources of Time-Life, Inc., to create the popular, influential series, the "March of Time." Designed to present the "news behind the news" for a mass audience, this monthly film magazine borrowed three important factors from other sources. From journalism, it borrowed the impartial, objective approach of the news story and the analytical approach of the editorial. From fiction films, it adapted the dramatic approach to the telling of current events. The "March of Time" series is famous for its histrionic style, its ironic presentation, its informality, and its stentorian "voice-of-god" narration. Despite its often slick and superficial approach, this series exerted a wide influence on the development of screen journalism and on the documentary film. Along with *The River* and its success at the Venice Film Festival in 1938, the "March of Time" series created worldwide interest in American nonfiction film making.

Perhaps most influential in the "March of Time" format was the use of personal interviews and personal portraits of important people, the use of diagrams and charts, and the "authority" of its narrative presentation and interpretation of the news. Some scenes were reenacted, and some footage was shot directly for the films, but whatever the source, the "March of Time" had the undeniable stamp of research and authority that mass-produced journalism can often bring to a story. The marks of research and the tone of authority do not always equal honesty and objectivity, and the films had no reservations about making drama out of fact.

Typical of these films is *Progressive Education* (1936), a tribute to the "late, great Horace Mann" and the new schools where fun and relevance, not facts and recitations, prepare children for the future. Or *The Movies March On* (1939), a brief history of the movies, less notable for its historical coverage than for its support of the Hays Office and the idea of Hollywood's responsibility to the public. Or *Story of the White House* (1936), another mistitled film, an account of the New Deal and Franklin D. Roosevelt, not an architectural or cultural history of the home of the nation's first family. Or *Problems of Working Girls* (1936), an alarming account of the exploitation of small-town girls by New York City businessmen.

To compete with "The March of Time" for mass audiences across the nation, and to provide the thousands of theatres in the RKO chain with a screen magazine, Frederic Ullman, Jr., developed "This Is America" (1942–51), a lively, engaging, and sentimental series devoted primarily to the values of small-town America. Its 112 issues cover a vast range of topics, but the emphasis is almost always on traditional America, not—as with its more famous competition—on bigness and growth. Although its overall tone is equally optimistic, its focus is considerably narrower, but nonetheless effective.[41] To counteract the "March of Time" series, a group of liberal and progressive film makers formed Nykino and undertook a series known as "The World Today." Less successful than the Time-Life, Inc., venture, and limited in funds and staff, they reached only a small audience, but from Nykino, the Frontier Film Group was born.[42]

The Frontier Film Group

While Lorentz and the producers of the "March of Time" worked within the system to change public opinion, the Frontier Film Group took a more radical and more militant stand.[43] As a group, they made only a few films, but in that effort they managed to attack major social evils at home and abroad.[44] Two of their films—*Heart of Spain* and *Return to Life* (both 1937) —deal with Spain; like Ivens' *The Spanish Earth*, they were made for fund-raising purposes. Both films are chiefly the work of Herbert Kline, but *Return to Life* is distinguished by the photography of Henri Cartier-Bresson. Kline also directed *Crisis* (1938), a record of the struggle of the Czech people for freedom from Nazi terrorism, but this was not a Frontier film. *China Strikes Back* (1937), similar in intent but even less interesting than Ivens' *The 400 Million*, takes a pro-China side in the Chinese-Japanese conflict. *People of the Cumberland* (1938) concerns the work of restoring economic security to the Tennessee mountain region. Other Frontier films include *The White Flood* (1940) and *United Action* (1939), a record of the striking automobile workers in Detroit.

The final and most distinguished release of the Frontier Film Group is Paul Strand's and Leo Hurwitz' *Native Land* (1942). Like Lorentz' *The Fight for Life,* it is a reenactment, using professional actors, and like the Lorentz film, it is an angry indictment of social injustice. In 1935, Strand had supervised the first Mexican documentary film for the Mexican government, a film titled *The Wave* (*Pescados*). This impartial presentation of the conflict between fishermen off the Vera Cruz coast of Mexico and the vested interests that were interfering with their livelihood is directly in the documentary tradition, but its failure to take a firm stand weakens its force. But with *Native Land,* Strand and Hurwitz tackle a grave problem with determination and conviction.

Native Land takes the whole question of personal and civil rights as its concern, and depicts the brutal violations of the Bill of Rights as recorded in actual testimony before the Senate Civil Liberties Committee hearings in 1938. The film's theme is the irony of injustice in a land of independence and freedom, the irony of tyranny and conspiracy in the land of the Bill of Rights. But this broad focus is quickly narrowed to the American labor movement in its struggle to organize in the post-Depression years. In four separate episodes (Midwest farm, big city, southern village, and industrial town), the film depicts actual incidents of murder and brutality, atrocities committed against the "little people . . . who take the Bill of Rights for granted." It is in these episodes that the film shows its strength, yet it is in the lack of cohesiveness between these sequences that the film's focus dulls and weakens its message. The episodes are related in theme, but the argument is not always clear. The "enemy within" includes spies, private armies, strike breakers, militant and armed groups such as the Ku Klux Klan, and profit-hungry industrialists. The film does not name these forces, and only identifies them as "the big shots," "the interests," and the "powerful corporations." At the same time, it depicts the union members as the "new pioneers" who "put the Bill of Rights into action." Made as a tribute to the common working man, *Native Land* is a gripping, patriotic film; but as an indictment of the "handful of fascist-minded corporations," it is uneven despite its realism.[45]

Native Land is a strong and powerful documentary film, and it narrowly misses being a great one. It recalls the strengths of the past, opens the wounds of the present, and calls a challenge to the future. Paul Strand's photography creates a dark, brooding mood, full of suspicion and suspense; his restless and constantly moving camera records the ironic duality of exterior growth and interior decay. If there can be such a thing, it is paranoid photography, infusing every frame with a fearful and suspicious mood. In the prologue, especially, the photography is matched by the superb editing rhythm; but in the sequences featuring the professional actors, another directorial hand is evident, and the visual exposition is often slow and clumsy. But in Strand's sequences, there is superb experimentation and creative photography. David Wolff's narration, spoken by Paul Robeson, is stirring, not only in its recounting of past terrors, but also in its reassurance that honest men are joining together, cooperating, to combat the "enemy within."

With *The Fight for Life,* this feature-length documentary deserves a special place in the history of the nonfiction film, and although its use of professional actors might actually detract from its "reality," its ability to combine music, narration, and photography make it an eloquent statement for freedom and democracy.

Influenced by *The Plow That Broke the Plains* and *The River,* as well as by the militancy of the Frontier Film Group, is John Ferno's and Julian Roffman's *And So They Live* (1940), an indictment of an outdated school in a backward mountain community. While it is neither so poetic as the Lorentz films, nor so direct as the Frontier films, it is effective in leaving an overall impression of despair.[46] Another more effective film on the same subject is Willard Van Dyke's *The Children Must Learn* (1940).

Willard Van Dyke and the Continuing American Tradition

As photographer, writer, director, and producer, Willard Van Dyke has been a leader among American documentary film makers since 1939, when *The City* became the link between the politics of Ivens, the poetry of Lorentz, and the nonfiction films of the 1940's.[47] Van Dyke studied with Edward Weston and began his career as a still photographer, but he soon learned the motion picture art. In 1936, he joined Stacey Woodward and Floyd Crosby as a cameraman on *The River,* and he served as an assistant director for some sequences in Lorentz' frequent absences from the shooting.[48] He was also briefly involved with Nykino, the group that later became Frontier Films, and he photographed the opening sequences of an early version of *Native Land* discarded in favor of the extant film.[49]

Van Dyke has made more than fifty films, most of which are marked by two distinguishing characteristics: an interest in experimentation and an instinctive feeling for the poetry in common, ordinary lives and events. Where Lorentz is best with the epic sweep and scope of national problems, Van Dyke excels when depicting the virtues in individual lives. Where Lorentz sings of America in the Whitman tradition, Van Dyke speaks in the tradition of Carl Sandburg. And where Lorentz works for an operatic blend of photography, narration, and music, Van Dyke works with the incisive skill of a great photographer for whom the image is all.[50] The films of Pare Lorentz were created out of a particular blend of politics and poetry; they evoke the hopes and aspirations of the New Deal, and must be seen and evaluated within that context. The films of Willard Van Dyke reflect his continuing interest in the changing scene, from the problems of education, agriculture, and communications to those of city planning, labor relations, and newspaper photography. Van Dyke's approach to each subject is fresh and unique, but visual sensitivity, humorous insight, and reportorial objectivity are almost always present in his work. The films of Van Dyke are the films of a craftsman committed not to one ideology or vision, but to an imaginative joy in the world around him.

Van Dyke's first important work is *The City* (1939), a film made with Ralph Steiner specifically for the 1939 New York World's Fair.[51] *The City* is about "the spectacle of misapplied human power," or, more specifically, the mess of American cities. A visionary film sponsored by the American Institute of Planners, it seeks to arouse public interest in the quality of city life by showing the evolution of city planning in four phases from the New England town, to the unplanned industrial community, to the congested metropolis, to the "new city" of the sponsor's dreams. It is a true social documentary in its subject matter, its problem-solution structure, and its attitude: "There must be something better. Why can't we have it?" But *The City* is primarily a film of distinguished photography and editing, of feeling for the common man, and for the experiences shared in common by all Americans. Its conclusion is as visionary as its subject, and if it evokes a future city where there are no slums, no consciousness of war or race, it must be remembered that its sponsors and its first mass audience were not so much interested in the present as they were in the future.

The City is rooted in the American Dream tradition by three factors: by its regret that cities have grown away from the harmony between the soil and the people so evident in New England towns; by its optimism ("Just watch us grow. The scales won't hold us.") ; and by Aaron Copland's musical score, a delightful piece of Americana. In *The City*, the visual images are alive and constantly changing, but they would not have their vitality without the imaginative editing by Theodor Lawrence and Henwar Rodakiewicz. The photography and editing are memorable, especially in the much-copied comic lunch-hour montage. The sound accompanies the photography and the editing in a dramatic and often humorous way to contrast planned and unplanned cities. A successful collaborative film, *The City* remains a sophisticated and mature approach to a complex problem, marred only by an oversimplified solution; as the group effort of several major talents, it deserves study in relation to its contemporary collaborative productions: *Night Mail, The River, The Spanish Earth,* and *Power and the Land.*

The first part of *The City* is devoted to the New England town, built around a central plaza and marketplace, and dependent on the town meeting for harmony and balance: "The town was us and we were part of it." At this point, the mood and music of the film are idyllic, but the mood does not last long; railroad, steam, and steel change the picture rapidly, and the emphasis becomes the dirt, smoke, and crowded living conditions of an ugly mining town: "Smoke makes prosperity, no matter if you choke on it." Here the film is topical and relevant, as it points out problems that still plague American cities: poor education, congestion, pollution, and a sense of uselessness in many people's lives. And it is here that the film's theme becomes distinct: "There must be something better. Why can't we have it?" The third episode of the film pictures the large metropolis of New York City; here the ironic theme is "The people, perhaps," not the American Dream evoked by Sandburg's famous words, "The people, yes!" We see rush hour traffic, regimented office work, garbage and congestion, much of it in photography that has the graphic qualities of postwar neorealism. Then, as now, it is difficult to cross the street, to get a cab, and to find a peaceful spot for a picnic. Here also the film's most famous sequence depicts a lunch hour on-the-run, a rapidly cut montage emphasizing the delightful humor of efficient lunch counters, mechanized sandwich assembly, and inevitable indigestion. In the tradition of the "city symphony," Van Dyke and Steiner capture the rhythm of New York with humor and insight. In a concluding montage of signs, New York, a "new city" once, seems to be transformed into "No York," a dead city.

As the second episode was preceded by a sequence depicting the early industrial growth brought by steam and steel, the fourth episode is introduced by the more sophisticated methods of construction, transportation, and, of course, city planning. The "new city" represents a move back to nature, a cooperation between man, machine, and nature. Man commands his technology, and the emphasis is on cooperation between the various elements of power, communications, and industry. Freeways bypass the planned town, the greenbelt concept provides plenty of space in which to play, and children swim in a clear pond instead of a dirty city river. The film takes a visionary look into the future, and overlooks the imminent destructive reality of World War II. In the "new city," there is no poverty, no race or class distinction, no misused human resources. The viewers are challenged to take a choice between the new city and the old. While there is little doubt that they would choose the new city, we can only look back and be wistful; in the thirty years since the film was released, the problems it depicts have only gotten worse. Megalopolis replaced metropolis, while the "new city" remained on the drawing boards of city planners. But we, not Van Dyke and his collaborators, must take the credit for that condition.

Van Dyke's early career was prolific. In 1940, a year after *The City,* he released five films: *Valley Town,* a study of the human consequences of automation in a steel town; *The Children Must Learn,* the story of an experiment in education in the Kentucky mountains; *Sarah Lawrence,* the brief biography of a typical student at Sarah Lawrence College; *To Hear Your Banjo Play,* a study of several folk songs by Pete Seeger; and *Tall Tales,* an account of three songs by Josh White and Burl Ives. Of these five films, *Valley Town* and *The Children Must Learn* are the most important.

The question of narration in social documentary has always

The City: Crowded city streets and unhealthy playing conditions for children represent some of the social ills to be corrected in the Steiner–Van Dyke cross examination of the development of American cities. Photograph courtesy The Museum of Modern Art Film Stills Archive.

posed a problem to film makers. The director can choose, among others, the omniscient narrator, the poetic commentator, the authoritative "voice of god," or the first-person narrator; he can, in addition, use prose, poetry, free verse, song, chant, or a combination of these. In *Valley Town*, Van Dyke chose the folksy mayor to deliver the first-person narration, and although this narration (by Spencer Pollard and David Wolff) bears certain resemblances to Lorentz' style of narration, in its feeling for America, it is neither as poetic nor as effective. The emphasis in this film is on the problem, not the solution. As automation revolutionizes American industry, it creates a pool of trained men without jobs; and while training for new jobs is one of the solutions suggested by the film, it is more concerned with presenting a bitter picture of men out of work, waiting without hope for some answer to their problem. This theme is emphasized and distinguished by its imaginative use of song soliloquy to record the disillusion and despair of a typical miner and his wife. This is an original approach to the problem of narration, but it is more successful as experiment than as communication. This soliloquy is part of a musical score by Marc Blitzstein that is an integral part of the film, but neither the narration nor the music sharpen the focus on the individual lives of the miners. *Valley Town* makes more contributions to the development of American documentary film than it does to the solutions of the problems it tackles. In *The Children Must Learn*, Van Dyke used a spoken narration of an omniscient, but soft quality, coupled with folk songs, sung by a chorus. Overall, the sound here solves the narrative problems of *Valley Town*, especially when the images are ironically juxtaposed with the music.

During World War II, Van Dyke worked with the U.S. Office of War Information in creating a series of films designed to project the American way of life to audiences abroad.[52] Van Dyke's films for the OWI include *Oswego* (1943), the study of a small American city as seen through the eyes of French visitors during wartime; *Steeltown* (1943), a picture of the life and work of American steelworkers; *Pacific Northwest* (1944), a film about the importance of Oregon and Washington to world trade and transportation; and *San Francisco* (1945), the official film record of the establishment of the United Nations. Like Ivens, but unlike Lorentz, Van Dyke continued to produce and direct films. In 1965, he became Director of the Department of Film of the Museum of Modern Art in New York.

* * *

The nonfiction film flourished during the 1930's, not only in England and the United States, but also in Holland, Germany, France, and Belgium. Within a few years, national efforts were producing large numbers of films, and as style developed and vision focused, various directors emerged as leaders. The social documentary advanced under Grierson and Van Dyke; the political documentary under Ivens; the poetic-political documentary under Lorentz; the romantic documentary under Flaherty; and the propaganda film under Riefenstahl. And across the world, film makers were discussing the possibilities and discovering the potentialities of the nonfiction film.

Experiments with photography, sound, narration, music, and color revolutionized film making. Advancements in financing and distribution made films readily available to mass audiences. And mass audiences increased their interest in films that broadened their knowledge and helped them to form opinions about contemporary events.

The nonfiction film developed as much during the 1930's as it was to develop in the following twenty years. In 1940, nothing stood in the way of further expansion, development, and success, except World War II.

NOTES

1 A much better earlier example of Eisenstein's influence remains in Grierson's *Drifters* (1929) .

2 For a brief study of the compilation film, see Jay Leyda, *Films Beget Films* (New York, Hill and Wang, 1964) .

3 Its influence can be seen also in the Van Dyke-Steiner production *The City* (1939).

4 As yet, there is no wholly satisfactory study of the films of Nazi Germany. The most widely acknowledged study is Siegfried Kracauer, *From Caligari to Hitler* (Princeton, New Jersey, Princeton University Press, 1947), especially pp. 275–307. A more recent study, but a very general one, is David Stewart Hull, *Film in the Third Reich* (Berkeley, California, University of California Press, 1969).

5 Specific Nazi propaganda films about World War II are discussed in Chapter Seven.

6 Kracauer asserts that the rally was staged for the cameras, but the rally was an annual event; it is true that Riefenstahl had cooperation from the authorities ,in placing her equipment, but it is also apparent from her accounts that Goebbels was opposed to her work and placed obstacles in her way. It is understandable that Kracauer's own political feelings hindered his judgment of this film, but it is regrettable that succeeding film historians have accepted his theories without much question.

7 There have been many varying estimates of the size of Riefenstahl's camera crew, but Nazi promotional material seems reliable in listing Sepp Allgeier as the Director of Photography, a crew of eighteen cameramen, and twenty-two assistants.

8 Three sources of information on Riefenstahl are (1) the special issue of *Film Comment* (Winter 1965) devoted to her; (2) D. Gunston, "Leni Riefenstahl," *Film Quarterly*, 14, No. 1 (Fall 1960), pp. 4–19; and (3) Richard Corliss, "Leni Riefenstahl: A Bibliography," *Film Heritage*, 5, No. 1 (Fall 1969), pp. 27–36.

9 Gordon Hitchens, "An Interiew with a Legend," *Film Comment*, 3, No. 1 (Winter 1965), p. 9. Another, more illuminating interview is that by Michel Delahaye in *Interviews with Film Directors*, ed. Andrew Sarris (Indianapolis, Indiana, The Bobbs-Merrill Company, Inc., 1967).

10 The figures estimating the size of Riefenstahl's camera crew at one hundred are apparently unfounded, for she says that she had only thirty men, of whom only six were truly professional—Hitchens, p. 9. A companion film to *Triumph of the Will* and *Olympia* is *De Kamera Fährt Mit* (*The Camera Goes Along*, 1936), an interesting behind-the-scenes account of the architectural and photographic preparations for these and other Nazi films. A folio-size collection of stills from *Olympia* and candid shots of all camera setups and of Riefenstahl at work can be found in Leni Riefenstahl, *Schönheit im Olympischen Kampf* (Berlin, Im Deutschen Verlag, 1937).

11 Riefenstahl says the diving sequence was "a simple idea," and that the "secret" of *Olympia* is the sound—see Hitchens, p. 9.

12 Joris Ivens, *The Camera and I* (New York, International Publishers, 1969), p. 138.

13 Ivens, pp. 136–37.

14 Pare Lorentz' unfinished *Ecce Homo!* (1939–40) contains what he called an "industrial symphony" sequence.

15 Ivens, p. 81.

16 See Ivens, pp. 81–93, for a discussion of the film.

17 Ivens, p. 87.

18 Ivens, pp. 87–88.

19 For a discussion of Ivens' editing principles, see Ivens, p. 95.

20 Ivens, p. 99.

21 For a discussion of the shooting and Hemingway's active role in it, see Ivens, pp. 103–38.

22 Ernest Hemingway, *The Spanish Earth* (Cleveland, Ohio, The J. B. Savage Company, 1938) , p. 19.

23 For a summary of the critical response, see Ivens, pp. 130–38.

24 *Power and the Land* was the last film to be finished by the United States Film Service; there is no mention of Lorentz by the Film Service in the title credits of the print in the collection of the Museum of Modern Art.

25 For differing views on Ivens' accomplishments, see Cynthia Grenier, "Joris Ivens: Social Realist and Lyric Poet," *Sight and Sound* 27, No. 4 (Spring 1958) , pp. 204–07; and R. Stebbins and J. Leyda, "Joris Ivens: Artist in Documentary," *Magazine of Art*, 31 (July 1938) , pp. 392–99ff.

26 For a biography and detailed account of Lorentz' career from about 1930 to 1941, see Robert L. Snyder, *Pare Lorentz and the Documentary Film* (Norman, Oklahoma, Oklahoma University Press, 1968) , a study which owes more than Snyder acknowledges to MacCann's work, cited below.

27 For a full discussion of the background, see Snyder, pp. 79–95.

28 While the philosophical implications of the whole question of government propaganda are of vital importance, they are not directly relevant to this critical history. For further information, see (1) Richard Dyer MacCann, "Documentary Film and Democratic Government: An Administrative History from Pare Lorentz to John Huston" (unpublished Ph.D. dissertation, Harvard University, 1951) ; and (2) Snyder, pp. 79–95, 145–76.

29 Snyder gives correct production data, pp. 213–14.

30 There are some obvious visual influences from *Plow* on John Ford's screen version of *The Grapes of Wrath* (1940) . It might also be worthwhile to study *Plow* with King Vidor's *Our Daily Bread* (1934) .

31 For a study guide to the film, see U.S. Film Service, *The Plow That Broke the Plains* (Washington, D.C., 1938) .

32 Lorentz is quoted in Snyder, p. 37.

33 Ironically, *The River* supports a kind of conservation project (flooding of vast valleys to create dams and cheap hydroelectric power) that would not be accepted by today's conservationists.

34 Pare Lorentz, *The River* (New York, Stackpole Sons, 1938) , n.p.

35 For a personal glimpse of the production, see Willard Van Dyke, "Letters from *The River*," *Film Comment*, 3, No. 2 (Spring 1965) , pp. 38–60.

36 Of the narration, James Joyce said, "the most beautiful prose I have heard in ten years."—William L. White, "Pare Lorentz," *Scribner's* (Jan. 1939), p. 10; Carl Sandburg commented, "It is among the greatest psalms of America's greatest river."—Snyder, p. 184.

37 For a discussion of the problems of release, see Snyder, pp. 63–78.

38 It was not particularly influential on succeeding film makers, but was well-received by both the medical and the lay communities. See Snyder, pp. 112–20.

39 For Lorentz' instructions to Gruenberg, see Snyder, p. 211.

40 After *The Fight for Life*, Lorentz entered the U.S. Air Force and made almost three hundred training films; after the war, he formed his own independent consulting and producing company, but never equaled his early achievements.

41 The full study of the "March of Time" has not yet been written; valuable assessments can be found in: A. William Bluem, *Documentary in American Television* (New York, Hastings House, 1965) and Robert T. Elson, *Time Inc., The Intimate History of a Publishing Enterprise, 1923–1941* (New York, Atheneum, 1968). My introductory study of "This Is America" will appear in the Fall 1972 issue of *Cinema Journal.*

42 John Howard Lawson, *Film: The Creative Process* (New York, Hill and Wang, 1964), p. 128.

43 At one time or another, the staff of Frontier Films included Paul Strand, Ralph Steiner, Joris Ivens, Leo Hurwitz, Willard Van Dyke, John Howard Lawson, Philip Stevenson, Albert Maltz, Elia Kazan, Margaret Murray, Kyle Crichton, George Sklar, Herbert Kline, Lionel Berman, David Wolff (also known as Ben Maddow), Robert Stebbins (also known as Sidney Meyers), Irving Lerner, and Louis Kamp. The advisers included Carlos Chavez, Aaron Copland, John Dos Passos, Lillian Hellman, Archibald MacLeish, Clifford Odets, S. J. Perelman, and Muriel Rukeyser—from printed prospectus of Frontier Films.

44 Earlier attempts in the 1930's to attack social problems in America through film include Seymour Stern's *Imperial Valley* (1931) and *Taxi, Sheriff,* and *City of Contrasts.*

45 In his definition of realism, Paul Strand writes,

> To begin with a negative statement, realism is not the mere recording of things as they are, seen through dispassionate eyes in which all things are of equal value, of equal interest—the eyes of a man who thinks he stands above life, above good and evil. Neither does realism consist in the description, no matter how honest, of the exceptional and sensational in life. . . . On the contrary, we should conceive of realism as dynamic, as truth which sees and understands a changing world and in its turn is capable of changing it, in the interests of peace, human progress, and the eradication of human misery and cruelty, and towards the unity of all people. We must take sides. In Paul Strand, "Realism: A Personal View," *Sight & Sound,* 19 (Jan. 1950), pp. 23–26.

46 It was to have been followed by another film, fifteen years later, showing the results of educational reforms that were being introduced by its sponsor (the Alfred Sloan Foundation), but this second film was never made.

47 See Harrison Engle, "Thirty Years of Social Inquiry: An Interview with Willard Van Dyke," *Film Comment*, 3, No. 2 (Spring 1965), pp. 24–37.

48 Van Dyke, "Letters from *The River.*"

49 Interview with Willard Van Dyke, at Museum of Modern Art, New York, July 16, 1971.

50 For an interesting comment on photography in American documentary films, see Willard Van Dyke, "The Interpretive Camera in Documentary Films," *Hollywood Quarterly*, 1, No. 4 (July 1946), pp. 405–09.

51 For a detailed critical catalog of the hundreds of films shown at the fair, see Richard Griffith, *Films of the World's Fair: 1939* (New York, American Film Center, 1940).

52 See Chapter Seven.

CHAPTER 6

The Humanistic Vision
of Robert Flaherty

In the temperamental world of nonfiction film, Robert Flaherty seems to have come closer than any other film maker to achieving an indestructible reputation. Of course, no artistic reputation is ever indestructible, and Flaherty's achievement presents something of a paradox, for he was always the great individualist. He did not participate for more than a brief time in any particular film-making movement; he did not write theories or manifestos; and he made only five major films. Yet he is a legend among all film makers, perhaps one of the very few of them who preserved his integrity while making films which expressed his individual beliefs.

Robert Flaherty was the father of the factual film, the first important film maker to document real life using real people and real locations.[1] Although John Grierson first used the word *documentary* to refer to Flaherty's *Moana* (1926), it would be misleading to think of Flaherty as the originator of the documentary film as we know it: the sociopolitical didactic film. Flaherty began the romantic tradition which freely, spontaneously, and poetically celebrates man and his life; his films are humanistic statements, not political ones. His purpose was to explore, to document, and to affirm life, not to make propaganda and not to educate, except in the broadest sense of acquainting people with other cultures. What the viewer learns from a Flaherty film, he learns from participating in the lives of people on the screen, not from listening to a narration about improved social conditions.

The distinction between the documentary and the factual film is an important one. As we have seen, the true documentary is founded on a social or political commitment; films such as *Night Mail* or *The River* record facts, but they also register opinions about those facts. And while it is probably impossible for any film maker (or any artist) to avoid registering his opinion, it is in the degree to which the documentary film maker registers his opinion that his films become more than just records of a person, time, or place. The factual film maker is more concerned with producing and preserving a factual record, a "document" to be sure, but one that is relatively free from the obligation to solve the problems it presents. As with any set of definitions, it is difficult to draw rigid lines, and with art forms it is undesirable to try. But if we are to understand Flaherty and his importance, we must understand his particular kind of nonfiction film making.

Flaherty is an *auteur* in every sense of the word, perhaps the first to acknowledge himself as such, for in the credit titles of his second film, *Moana,* Flaherty and his wife are listed as the "authors" of the film. *Moana* may be an old wave on the shores of the Godard-Truffaut school, but it joins Flaherty's other films as the highly individualistic creation of a man who would not yield to anyone or anything in his determination to make films. Critics of Flaherty might dismiss this *auteur* label as a rash attempt to make the work of such an innocent observer relevant to today's more sophisticated films, but such a dismissal would ignore the unique vision and personal stamp that mark each of his films.

Robert Flaherty was an innovator and an experimenter, an idealist and an innocent, a romantic man who fought the establishment with cunning and a naïve belief in the transcendency of art over money. He was an ecologist and an ethnologist, in love with man and the natural world, fascinated with the crafts of primitive man and appalled by the dehumanizing technology of modern man.

Flaherty's vision is often called *poetic,* a term that has negative as well as positive connotations. His work is poetic if that label suggests he created a lyrical mood, handled his subject with care, and avoided finding easy answers to large questions. His films are poetic if they help the viewer to transcend the everyday, to explore and even to escape, and finally to understand his own environment with a greater sensitivity to human problems and relationships between man and nature. And they are poetic because Flaherty was a poet—an individualist, a romantic, a rebel, a visionary, and, in Shelley's sense, a legislator for mankind, for man's survival in the face of encroaching technology and progress. He was not a technician, however, and he sometimes lacked the greater poet's skill in balancing his images, in shaping his metaphors, and in controlling his material. Although he made several others, he is chiefly remembered for five films: *Nanook of the North, Moana, Man of Aran, The Land,* and *Louisiana Story.* What he brought to the new world of film making was his vision and his enthusiasm, and he left his mark on film makers as diverse as Arne Sucksdorff, John Huston, William Wyler, Pare Lorentz, and Richard Leacock. Flaherty was a pioneer in undeveloped country, and while he didn't clear many trails, he left a legacy to inspire others to conquer what he never intended to. A man of great artistic integrity who, like all pioneers, was of his time but also ahead of it, he serves as a model, an inspiration.

Robert Joseph Flaherty was born in Iron Mountain, Michigan, in 1884.[2] His father was the owner-manager of an iron ore mine, and young Flaherty grew up knowing the prosperity and the poverty which come to families who live on the unpredictable resources of nature. It was here that Flaherty learned to respect nature, to investigate man's relationship with his world, and to explore the resources of the world for answers to man's survival. A nomadic childhood forced him to develop his own strengths and his remarkable capacity for enduring the hostile elements of nature. After studying at the Michigan College of Mines, he went on several trips with his father and learned the practical aspects of exploring, map making, prospecting, and surviving in unknown country. Investigating the material resources of nature, he also learned to depend upon its spiritual resources; it is not ironic that he began his career as a prospector for iron ore and ended it as a conservationist deeply concerned with the ways in which technology affects the balance of nature.

There is much legend surrounding Flaherty's life, legend formed from anecdote, rumor, and the substantial style with which

Flaherty lived. Myth making in a man's own time is risky, and Flaherty's admirers and biographers seldom show restraint in expanding threads into skeins and skeins into tapestries when the color seems more important than the substance. But popular mythology often redeems the eccentricities of the human spirit which modern technology seems so determined to destroy. In 1910 Sir William Mackenzie, a Canadian mining power, commissioned Flaherty to explore the iron ore possibilities of the chain of islands outlying the eastern coast of Hudson Bay. Flaherty accepted the challenge with enthusiasm and energy. He traveled by foot and by canoe, recording his impressions in a diary. He made four expeditions in his efforts to chart the territory and to reach the Belcher Islands. What we know, but he didn't, is that he was training his eye for a task that would have sounded absurd at that time—the task of capturing Eskimo life on film.

The first two expeditions were in 1910 and 1911; they were marked with the usual achievements made by men charting virgin territory, and Flaherty was determined to go back again with proper equipment and, most important, a proper ship. When Mackenzie agreed to finance the third trip, Flaherty's career as a film maker was born. There are conflicting accounts of their conversation, but Flaherty's own words capture the spirit of the moment:

> Sir William said to me casually, "Why don't you get one of those new-fangled things called a motion picture camera?" So I bought one, but with no thought really than of taking notes on our exploration. We were going into interesting country, we'd see interesting people. I had not thought of making a film for the theatres. I knew nothing whatsoever about films.[3]

This is the stuff that legend is made of, and so it hardly matters what the exact words were. What does matter is that Flaherty got his first camera, a Bell & Howell, and took a three-week course in motion picture photography. Since this was the only formal training he received in photography, cynics can say that his years of practical experience added little to his ability in later years; his camera was almost always static, and it seems that he worked in ignorance of Pabst and Eisenstein, Pudovkin and Clair. But Flaherty's career began with a search for rocks, not with a desire to develop new techniques of camera movement, and his enthusiasm for the new gadget more than compensated for his lack of technical know-how. It should also be remembered that the real experiments with camera placement and movement, with editing and rhythm, and with film *as* film did not occur until the mid-1920's. *Nanook* was not released until 1922, but when Flaherty set off for the subarctic with his camera, lighting equipment, film stock, and portable developing and printing machine, it was still 1913.[4]

Flaherty began to use the camera first for amusement, to occupy his time between the profitable periods of exploring. From his journals, we learn that the Eskimos loved being photographed and often vied for prominent places in front of the camera; this first encounter with a "star" mentality taught Flaherty much about the handling of "actors." In his films, the people who appear are, of course, not professional actors; they act and react according to habit and instinct, not script; when they speak, they speak naturally, or they improvise, but they do not read printed dialogue. The highest testament to Flaherty's ability to understand and work with people is that lack of self-consciousness which is so apparent as Nanook goes about his labors or as the Cajun boy in *Louisiana Story* sails quietly in his canoe.

In 1914, Flaherty returned to New York, married Frances Hubbard, and edited the crude footage he had shot in Baffin Land. When he went back again in 1916, at the age of thirty-two, to the islands which he had charted, he concentrated as much on film making as he did on prospecting. It is difficult to say exactly when Flaherty became aware that the remainder of his life would be devoted to the making of films, but his own words underscore his sense of himself: "First I was an explorer; then I was an artist."[5] The essentials of Eskimo art are an apparent influence on Flaherty's aesthetics. From the Eskimos, Flaherty learned that art is more than just an expression of life's values, that art enables man to understand his relationship to life, and that art is also artifact, a utilitarian record of the moment. The Eskimo sees life clearly and simply, in terms of existence and action, and from the wastes of snow and ice, he makes his statement as an act of conquest and affirmation. In his carvings, he reveals form so that he might protest against the formlessness of his environment. The Eskimo's approach is to explore, conquer, and record; for Flaherty, too, film making was an act of exploration first, and affirmation second.

Flaherty shot seventy thousand feet of film (approximately 17 1/2 hours of screening time) on this third expedition, and he assembled it into a print which was first shown at Harvard. Later, while packing the negative for shipment to New York, he dropped a lighted cigarette into it and the film went up in flames. This accident proved to be the best thing that could have happened to Flaherty's career as a film maker, and he wasn't sorry. He says,

> It was a bad film; it was dull—it was little more than a travelogue. I had learned to explore, I had not learned to reveal. It was utterly inept, simply a scene of this and that, no relation, no thread of a story or continuity whatever. . . . Certainly it bored me.[6]

With the partial print made from the burned negative (the so-called Harvard print), Flaherty went to New York, where for two years he arranged screenings of the film and attempted to gain support and financing for another film and expedition. World War I convinced him that film could open up avenues of communication and establish patterns for understanding that might help to avoid future confrontations. And he felt, most of all, that a film about an Eskimo, a man who has fewer resources than almost any other man in the world, who lives in a desolation that few can survive, and whose life is a constant fight against starvation and death, could be a film that would reawaken so-called civilized man's consciousness of his own resources and values. In 1920, when Flaherty was thirty-six, he convinced Revillon Frères, the French furriers, to back him. For them, it was not a wholly altruistic gesture; they had competed for years with Hudson's Bay Company and saw the film as a fresh, new kind of publicity. But for Flaherty, it was the opportunity he had waited for, and the fact that he knew less about film distribution than he did about production did not daunt him.

This time, however, Flaherty proceeded with considerable practical experience behind him, and he matched his equipment to the conditions he would face on location. Because of the extreme cold in which he would be working, Flaherty chose cameras which were lubricated with graphite instead of oil or grease. He made another significant decision in choosing a gyro-head tripod which would enable him to pan horizontally or to tilt the camera up and down. In addition to this relatively more sophisticated and flexible equipment, he took full developing, printing, and projection equipment. If this was to be a film about Eskimos, thought Flaherty, then it should also be a film by them. This decision formed an integral part of his production philosophy, and the Eskimos were involved in every phase of his operation from working in front of the cameras to carrying water for developing the film, even though they did not know what it was all about. They had never seen a motion picture, and they had difficulty understanding that the rushes Flaherty projected for them were only an imitation of their lives. When they finally comprehended the process, they enthusiastically learned the subtleties of washing, developing, and printing film. Such involvement proved beneficial, of course, because as they saw their progress on the screen, they were able to develop a better sense of themselves and to lose whatever self-consciousness they might have had working with a director who exploited rather than understood them.

From the very beginning, *Nanook of the North* was an extraordinary film production. Not only was it the first commercially financed film of its kind, but it was being made under the most adverse conditions by an amateur with a nonprofessional cast and crew. Although Flaherty had the advantage of his earlier experiences in filming these people, and knew what to avoid on the second try, he hadn't prepared any shooting script. Moreover, the intrusion of a film maker on the daily struggle for survival of a group of Eskimos presents other problems. The film maker could have entered as the "White Man," given the natives some compensation, and told them to go about their daily activities as if he were not there, hoping to capture whatever he could and, thereby, to document their lives on film. But the Flaherty philosophy was to engage their interest, understand their problems, obtain their cooperation, and then make himself one of the group by agreeing to live and to suffer with them. Although this approach was clearly the successful one, it was not without hardship; for a long time, there was no food for the sled dogs or the men; and when he wanted to film a walrus hunt, the walrus was not always cooperative. Often Flaherty had to stage certain sequences, but after a year of shooting under these conditions, he finished, and in August, 1921, returned to edit the exposed stock.

Flaherty edited the film with the assistance of Charles Gelb, but perhaps it is more accurate to say that they assembled the film; they knew little of modern editing techniques, a deficiency which is made all the more obvious by the titles supplied by Carl Clancy. But this was not important to Flaherty, although it must have been to the executives of Paramount and First National (later Warner Brothers) who rejected it after screenings. Dejected, Flaherty turned again to Revillon Frères, which, along with the Pathé Company of New York, was controlled by a parent company in Paris. Another screening was scheduled for the Pathé executives, but nothing happened until later when Roxy Rothafel, the impresario of New York's Rialto Theatre, was impressed. The rest is film history. *Nanook* opened at the Capitol Theatre in New York in 1922 to good business and good notices, although film criticism then was hardly what it is today. *Nanook* did not continue to do good business in the United States, but it went on to considerable success in London and Paris. Distributors thought the film was too special for a roadshow engagement in the United States, and despite the fact that it had cost comparatively little to make and that those costs had been covered by a furrier, not a film company, there was little inducement for the American film industry to give it the special distribution that it required.

What gives *Nanook* its power and charm? What saves it from being an educational film for grammar school children or a travelogue for armchair travelers? What makes it a landmark in film history, as well as a useful tool in the studies of anthropology and ethnology? Perhaps the most genuine reason for the film's power is that indefinable chemistry that occurred between Flaherty and Nanook. The film maker and his subject were admirably suited to one another, not as master and material, but as men who understood one another. Both were individualists, poets, technicians;

both had a light sense of humor; both approached the elements of their respective lives with gentleness, warmth, and affection. Flaherty did not document Nanook's life so much as he ennobled it. Nanook is larger than life, not because he triumphs over it, but because it does not neglect him. Nanook is more than the master of his environment; he is the master of himself, a hero who endures and prevails and who, without pride, has the humility that comes only to a man who lives close to nature. The power of the film, and the charm, lies in Nanook and his way of life, but it lies, as well, in Flaherty's respect for that life.

Critics have charged Flaherty's film with exploiting Nanook, with overemphasizing the hardship and severity of his life for theatrical purposes without offering him any help. The charges raise the question of an artist's moral responsibility, but it is not a wholly relevant question here. That Nanook died two years after the film was released, as so many of his people did, was due to starvation, not to any neglect on Flaherty's part. The adversity seen in the film is Nanook's; it belongs to his culture, not ours. He has never known enough warmth to know how bitterly cold his world is. Nanook knew no other life. It is we who suffer by empathy and by the knowledge of how much one man will give in order that he and his family may live. If Flaherty had to stage certain sequences, he staged them because physical conditions would not permit him to film otherwise. Clearly cultures differ, but the film does suggest that the white man could spoil Nanook's way of life. When Nanook's family visits the trading post, his child is made sick by the trader's food.

Nanook of the North is a very simple picture about an ordinary man in circumstances which are ordinary to him, but which seem extraordinary to us. The slow rhythm of the film matches Nanook's own pace of determination and control. We see how Nanook and his family live, their eating habits, sleeping arrangements, and hunting expeditions. We see them at the trading post, on a walrus hunt, fishing for food, building an igloo, and feeding the sled dogs. Most of this is shown for its factual value, not for any theatrical purpose, although Flaherty does capture the excitement of the walrus hunt and skillfully relates the suspense of the hunt to the hunger of the family. Men are fighting for food and for their lives, and this is both natural and dramatic.

Flaherty achieved a nice balance between showing those things that the Eskimos must do when nature is in control—such as hunting the walrus or trapping a fox—and those things that they do when they are in control, such as building an igloo. A central episode in the film shows the seemingly effortless way in which Nanook cuts blocks of frozen snow and fits them together to make an igloo; this episode emphasizes his skill and assurance with only the simplest of tools. And audiences still applaud when he fits a block of clear ice into the structure to make a window; his control over nature seems so masterful that one wonders how survival could ever be a problem. But before he, or we, feel assured, Nanook is shown teaching his young son how to shoot a bow and arrow; this is a tender sequence of great warmth, but it serves to emphasize the necessity of one generation's passing on its skills to the next. The film is not without its humor, especially in a long struggle between Nanook and a seal under the ice. We do not know what is struggling on the other end of the line, what makes Nanook exert so much energy, until the seal is finally hauled out onto the ice. The seal that was landed was, of course, a dead one, but Flaherty made no pretense here of actuality: "Sometimes you have to lie. One often has to distort a thing to catch its true spirit."[7] In his tug-of-war with the seal, Nanook loses his balance and falls head over heels, much to the amusement of other members of his family and the audience.

Flaherty creates suspense by showing the day coming to an end, with the dogs getting hungrier and more violent, the weather getting colder, and no shelter yet apparent for the family. The precariousness of their life is emphasized as the dogs cause a delay by tangling their lines. The family is forced to take shelter in an abandoned igloo, but they sleep warmly as the blizzard outside turns the landscape into a white fury. The film ends here, but it is not a happy ending; the family is lost, the dogs are shown sleeping under a heavy blanket of snow, and there is no suggestion that morning will come, or, when it does, that it will be good. But Flaherty is not concerned with happy endings, and if the previous

Nanook of the North: A tender moment as Nanook warms his son's hands after teaching him some tricks with the bow and arrow. Photograph courtesy The Museum of Modern Art Film Stills Archive.

footage has not suggested that Nanook and his family have the strength to get through such a night, then no tacked-on ending would do it anyway.

It is both difficult and unfair to discuss the technical aspects of *Nanook* as a film, for it was the first effort of a man who knew less about film making than most beginning film students know today; he had experience, of course, but that experience lay in shooting, not shaping, a film. *Nanook* has many faults, not the least of which are the introductory titles and those that distinguish between the various episodes. The camera is always stationary, although it pans and tilts. But the flaws one might expect in a first film are not there. Nanook and his family prove to be good actors, and there is a lack of self-consciousness in their behavior. Flaherty has a nice sense of the visual gag, especially when he shows the family emerging from their kayak in surprising numbers or when Nanook is fighting the seal. The images are nicely framed, although Flaherty lingers on some moments to the point of loving. But we must evaluate *Nanook* in the context in which it was filmed, and grant Flaherty his approach. The film is a social document embodying the clear vision of a romantic idealist. It is not a documentary in our understanding of that word, for it does not help, for example, to solve the problems of people living in the wilderness, nor does it have any immediate social value. Its value is the value of any work of art that illuminates man's nobility. There is, of course, much to be learned from the film, much of great relevance to everyday life. The immediate environment is cold and foreign, but the broader implications are universal. The film is still being shown in theaters, in classrooms, on television. As long as we identify with each other, and with the life force itself, we shall identify with Nanook and with Flaherty's simple, genuine, and true evocation of his life. We participate in his life, as he does in ours, through film, but we are the richer for it, and we never forget the experience.

* * *

The success of *Nanook* caught the attention of Jesse Lasky, then head of Famous-Players-Lasky, the predecessors of Paramount

Pictures. Flaherty was offered the opportunity to go anywhere in the world to make a film so long as he produced one comparable to *Nanook*. He chose the South Seas, partly out of interest in the people and their life, and partly because he could take his wife and children to a pleasant climate. Flaherty spent almost three years in making *Moana,* his response to Lasky's challenge, but from the beginning it seems clear that he had no intention of supplying another *Nanook*. First of all, he had no first-hand experience with the territory, as he had with the Eskimo country, although he had read about it. Second, he found that the Samoan island of Savaii, where he made the film, was so beneficent, so rich in natural resources, and so obviously a tropical paradise that it was impossible to imagine a Nanook-like conflict in which the natives must fight for their very existence. Here the sea was brimming with fish, the land was rich, and the weather was almost always warm; people wore loincloths and rarely came near any natural danger. Clearly the problem for Flaherty was to make a film about an unfamiliar subject, to translate his personal experiences with these people into some cinematic vision of their existence, and to allow his observations to succeed where his preconceptions would not. But Flaherty was a novice, and instead of waiting for his film to come to him, he sought for a theme and a set of characters that would, without direct imitation, remind him of the struggles he recorded in *Nanook*. What was so hard for Flaherty to learn was that the Samoans had an easy life and that the preconceived film was not going to be made. But his amateur approach was lucky, for in the process of searching for a theme, he made a more important discovery in the use of the camera and film stock.

After shooting some forty thousand feet of orthochromatic stock, Flaherty tried some of the new panchromatic film supplied by Kodak. Immediately he was struck with the contrasts between black and white, with the overall realism of the images, and with the depth and dimension that it was possible to capture on the new stock. After a year, Flaherty discovered the proper methods of shooting and developing the panchromatic film, but he still had not found a suitable subject around which to develop a film.

Moana was finished and released in 1926, and while it was the

Moana: Dressed with the garlands and beads that represent his coming-of-age, Moana waits for the ceremony to begin. Photograph courtesy The Museum of Modern Art Film Stills Archive.

film to which John Grierson first applied the term *documentary,* the film is clearly a factual account of the lives of the Samoans. The film begins with a light dramatic situation, showing the natives gathering roots. From that point, the narration is strictly episodic, moving from a sequence in which the natives trap a wild boar, to one of fishing, to another in which the mother is shown making cloth from bark. Following this, we see a young boy harvesting coconuts, a turtle hunt, preparations for a tribal feast, and finally the climax of the film—the coming of age of Moana in a ritual of tattoo, dance, and drinking. To give personal focus to the film, Flaherty chose this ancient ritual, a lengthy and painful one, but a moment in a boy's life which, if successfully captured, might have illuminated the whole race for the audience. Flaherty missed, however, and in his close-up fascination with the intricacies of the painful needlework, and with Moana's facial anguish, he lost sight of the cultural meaning of the ritual and of its significance beyond personal discomfort. The film is an idyll, closer to a travelogue than anything else, and its unimaginative attention to the facts of local color and daily life provide none of the insights into human strength and behavior which made *Nanook* such a powerful statement. An anthropologist with a camera, Flaherty possessed all of the vices of the scholar, but, at the same time, he remained an artist. He belabors a point and then enlivens his film with a brief shot or episode of matchless beauty, clarity, and brevity. However, a disproportionate balance remains and the tension is not always resolved so nicely as one would want.

Moana remains important in Flaherty's canon because it allowed him more experimentation than was possible in the relatively confined circumstances of the Arctic. Not only was he able to shoot with a more responsive film stock, but he was also able to make use of a larger variety of lenses and camera techniques. While Flaherty seemed more aware of the camera's flexibility, he did not really understand how to pan or tilt or how to use the long shot and the close-up for maximum effect. Indeed, there are sequences in *Moana* in which the camera work is crude. For instance, as the young boy climbs the coconut tree in search of fruit, Flaherty tilts the camera upward to record his progress, but invariably he allows the boy to climb out of the viewfinder, only to jerk the camera upward, once again, to continue the shot. And while the new stock gives the film a much more realistic appearance, the static quality of the photography does little to redeem the subject. As with *Nanook,* the episodic structure of the film determined its editing; Flaherty and Julian Johnson wrote the titles, but a title such as "Meanwhile, what has happened at the snare?" does little to enhance rhythm or to focus interest.[8] We must assume that Flaherty was in control and that the pace and rhythm of the film are his. There is no conflict, no hostile elements of nature, no sex; in fact, there is precious little to interest the moviegoer.

Paramount's executives realized that the film had little theatrical appeal, but they agreed to let Flaherty try it in the six American towns with the hardest audiences. In these towns, Flaherty was successful in attracting the right people, but they were not regular moviegoers; their names had been secured through the mailing lists of special-interest organizations, and their interest was more in the subject matter than in the film itself. Paramount was not convinced, and despite Flaherty's objections, the film opened on an ordinary release in New York at the Rialto Theatre, where the marquee had been decorated with fake palm trees and the slogan: "The Love-Life of a South Sea Siren." The audiences which came to see it did not get the love life of Dorothy Lamour's ancestors, but rather a harmless sequence in which Moana and his fiancée dance before members of their families. The film is about as erotic as similar picture stories in the *National Geographic,* and, if nothing else, Paramount learned something about advertising as *Moana* died a quiet and deserved death in the United States even though it enjoyed some success in Europe.

Moana is a failure, but an interesting one, if only because it failed to fulfill the promise suggested by *Nanook.* As "The Moviegoer" of the *New York Sun,* John Grierson wrote, *"Moana,* being a visual account of events in the daily life of a Polynesian youth, has documentary value."[9] He was not using the term as he was later to use it to mean a film with a particular sociopolitical statement, but in the sense of the French word *documentaire* used to describe travel or expedition films. *Moana* has a lyrical intensity which

Moana: During the filming, Robert Flaherty was briefly incapacitated by a stomach ailment; here, in a rare photograph, he is seen being carried on a litter by native islanders. Photograph courtesy The Museum of Modern Art Film Stills Archive.

shines through its static and beautiful images, but it is a remote film, not one like *Nanook*, which redeems the human spirit, and not one like *Man of Aran* (1934), in which Flaherty once again captured man and nature in an archetypal contest of will.

* * *

Between 1925 and 1932, Flaherty was occupied with a number of projects, none of which appear to have given him much satisfaction or to have advanced his career in the art of film making. In 1925, under a commission by the actress Maude Adams, he produced *The Pottery Maker* for The Metropolitan Museum of Art in New York. This fourteen-minute film is not an important one, although it shows Flaherty's appreciation of an artisan's handwork, a concern that is evidenced in all his films; it is also interesting to compare its treatment with the pottery-making sequence in Flaherty's next film, *Industrial Britain* (1931). In the same year, he worked on an experimental film called *Twenty-Four Dollar Island*, again on a commission, but the film was never released commercially and died as a backdrop for a stage production at the Roxy Theatre.[10]

In 1927, Flaherty was approached by M-G-M with an offer to return to the South Seas and make a film to be titled *White Shadows*, based on a book by Frederick O'Brien, the man whose work had suggested *Moana*. The project proved to be a disaster, and Flaherty was back in Hollywood within the year. In 1928, Fox sent him to make a film about the Pueblo Indians in New Mexico, but this project too ended when Flaherty was recalled to Hollywood and assigned to make a picture in Tahiti with the German director F. W. Murnau. But when *Tabu* was released in 1931, it was Murnau's film, although Flaherty's influence can be seen.[11]

After the *Tabu* experience, Flaherty took his family to Berlin in 1930; there he met Joris Ivens and studied the films of Eisenstein and Dovzhenko. During this time he also conceived a film about the dying civilizations of Central Russia, but this project was never realized, although there were cooperative discussions with officials in the Soviet film industry. At a time when Flaherty's future as a film maker looked very unpromising, he was called to London by John Grierson, then head of the E.M.B. Film Unit, to make a documentary about British industrial craftsmanship. The budget was considerable, but Grierson knew that it would probably not be sufficient to meet the expenses incurred by Flaherty's extravagant production methods.[12]

Flaherty was obviously interested in the simplicity and the individuality of British craftsmanship, but this was not his idea of film making, and he could not accept the short-range social implications of the British school of documentary.[13] Flaherty's interests were timeless. Grierson wanted to praise the working class, to improve social conditions, and to use the dramatic possibilities of film to inform and to educate, while Flaherty wanted his films to ennoble mankind, to show tradition and culture, and to inform and to educate for such broad and abstract goals as human understanding and world peace. While the British documentary was to move forward in the direction of *Night Mail,* Flaherty wanted to continue in the tradition of *Nanook.* He was soon to get his chance in the primitive islands off the west coast of Ireland.

* * *

Following a suggestion that he make a film about the lives of the Aran Islanders—a film which could realize the "man against the sea" theme that he had failed to find in the Samoan Islands—Flaherty read John Millington Synge's *Riders to the Sea* and *The Aran Islanders.* With the backing of Michael Balcon, head of production for Gaumont-British, the major English film company at that time, Flaherty arranged a budget—actually smaller than the total cost of *Nanook*—and set out for Ireland undisturbed by the meager financial backing. After two trips to the Aran Islands, Flaherty had seen enough to begin planning his film.[14] The central theme, of course, was to be the conflict between man and the great natural force of the sea. He could have picked no better location in the world than the Aran Islands. The life of the islanders was not as primitive as Nanook's, or as simple as Moana's; their very existence was precariously balanced against the raging sea which isolated them on sharp, rocky bits of land. The islanders lived simply on what they could grow; since there was little natural soil, they had to grow their basic stock of potatoes in handfuls of soil fortified with seaweed that was harvested and then hoisted up the sheer face of the cliffs to the planting beds. To give a dramatic basis to his story, Flaherty revived a custom that had been dead for more than fifty years before he arrived. He wanted to film a hunt for basking sharks, a huge but harmless species that was still plentiful in the waters off the islands. At one time the oil rendered from the sharks lit the lamps in the humble cottages on the islands, but paraffin had long since replaced the oil and the custom of hunting. Now for a film, the men agreed to relearn the arduous task of working the boats and handling the harpoons. Perhaps it was Flaherty's conviction and energy that persuaded the islanders to enter into this work so cooperatively, and perhaps it was the very real fact that no particular danger was involved from the sharks since they lived on plankton, not men washed overboard. But whatever the motivation, the men performed with astonishing enthusiasm even though many of them could not swim.

The decision to film the shark hunt typifies a basic aspect of Flaherty's style. He always used images out of real life, of course, but he was never hesitant to stage an event, as long as it was probable, if this would enhance the scope of his vision. *Man of Aran* was made as he went along, not from a script. Flaherty was a poet, immersed in a genuine act of creativity, and he let his films grow organically out of the material at hand. Today we can criticize his inexperience with the grammar and rhythm of film, his inflexibility in camera angles and positioning, and his reliance on buildup and suspense for overall effect. It makes little difference, though, to talk of his films in this way. He seems to have been conscious of what he was doing, and every bit as conscious of what he was not doing and what he did not know; he was a genuine and original artist, an *auteur* in every sense of the word, and he must be judged on the basis of what he accomplished. There are considerable weaknesses in each of Flaherty's films; in *Man of Aran,* for instance, there is no awareness of the economic depression that was sweeping the world at the time, no attempt to show whether or not these

Man of Aran: Weary, but safe, after the storm, the family struggles to save its boat and precious equipment. Photograph courtesy The Museum of Modern Art Film Stills Archive.

problems affected the islanders. With equal obliviousness, Flaherty avoided the very real conflict between the Catholics and the Protestants on the islands. It may also be that his characters do not exist as personalities, that they are not particularly distinguished by their environment, that he did not succeed in his attempts to dramatize the conflict between man and the sea, that he did not take any attitude—whatever it might have been—toward their life, and that he actually distorted their present life by including the shark hunt.

Like Flaherty's previous films, *Man of Aran* is simple in construction. It recounts the typical activities of the islanders with careful, quiet observation. The problem inherent in such an episodic approach is that Flaherty relied on music, rather than narration, to unify his story. The use of Irish folk tunes is effective, but the music in general is overly insistent and, in one episode, it becomes silly—but not by intention—as it accompanies the sequence showing a man splitting rock with a pick. Subtitles were considered obsolete by 1934, but Flaherty continued to use them in spite of the arguments by his editor John Goldman that they weakened the rhythmic principles on which he was trying to edit the film. There is a great deal of suspense in Flaherty's technique, and it is established early as the boy is seen fishing from the edge of a very high cliff. He is so oblivious to the danger involved that the danger is increased that much more for the viewer. After some moments of quiet pleasure, the boy sees a huge shark in the waters far below him; his first reaction is not fear, even though the shark appears threatening, but rather he is full of wonder and fascination. Here and in *Louisiana Story,* Flaherty observes menacing aspects of nature through the cool detachment of a boy's vision. The central focus of the film is on the two shark hunts. The first ends with a man overboard, a momentary scare, and the eventual escape of the shark, but it is successful in showing the activity of the men in the boat, captured in a beautifully edited sequence. In the second hunt, the men approach the shark quietly, but once the animal is harpooned, it fights angrily and drags the boat out to sea. There is excitement and suspense here as the shark dives to the bottom and rests. This sequence is overly long, but Flaherty apparently wanted to convey the anxiety and tedium of the two-day hunt. For con-

trast, he cuts back to shore to show the warmth and comfort of
the cottage, the woman and child watching the men from shore,
and the community activity as the kettles are prepared for the
rendering. Throughout, Flaherty has kept the focus on the boy's
activity and longing to go to sea with the men. Although Flaherty
might have ended the film with the dramatic shark hunt, he placed
it within the story, and went on to some of the most spectacular
nature photography ever presented: the storm. The dark and
powerful poetry of these frames affirms better than anything else in
the film the brutal power of the sea and the ruggedness of the
islanders. The storm builds slowly, and the animals are the first to
react, but the woman continues to gather seaweed; it is not until
the magnitude of the storm is established that we are reminded that
the men are still far out to sea in a boat which seems useless against
the size of these waves. The emotional excitement of this episode is
breathtaking as the men fight towering waves in their attempt to
land the boat while the woman and the boy try helplessly to guide
them with shouts. Eventually the boat is sacrificed as the men swim,
wade, and jump to safety, but the woman's keening, broken by her
thanks for the men's safe return, adds a touch of tragedy that sur-
passes the visual poetry of this experience. Even though her men are
safe and her cottage is warm, she cries out helplessly against their
eternal enemy, the sea, in a mournful, unforgettable moment.

Man of Aran was attacked by most British critics, yet it received the Mussolini Cup for the Best Foreign Film at the 1934
Venice International Film Festival. In the 1930's, economic disaster
forced men to examine the immediate patterns of their lives. That a
film crew should spend two years producing a poem of isolation and
strength was simply an indulgence that nobody could seemingly
afford. In Flaherty's world there were no class struggles, no apparent hunger, no bombings, and no lines of unemployed men. There
was just the impersonal observation of man's eternal struggle
against the elements, an observation that was ironically anachro-
nistic. The world had lost its innocence, and if it could not relate to
Flaherty's film, that was its problem, he thought, not his. But the
documentary film titles of those early years—*Night Mail, Coal Face,
Housing Problems*—show that Flaherty might have to make some

compromises if he wanted to continue his career. He never lost his innocent vision or his sense of wonder at the natural world around him, and it is only when he tried to make the kind of documentary film that Grierson wanted that he was untrue to himself and a self-acknowledged failure.

*　*　*

Flaherty's activities between 1934 and 1939 are not of direct interest to the scope of this study; he was engaged primarily in directing *Elephant Boy* for Sir Alexander Korda. Although the film was honored for its direction at the 1937 Venice International Film Festival, it is clearly a Korda production incorporating some Flaherty footage and is perhaps most notable for its introduction of Sabu.

At the invitation of Pare Lorentz, Flaherty returned to the United States in 1939 to make a film about soil erosion and agricultural displacement for the government. This was a new challenge for Flaherty, and one that he accepted eagerly. Not only would he finally have an opportunity to explore and learn his own country, but he would be working with a new producer and a generous budget. The various film units of the U.S. government were comparatively new and not nearly as organized as those of the British. No businessman himself, Flaherty was at the mercy of a disorganized and chaotic operation. With another producer, Flaherty might have accomplished more, at least in financial terms, but Lorentz was too busy making a film of his own and not able to orient Flaherty to the bureaucratic complexities of Washington. Furthermore, Lorentz and the government took an approach to film making that was basically unfamiliar to Flaherty. Revillon Frères wanted publicity and got it with *Nanook;* Paramount and Gaumont-British wanted entertainment and got it with varying results in *Moana* and *Man of Aran;* but the U.S. government wanted New Deal propaganda. Such an expectation would have been an ordinary challenge to a film maker schooled in the Grierson approach, but for Flaherty it was both a challenge and an obstacle. His film *The Land* is his most controversial, as well as his most untypical achievement.[15] After it was completed and kept from general release, Flaherty admitted that he did not like it either and that he would have made it differently if he had had a second chance.[16] But *The Land* is not nearly the mistake that its reputation suggests. It has an epic theme, stunning photography, a realistic grasp of the social problem, and the undeniable stamp of its maker.

Made in the years preceding U.S. involvement in World War II, *The Land* is Flaherty's war film, but it is not about guns and trenches or planes and submarines. It is Flaherty's personal war against the machines and technology that created hunger and unemployment in the land of plenty, the richest country in the world. But these were times in which social situations changed swiftly, and the labor and farm problems that Flaherty treated so objectively were neither the same nor as acute when the film was completed. It was out of date before it was released, even though its overall theme was timeless. This contradiction emphasizes Flaherty's problem. He was working in foreign territory—the province of the sociopolitical documentary film maker—not in the recognizable contours of his own art, the romantic nonfiction film. He did not know how to make a contemporary sociopolitical statement. He was not used to producing a film in a matter of months so that its political message would still be relevant to its viewers. And despite his enthusiasm for the project, his own method was to work slowly, to shoot first and to assemble second, to proceed without plan, and, most of all, to see things his own way.

The Land is about power, or more specifically, about the abuses of power; machines which save back-breaking labor are shown, ironically, as a force of destruction, not salvation. The mechanization of agriculture may save aching backs, but it creates sore feet for the displaced thousands out of work and untrained to accept different work. The problem was, of course, a very real one, but Flaherty's explanation seems simplistic. Certainly the people were victims of progress, but he seems more interested in lamenting the romantic past than in grappling with the means which were needed to improve the conditions. Again he made a film that captured a moment in time without doing anything to relate that moment to the future, although a quotation from the book of Job attempts to give the problem a historical precedent. Flaherty sees soil erosion as a failure to honor the promise that once characterized America: "We are wasting more than our land, we are wasting our promise as a people, as a nation." This incantatory narration, spoken by Flaherty himself, owes much to the magnificent narration of Lorentz' *The River*, but Flaherty's narration (written by Russell Lord and Flaherty) is never as poetic as that in *The River* although it has an honest, vitally concerned tone to it: "Nowhere in the world has the drama of soil erosion been played so swiftly and on so great a stage."

Flaherty's moving camera—a welcome development in his usually limited use of the camera—captures some vivid images, but they do not speak for themselves, and they never capture the despairing faces that Walker Evans did in his stark still photographs, or that Strand, Steiner, and Hurwitz did in *The Plow That Broke the Plains*. Flaherty has frequent opportunities to let the human plight come through, but he does not always succeed. When he shows a farm family forced to leave its home and join the procession on the roads to California, we are reminded of John Ford's poignant handling of the same incident in *The Grapes of Wrath*, in turn visually influenced by Lorentz' *The Plow That Broke the Plains*. There, with sentiment and music and an almost indescribable coupling of fear and hope, Ford accomplished what Flaherty could not with his straight photography and his ironic narration: "We had another name for these people once. We called them pioneers." Yet the film has moments which beautifully evoke the plight of these people, such as the boy moving uneasily in his sleep and his mother commenting, "He thinks he's shucking peas."[17] Ultimately, there is no sharpness in Flaherty's attitude toward the problems; the film might have been successful if he had been outraged or even as romantically sentimental as Steinbeck. Instead, there is just comment about working children, low wages, and hunger. While the film does not pretend to cry out for rebellion against the system, it does not really condemn the circumstances or even try to understand them.[18]

Contour plowing is suggested as one remedy for the erosion

problem. This technical suggestion is valid, but it offers little
comfort when measured against the faces of starving children.[19]
Richard Arnell's concluding triumphant music, from a score that is
consistently and insistently dramatic in the worst ways, is coupled
with Flaherty's enthusiastic remark: "The face of the land made
strong again, made strong forever." While both the narration and
the music underscore the theme of abundance *versus* poverty, we
are reminded that, as a nation, the United States has both the
power to survive its problems and the power to destroy itself. But it
is only in the last minutes that Flaherty asks, "What about the
people?" If he had asked that question in the beginning, and if he
had conceived a film that could have been made in a shorter period
of time, he would have found the answer. He knew the answer all
along: the prevalence of the human spirit. But he lost it in a haze of
government propaganda. *The Land* could have been a very powerful and very influential film; instead, it is a very beautiful, empty
film. Helen van Dongen did what she could to edit its sweep and
spread into something more than a cry of pain, and she was responsible for getting Flaherty to narrate the film and give it an even
more distinctive stamp, but there are times when honesty and simplicity are not enough. *The Land* is three separate films: an editor's,
a musician's, and a narrator's. That it fragments in such a way is
Flaherty's error in not knowing how to unite contemporary social
comment with human insight. But, after all, *The Land* stands as a
testament to one man's refusal to accept artistic compromise, and if
it is a failure as a documentary film, it succeeds as a Robert Flaherty
film, as a film of keen insight, rugged determination, and visual
beauty.

* * *

The war years marked a period of comparative quiet for
Flaherty, although he did some work for a War Department film
unit. Shortly after World War I, Flaherty had been commissioned by
Revillon Frères to make *Nanook,* and now, in 1943, on the twentieth anniversary of his first film and during World War II, he was
approached by Standard Oil with a new and very appealing chal-

lenge. Standard Oil would pay all the costs, and turn over all the theater revenue to Flaherty, for a film which would show the public the long and hard work which came before the company struck oil. Flaherty was to have complete artistic control, a generous budget (it eventually exceeded $250,000), and a complete crew including photographer Richard Leacock and editor Helen van Dongen. Flaherty began work in 1946, and the resulting film, his masterpiece *Louisiana Story*, was released in 1948. He never made a finer film, and he never made another, but if this had been his only film, it alone would have earned him a distinctive reputation.[20]

Louisiana Story is a soft, lyrical film of exquisite sensibility. Flaherty called it a "fantasy," referring no doubt to its dreamlike quality, but it is also an autobiography, the very essence of a romantic whose eyes, at the age of sixty-two, were still filled with the wonder of a boy as he explores the world around him. Among his other films are biographies of an Eskimo man and a South Seas island young man, but here is an autobiography of himself and, of course, of the young boy whose film it is. Everything is seen through the eyes of the Cajun boy—Alexander Napoleon Ulysses Latour— for the swamps and bayous of Louisiana are very much his private world. The outline of the film is a simple one; it records an oil-drilling crew's entering a quiet backwater region, drilling success-fully, and leaving. Standard Oil is never mentioned in the film, except for a brief credit title thanking the men on the drilling rig; but the film is no more about oil than *Nanook* is about snow. The film is about magic: the magic of youth, the magic of nature, and the magic of self-possession.

As are most of Flaherty's films, *Louisiana Story* is episodic, with fade-outs between the sequences instead of titles.[21] There are five distinct episodes in the film, but they are never obvious; the film is never insistent, for it unfolds leisurely for the viewer, catching him in an unreal world of shapes and shadows. Leacock's photography is a triumph of subtle images: shimmering light and water for the boy's world of nature, and solid light and dark for the men's world of machines. Circular in construction, the film moves from peace and quiet to activity and noise and finally back to peace and quiet; it opens with the boy and it ends with him, and while it centers on the noisy oil-drilling operation, it suggests that nothing, not even steel derricks and steam engines, can penetrate and alter his vision of the world. Flaherty knew different, of course; he knew what man could do to his natural environment long before ecology became fashionable. He knew that innocence was bankruptcy in a world of material power, and he knew that man's technology, especially when harnessed to an industrial giant, was rarely beneficent. He knew these things, and we know them, but somehow the realization of them is not relevant to *Louisiana Story*. The environmental protection groups can claim otherwise, and with unimpeachable justification, but if they argue that the film does not show Standard Oil to be an evil force in the disruption of the balance of nature (and such criticism has not been apparent), they forget that the film is seen through the eyes of a boy, a boy whose only friend is a raccoon and whose closeness to nature is so intense that he will fight an alligator to prove a point.

The film opens slowly and quietly, revealing the boy in his pirogue floating through the shadowy world of cypress trees, Spanish moss, birds, and alligators. As he is about to shoot a porcupine, he hears an explosion, followed quickly by another; this seems to be his first awareness of something outside the bayou, something he does not understand. The following images only suggest the size and power of some anonymous monster, and it is not until we see his father signing a contract with a representative of the oil company that we realize that the bayou will never be the same again. Soon the quiet waters will be split with the roar of speedboats and the incessant sounds of drilling. The family's attitude toward this activity is ambiguous; they are neither hostile, nor hopeful of overnight riches. It is only when the wake of a speeding boat swamps the boy in his pirogue that he realizes what is happening. Flaherty then establishes one of the important symbols in a film which is heavily symbolic. The surveying team locates a spot for drilling and marks it with a stake in the water; this stake is a recurrent symbol of their invasion, and soon it is surrounded by the debris brought down the river by the drilling barges, then by the derrick itself, and finally at the end by the "Christmas tree" or pumping unit which will control the flow of oil into the pipelines. Perhaps the most effective symbol in the film is the derrick itself, a steel structure of abstract force and almost spiritual grandeur. The boy first sees it as he is looking for his raccoon, and the moment in which it enters his sight is unforgettable. Gliding through the flat marshes on some unseen barge, it towers clean and powerful; the majestic music which accompanies it does not exaggerate the moment. But it is also foreboding and not unlike the quiet and menacing ships which glide through the canals in Antonioni's *Red Desert:* observable, but unexplainable; manned, but inhuman; powerful, but unnatural.

The second part of the film is a long, but brilliantly photographed account of the noisy drilling operations. Frequent cuts to the boy in his boat further emphasize the foreignness of the drilling rig. Here Flaherty's detailed interest in the industrial process is matched by Leacock's inventive photography; the drilling is seen from many angles—from the front, from above, from the men's eyes, and finally from the boy's. He is inside the derrick now, and as he becomes friends with the workmen, he tells them about his magic— his bag of salt and the "something else" hidden in his shirt and kept to frighten "them" if such nameless spirits should ever appear. This introduces the third episode of the film, and it seems then that the huge alligators are "them." The boy and his raccoon are drifting through the water, but when the boy beaches the boat and begins to explore, he leaves the animal tied in the boat. In a scene of tremendous suspense, he finds an alligator's nest and holds a newly hatched alligator in his hand; the mother sees him, leaves the water, and moves stealthily toward the boy. As the music heightens what could be a tragic moment, the alligator gives a warning hiss, the boy runs back, and the scene ends safely. It defies verbal description, so perfectly matched are the editing, the music, and the sense of drama in the scene. Here the alligator is man's real enemy—primeval, vicious, and destructive; it is only later that we realize that oil and oil drilling fit the same categories. At this point, Flaherty builds considerable sympathy for the boy by suggesting that the alligator has eaten the lovable raccoon, who has, meanwhile, disappeared from the boat. In an act of revenge that is more bold than believable, the boy traps an alligator, fights him in a tug of war, and loses; but soon after, we see him with the skin and a triumphant flexing of muscles. This long sequence is masterfully edited to capture the excitement of the fight—the boy on one end of a slim rope and the alligator on the other—and it almost conceals the fact that the fight was staged. Certain unavoidable clues give this away, but it seems unimportant; maybe it did not happen while the cameras were conveniently loaded and ready to shoot, but it could have happened that way, and would have, most probably, if Flaherty had never thought of it.

In the next episode, the father's teasing of the workers about their failure to strike oil is dramatically contrasted to the wildcat blowout of the drilling operation; we see the tremendous rush of gas and salt water, followed by the Lorentz technique of using newspaper headlines to "explain" the event. Following the blowout, activity at the rig comes to a standstill. Climbing around on the rig, the boy decides to evoke the spirit of the well as he drops his bag of salt down the shaft and spits after it. The men laugh when he tells them of his magic, and he is both bewildered and hurt. He believes in his own magic, not in oil, and he wants to prove himself and his ability against the strange and unsuccessful attempts of the men and their machines. The problem is eventually solved by slant-drilling, and soon the well comes gushing in. At this point, the themes of the film reach a climax as Flaherty juxtaposes tranquility and disruption, superstition and technology, confident youth and skeptical age.

In the concluding episode, the father returns from the city with the usual provisions and some presents for the family, purchased with money received in partial payment for the oil. There is a double boiler and a dress for the mother, and a new rifle for the boy; as he goes out into the yard to test the new gun, he sees his friend the raccoon for the first time since he, and we, presumed that it had been killed by the alligator. Rather than a heavy-handed suggestion that the oil company arranged the reconciliation of master and pet, this final sequence serves to round out the structure, for now the drilling barge leaves as quietly and as impersonally as it came. There is quiet once more on the water, the boy has a new gun, and the raccoon is back home. One thing is changed, however; the wooden stake has been replaced by the "Christmas tree" pumping unit. The boy sails out to the pipe sprouting from the water, climbs it, and in a final gesture, waves good-bye to the departing men as he spits into the water. It is a sign that his magic, not their

Louisiana Story: With his bag of "spirits," the boy investigates the quiet mystery of the bayou swamp. Photograph courtesy The Museum of Modern Art Film Stills Archive.

technology, brought in the well, as well as an age-old gesture of contempt; perhaps it is the boy's contempt for the noise and confusion of the drilling, and perhaps it is Flaherty's contempt, his last word against the machines he hated so much. Flaherty is not contemptuous of the industrial giant which made his film possible, but with a smile on his face—on the boy's face—he says good riddance as he waves good-bye.

* * *

After *Louisiana Story,* Flaherty was involved in many projects and activities. In 1948, he made plans to do a film on Picasso's *Guernica* painting in New York's Museum of Modern Art. This project was largely experimental and was left unfinished at his death, although it was completed by his brother David and has been released. In 1950, a German-Swiss film documentary directed by Curt Oertel and based on the life of Michelangelo was released as *The Titan;* Flaherty was originally approached to reedit the film—an assignment which Helen van Dongen, among others, also refused—but Flaherty merely allowed his name to be used in the capacity of producer for promotional purposes. In the same year, he went to Germany as a cultural ambassador for the U.S. Department of State and showed a selection of his films: *Nanook of the North, Man of Aran,* and *Louisiana Story.* Although he made some plans for a film on the split between West and East Germany (to be titled *The Green Border)*, nothing came of these plans, nor did anything come from a film project for the State Department on racial integration in Hawaii called *East Is West.* In 1951, the Museum of Modern Art offered a Flaherty retrospective, and Mike Todd and Lowell Thomas engaged him to travel around the world making films in the new process of Cinerama. He accepted, admitting that money was his reason, but all he completed was a sixty-minute newsreel on General MacArthur's return from Korea. Flaherty died in 1951.

* * *

The history of the development of film is marked with many great names and great accomplishments, but the truly innovative geniuses are few. John Grierson writes,

> I personally regard Robert Flaherty as one of the five great innovators in the history of film. I think that with him go Méliès, the first of the movie magicians; D. W. Griffith for developing the strictly movie terms in which a drama could be unfolded; Sennett for transferring comedy from the limited space and conventional props of circus and vaudeville to the infinite variety of the world about; and Eisenstein for his study of organized mass and movement and his great sense of the film's potential in both physical and mental impact. Flaherty, great personal story teller as he was, did not especially think of film as a way of telling a story, developing a drama, or creating an impact, either physical or mental. For him, the camera was veritably a wonder eye, to see with more remarkably than one ordinarily saw.[22]

Although Robert Flaherty's career spanned many years, the list of his films is short. He was his own man, and he made films his own way. He started a tradition, and he left a legacy. No study of nonfiction film can proceed without a consideration of his films, and yet it is difficult to assess his influence. This indefinable quality may be the defining measure of his greatness, and his influence is there, nonetheless, every time a film maker focuses his lens with innocence, wonder, and love. As Jean Renoir recognizes: "There will be no Flaherty school. Many people will try to imitate him, but they won't succeed; he had no system. His system was just to love the world, to love humanity, to love animals, and love is something you cannot teach."[23]

NOTES

[1] For a discussion of Flaherty as a maker of "naturalistic documentary," see Hugh Gray, "Robert Flaherty and the Naturalistic Documentary," *Hollywood Quarterly*, 5 (1950–51), pp. 41–48.

[2] Arthur Calder-Marshall, *The Innocent Eye: The Life of Robert Flaherty* (London, W. H. Allen, 1963). Most of the biographical material in this chapter is based on Calder-Marshall's study, the most reliable of many accounts of Flaherty's life.

Nonfiction Film

158

3 Calder-Marshall, p. 55.

4 One year before Flaherty was heading toward the North Pole, Captain R. F. Scott was leading a British expedition to the South Pole, a record of which is preserved in Herbert G. Ponting's film, *Ninety Degrees South;* see Chapter Three for a discussion.

5 Calder-Marshall, p. 72.

6 Calder-Marshall, p. 77.

7 Calder-Marshall, p. 97. As Jean Renoir noted, this method of engaging our curiosity makes it seem that Flaherty made the picture for each individual member of the audience (Calder-Marshall, p. 95).

8 A worthwhile project for film students might be the theoretical reediting of *Moana.*

9 Calder-Marshall, p. 118.

10 However, in its use of distorted city images, the film is a legitimate ancestor to Francis Thompson's fanciful color film *N.Y., N.Y.* (1957); in 1969, the Metropolitan Museum of Art commissioned Thompson to make films (related to its major exhibitions), reviving a tradition begun by Flaherty with *The Pottery Maker* over forty years before.

11 Flaherty resigned the picture before the final reediting was begun. The film's credit titles are: director, F. W. Murnau; producers, F. W. Murnau and Robert Flaherty; screenplay, Murnau; photography, Floyd Crosby and Flaherty.

12 When filming *Louisiana Story,* Flaherty asked Helen van Dongen, "What is the longest distance between two points?"; before she could answer, he replied, "A motion picture" (Calder-Marshall, p. 214).

13 The film is discussed more fully in Chapter Three. See Grierson's comments on Flaherty in *Grierson on Documentary,* ed. Forsyth Hardy (New York, Harcourt, Brace and Company, 1947), especially pp. 139–44.

14 A fascinating account of the Aran Islands and of Flaherty's work there is Pat Mullen, *Man of Aran* (Cambridge, Massachusetts, The M.I.T. Press, 1970).

15 *The Land* was begun for the U.S. Film Service, but finished under the auspices of the Agricultural Adjustment Agency.

16 It has been shown nontheatrically, but has never been in general commercial release.

17 John Huston reportedly said that the moment was worth all of *The Grapes of Wrath* (Calder-Marshall, p. 196).

18 When Flaherty comments, "We fed the world, but now we can't feed ourselves," he pictures the incredible farm surplus stored in silos but does not suggest that this surplus can go to the poor. Such a suggestion may not have been within the scope of the government's plans, even though we earlier hear a man on a breadline comment that government food is keeping him from starving.

19 An effective film on this same subject is Alexander Hammid's *Valley of the Tennessee* (1944); see Chapter Five.

20 After Charles Chaplin, Jean Renoir, and Dudley Nichols saw the film at the Hollywood premiere, they wired Flaherty: "DO THIS AGAIN AND YOU

WILL BE IMMORTAL AND EXCOMMUNICATED FROM HOLLYWOOD WHICH IS A GOOD FATE" (Calder-Marshall, p. 229) .

21 Helen van Dongen's diary of the filming shows that the structure of the film is hers, imposed upon Flaherty's usual mass of unrelated footage; but the film is also the collaborative effort of several key artists, including Virgil Thomson and Richard Leacock. See Helen van Dongen, "Robert J. Flaherty: 1884–1951," *Film Quarterly*, 17, No. 4 (Summer, 1965) , pp. 2–14.

22 John Grierson, "Robert Flaherty," n.d., n.p. From an essay by John Grierson, in the files of the Film Study Center of the Museum of Modern Art. Grierson's editor, Forsyth Hardy, cannot identify it.

23 Calder-Marshall, pp. 248–49.

CHAPTER 7

World War II on Film

During the 1930's, nonfiction film makers were finding a voice, a
style, and a vision; their work was almost always experimental—in
the sense that they were creating new forms—and while they were
sometimes unsure of the purposes behind their work, they were
encouraged by their success with the public. Still an emerging art
form, nonfiction film was overshadowed by the great fiction films of
the major studios; still something of an oddity, it was misunderstood as educational, mistrusted as propaganda, and misused as
advertising. In most countries, documentary and factual films were
a force for social reconstruction, but the dark threat of a destructive
second world war gripped free nations and everywhere turned
people's attention from national to international problems. Such
matters as education, housing, and pollution became secondary to
such matters as treaties, armaments, and battle plans. The colossal
scope of the war made it necessary to engage all the natural resources of each involved nation in the fight for freedom. The
reluctance of people to fight another world war made it necessary
for governments to inform and to convince them of the need to
fight. Supplies had to be produced, funds had to be raised, men and
women had to be drafted for the armies in the factories and in the
fields. Civilians had to feel that they were involved, too. There
would be a thousand new things to learn, a thousand new pieces of
equipment with which to become familiar, dozens of new places and
peoples to encounter for the first time. Clearly, it was a massive task

to prepare for the global effort that would save the world from conquest.

Military and civilian strategists on both sides of the conflict realized, from the beginning, the important role which motion pictures could play in modern warfare. Films could train soldiers and industrial workers; they could build opinion, strengthen attitudes, and stimulate emotions; they could be invaluable in reconnaissance and later in combat. With the new, portable projection equipment, films could be shown in the field, in military hospitals, in jungle outposts, in industrial plants, and in civilian theaters. As barbers, lawyers, and insurance salesmen were drafted into the field, photographers, editors, and writers were drafted into the film units of the various armed forces. And although none of them had been preparing for war, they were ready for it when it came.[1]

In technical terms, World War II was probably the single greatest stimulus to the development and proliferation of film making around the world. In the United States alone, the budget for documentary and factual film production and distribution exceeded $50,000,000 a year during the war, and comparable amounts were spent by the Allies.[2] On both sides of the Atlantic, major directors such as Frank Capra, John Huston, Carol Reed, and William Wyler joined Pare Lorentz, Robert Flaherty, and Willard Van Dyke in the war-film production units. The resources of major studios, film archives, and motion picture equipment manufacturers were put at their disposal.[3] With abundant resources of men, money, and equipment, these directors, and others, produced an astonishing number of films of all kinds, for all purposes. These films are a record of conviction and achievement, but they are also a grim record of free nations at war, of horrible atrocities, and of casualties beyond belief.

The viewing of war films during the actual war in which and for which they were made imposes special burdens on the audience, whether they are civilians or members of the military. Faced with the unpleasant task of viewing and reviewing war films, James Agee wisely observed near the conclusion of World War II that,

> for all that may be said of our seeing these terrible records of war, we have no business seeing this sort of experience except through our presence and participation. . . . If at an incurable distance from par-

ticipation, hopelessly incapable of reactions adequate to the event, we watch men killing each other, we may be quite as profoundly degrading ourselves and, in the process, betraying and separating ourselves the farther from those we are trying to identify ourselves with; nonetheless because we tell ourselves sincerely that we sit in comfort and watch carnage in order to nurture our patriotism, our conscience, our understanding, and our sympathies.[4]

While neither the American nor the British films idealize war, they do explain it in an attempt to justify it. While men are not by nature eager to sit in darkened rooms and watch films which train them to drop bombs on foreign cities, they did it. And while mothers and fathers do not usually go to the local movie theaters to watch battles on strange soil in which their sons risk their lives, they went. Bound together by a common goal—freedom from aggression and tyranny—these people often set aside logic, morals, and values to support the overriding idea of victory over the enemy. It has been said that some wars are necessary, are worth fighting. A war to save the world from Hitler was necessary and was supported. Looking at the film records which preserve its efforts and battles, one senses not only history, but also civilized values being tested. Since World War II, Americans have been engaged in a "cold war," and the specter of nuclear holocaust and the Korean and Vietnam conflicts have changed attitudes about the need to fight. The films made about and for the Korean and Vietnam wars were mainly official ones for military and television purposes; we still need to learn the full story about the government's film production units. However, the public has been well-informed, for television documentaries, news programs, and "specials" have taken the place of earlier government films and newsreel accounts of war. As the Vietnam war developed, more and more Americans retracted their support for the effort. And as it plainly became a war of politicians and diplomats, not a war supported by a majority of the people, it became an underground war, as far as propaganda forces were concerned. A few sponsored films were made to support and to oppose its course, but they do not seem important as film or as propaganda. And while this may be politically naïve, it helps to prove a point about war films, for the majority of the people support them and participate in them only to the extent that they believe a particular war is being fought in the name of freedom and justice. The majority of free people everywhere do not fight for shallow patriotism, or for mindless aggression; when they unite in battle, it is to preserve the freedoms of life for them and for the world. American and British war films are a magnificent record of free people fighting to preserve their freedom.

Patterns in War Film: America and England

Wartime nonfiction films were not directly influenced by the theories of men like Grierson, although they do deal with moral, social, and economic issues insofar as they are related to war, and insofar as they suggest conclusions, stimulate ideas, and change or affirm attitudes related to war. The functions of war films are broad and varied, dependent upon the nature of the audience, the task to be performed, and the necessities of production. There are, of course, certain basic types of films: training films, incentive films for industrial workers, propaganda films for domestic and foreign purposes, reconnaissance films for strategy, combat films for study and archives, and, finally, the few and very special films which transcend the immediate war and become works of art in themselves. And there are certain patterns which are discernible within these larger categories.[5] First, there is a tendency toward personalization of subject matter, the showing of incidents which would lead to a viewer's identification with the participants in the film. Such a film (*Memphis Belle* or *The Battle of San Pietro*) might show fighting men before battle and then during battle to build an empathy for their risk and efforts. Second, there is a tendency in films produced primarily for domestic propaganda to show the common bonds of people engaged in a united effort and the value of teamwork. Some of these are incentive films (*The Story of Big Ben*) to inspire increased industrial output, while others are emotional appeals to unity (*Fellow Americans* or *They Also Serve*). Third, there is a tendency to show the need for war, the justice of the cause, the essentially pacifist nature of the free people, and respect for the dignity of man. These films are also in the category of domestic propaganda, and most of them are elaborately produced (*Know*

Your Ally, Britain; Men of the Lightship, or *Listen to Britain*).
Fourth, there are films which emphasize the justness of the fight
against a ruthless enemy, forceful films which leave little doubt
about the reasons for war (the "Why We Fight" series or *Desert
Victory*). Finally, in the later stages of war, films tend to stress the
terrible price of war, in human terms, by portraying the refugee
problems, the physical and psychological casualties, and the im-
mense task of reconstruction (*Let There Be Light* or *Le Retour*).

It is a difficult task to make a general assessment of the technical quality of films produced during wartime. Each film must be
qualified by the conditions under which it was made, the audiences
to which it was shown, the distribution requirements that often
made technical polish and perfection impossible, and the overall
function of the film. The distinguished films in the "Why We
Fight" series were, for the most part, edited compilations of existing
footage from combat cameramen, newsreels, documentaries, factual
films, and even some fictional films. Other films have the immediacy
of combat (*With the Marines at Tarawa*), and others have the
immediacy of today's direct cinema (*Let There Be Light*). Some
films lack narrative structure, while others are carefully planned
treatments (*Report from the Aleutians* or *Listen to Britain*). And
while many war films lack the careful composition, focus, and lighting which characterize the photography of most nonfiction films
made before and after the war, they make up in immediacy and
excitement what they lack in technical perfection. With a few
notable exceptions, wartime films are black-and-white, with spoken
narration, and make heavy use of patriotic, martial, and folk music.
Finally, in contrast to the typical problem-solution structure of the
true documentary film, war films tend to assume the justice of the
cause and the imminence of victory, so that they are infused with a
particularly uplifting spirit—one of the major characteristics of
propaganda—rather than with the spirit of reasonable thought that
accompanies the solutions presented in social documentaries.

While the question of "success" is not particularly relevant to
films made specifically for the war effort, some did enjoy commercial
success when released for the general public; in these instances, they
were most often on a double bill with the featured fiction film, and

it is difficult to gauge their particular success. It is apparent, though, that American audiences were as receptive to nonfiction films as they were to the Hollywood products.[6] Despite audience response to such films as *The Fighting Lady, Desert Victory,* and *To the Shores of Iwo Jima,* the public was prevented, for reasons of morale, from seeing *Let There Be Light,* a film about the psychological casualties of war that is more powerful than all the combat footage ever shot during World War II. But "success" in commercial terms is not the point; "victory" in military terms was the aim and, it was hoped, the ultimate effect of the films. Early in the war, a German general commented that the opponent with the best cameras, rather than the best armaments and armies, would be the winner.[7] Fortunately, he was right.

Nazi Films

The Nazis began their propaganda campaigns long before World War II was discussed as a possibility by the rest of the world.[8] As early as 1933, the Ministry of Propaganda, under Paul Joseph Goebbels, controlled radio, newspapers, theater, and film. Later, all German art was regimented in the "national chamber of culture" for the benefit of psychological warfare. Goebbels' theatrical flair and brilliant insight into mass psychology influenced a series of films that included *Triumph of the Will, Baptism of Fire,* and *Victory in the West.* The Nazis used large quantities of newsreel material, especially shots taken at the front, for newsreels and features.[9] They aimed at repressing thought and manipulating conclusions. In their use of commentary, they told what the visual images did not, impressing rather than instructing. In their use of maps, they exploited the graphic similarities of maps and the human nervous system to arouse a "natural" sense of encircling conquest. They also contrasted facial shots of Negroes with those of Germans to support their master race theory; however, the camera couldn't lie when Jesse Owens and his black teammates won the events filmed for Riefenstahl's *Olympia.* They used captured enemy film to work against the country from which it was seized. The

Nazis used music to intensify and manipulate, much as it was used in British and American war films; but in the Nazi films, the handling of music alone can transform an English tank into a child's toy, can erase the fatigue from a German soldier's face, and can exaggerate a few men into an advancing German army.

When the Nazis pictured Hitler, they did so with little restraint. In the early films, such as the semibiographical *Triumph of the Will,* he is continually on the screen, ranting, marching, saluting, a forbidding public figure. Later, in *Baptism of Fire,* this approach is lessened, in image and in content, to picture Hitler as a more magnanimous leader. Finally, in *Victory in the West,* warlord becomes wargod. To relieve the stridency of these political aspects, the films often picture common events and people with a false sentimentality about home, family, and religion. But the common people are never given the vitality that they possess, for example, in *Potemkin.* There is a quality of Utopian fantasy about these films that is suggested by their formality, grandeur, and unrealness. In *Triumph of the Will,* people are portrayed not as individuals, but as tiny parts of a vast superhuman machine. The only individual shots in this film are those of Hitler and his immediate staff; when we see the people, we see thousands of them at one time, standing at rigid attention, in massed columns, listening to their leaders. Finally, the Nazi manipulation of truth carefully avoided references to the attempted extermination of the Jewish people and to the concentration camps.[10]

The earliest Nazi films include *Blutendes Deutschland; Hans Westmar, Einer von Vielen; Triumph of the Will; Bilddokumente; The Camera Goes Along; Pilots, Gunners, Radio Operators;* and *We Conquer the Soil.*[11] Riefenstahl's *Olympia* was certainly a product of Nazi propaganda, and useful around the world as a demonstration of German athletic skill, but it is not directly related to war.

Other European War Films

The largest number of war films were produced in England, America, and Nazi Germany. French film making during the war was halted by the German Occupation, but after the Liberation, the French made several memorable films, including *La Bataille du Rail* (1946), *Le Journal de la Résistance* (1945), *Farrebique* (1946), *Les Maudits* (1947), and *Le 6 Juin à l'Aube* (1946).

The Russians made the familiar variety of war films, from training films to those recording great battles. Memorable among these are two newsreel compilations—*The Siege of Leningrad* and *Stalingrad*—and *The Battle for the Ukraine* (1943), produced by Dovzhenko. Of contrasting interest here is the "Why We Fight" film *The Battle of Russia* (1944). In Canada, the "World in Action" series provided informative documentaries.[12]

British War Films

As early as 1939, the British were making nonfiction films related to war. With their excellent background in documentary film making, with wide government support, and with a public favorable to their work, the British nonfiction film makers entered war production with considerably more experience than the Americans. Even before the major fighting began, they produced *Squadron 992* (1939) to familiarize the public with the balloon barrage being set up as defense against bombing. In 1939, the G.P.O. Film Unit came under the supervision of the Ministry of Information, and in 1940 it was renamed the Crown Film Unit.[13] The Crown Film Unit was particularly successful in securing facilities, staff support, and subjects with which to work.[14] Its achievements include training films, films to bolster British courage in the face of Nazi aggression, and films to project British strength abroad.[15] For audiences in the United States, the British prepared *London Can Take It, Floating Elephants* (the retitled *Squadron 992*), *A Letter from Home,* and *Men of the Lightship.* The Colonial Film Unit made special movies for instructional work among the African natives, short films to train white-collar workers for industrial jobs, to familiarize citizens with the social services available to them, to instruct people in maternity and child-care matters, to acquaint people with London transportation, to explain the medical services, and to show general conditions and the mood in British cities, towns, and villages.[16]

Agriculture and nutrition were major domestic problems for England during World War II. A skillful documentary depicting the efforts of British farmers in supplying food for people at home and for troops abroad is Humphrey Jennings' *Spring Offensive* (1940). Primarily an information film, although it can be classed as "lyrical propaganda," it is a relaxed and casual film which makes the wartime agricultural effort seem an easy task, one that hardly alters the lives of men in the country. *Spring Offensive* emphasizes the geniality and spirit of the British people, but served a more emphatic propaganda function by warning that British farmland had been neglected since World War I. While the human and natural obstacles seem easily overcome, the film is careful to point out that a nation must keep its farms in full production if it is to remain strong. Secondarily, this film pays tribute to country people for providing shelter for city children during the bombing. Wholly British and thoroughly charming, Ruby Grierson's *They Also Serve* (1940) is a good-natured, affectionate study of the role British housewives played during the war. Without pretense, this brief, simple film touches human moments that crystallize the entire war effort at home. In a different way, Arthur Elton's *Airscrew* (1940), like his earlier *Aero-Engine* (1933) or *The Transfer of Power* (1939), is a brilliant explanation of a technical process, the manufacturing of a metal airplane propeller. Of basic informational interest, it functioned also as an incentive film to raise pride among British industrial workers.

Living on a small island and dependent upon the sea for trade, transportation, and defense, the British were keenly aware of their strategic vulnerability to bombers flying from the continent and to submarines in surrounding water. Among some of the films dealing with the sea and the men who make their livelihood on it are *Merchant Seamen* (1941), *Coastal Command* (1942), *Ferry Pilot,* and *Western Approaches* (1944), and *Men of the Lightship.* In the tradition of *Drifters, Granton Trawler,* and *North Sea,* David MacDonald's *Men of the Lightship* (1940) is the first and the best of the British wartime films about the sea. Designed to arouse humanitarian feelings everywhere, this film depicts the Nazi bombing of a lightship patrol boat. In excellently reenacted scenes, it

Target for Tonight: Conviviality is silenced as members of the British bomber squadron receive their assignments for the evening's attack. Photograph courtesy The Museum of Modern Art Film Stills Archive.

portrays the informal life of the men on the ship, their survival tactics after the bombing, and, finally, their deaths by exposure as their lifeboat is lost in the fog. As a tribute to the defenseless heroes of the lightship service, this is a dramatic but controlled piece of propaganda demonstrating the Nazis' ruthlessness in attacking anything and everything. Followed by *Target for Tonight*, it helped prepare the British and their allies for the blitz attacks that were soon to devastate London, Coventry, and other British cities.

Like *Desert Victory*, Harry Watt's *Target for Tonight* (1941) is about offensive operations and was very popular with civilian audiences. It remains one of the most widely mentioned British war films, probably because it, like *Fires Were Started*, sees war operations through the eyes of the men involved, rather than through the filter of politics or propaganda. *Target for Tonight* details a typical Royal Air Force bombing raid on Germany; we see and hear the crew of one bomber discussing the plan, carrying out the mission successfully, and returning their damaged craft to a safe landing in a heavy fog. The approach is not dramatic, but rather a routine, descriptive attempt to show the careful planning and apparent ease with which the offensive operation is handled. There is a sequence which shows the reaction of German soldiers to the bombs and the destruction that occurs as the bombs fall, but these scenes appear to be reenacted. Beneath this surface we see the British: confident, but afraid; humorous, but wary; convivial, but alone with their thoughts. Watt does not dramatize the ordinary, as he did in *Night Mail*, but he does provide an intimate, natural picture of men at war. Unlike Capra, who, in his "Why We Fight" films, sees war as a vast struggle between forces of right and wrong, Watt sees war as the combined operations of many small units of men. He sees war in human, not global terms. Generally, this approach is characteristic of British war films, where people, not battles, are the concern, where defensive planning, not propaganda, is the focus, and where the war effort is a sense of mission, not destiny.

J. B. Holmes' *Coastal Command* (1942) is a dramatic, intimate picture of the work of the Royal Air Force and the Royal Navy in protecting British shores during World War II. Pat Jackson's *Western Approaches* (1944) records the story of wartime convoys on

Coastal Command: A bomber pilot scans the coastal waters in this tribute
to the forces that protected British shores during World War II.

the Atlantic, contrasting American and British methods for transporting men and materials around Nazi traps. While the film is somewhat similar to *North Sea,* Jack Cardiff's color photography (color is very rare in British nonfiction film history) enlivens an otherwise routine film.

With *Spare Time* (1938) and *London Can Take It* (1940), Humphrey Jennings expressed his feeling for ordinary people and activities. With *Listen to Britain* (1942), he captured a broad impression of a nation resolute in its stand against Nazi aggression. The key to this outstanding cross-section view of British life is not sight, but sound. *Listen to Britain* continues the tradition begun with *Night Mail* in its exploration of the uses of sound in the documentary film, and it includes directly recorded natural speech, poetic commentary, music, and the natural sounds of life. Similar in approach to other cross-section war films (*The Ramparts We Watch* and *War Comes to America*), *Listen to Britain* attempts a "symphony" of the sounds of Britain at war. From its fervent spoken patriotic narration, to its use of dance-hall and folk songs, to its recording of mechanized military vehicles, to a concert by Myra Hess in the National Gallery, the sound track underscores the sense of anticipation and waiting that is visible on every face. Ironic notes are recorded throughout in shots of dirigibles keeping watch, in a mix of traffic and factory sounds over a Mozart piano concerto, in shots of empty galleries and empty frames in the National Gallery, now evacuated of treasures. In its mixture of these various sight and sound elements, and in its recognition of the power of sound to provide not just accompaniment but counterpoint to the images, *Listen to Britain* is an important contribution to the use of sound in nonfiction films. With characteristic British understatement and reserve, the film provides a careful portrayal of a strong nation, ready for war, but continuing in its traditional activities. Children dance in a ring at school, miners go down into the pit, the Queen appears at a lunchtime concert for office workers. All are aware that, sooner or later, they will become the "target for tonight." Through the film's artistry and candor we become familiar with the solid human strength that was to preserve England through the war. In *Fires Were Started* (1943), Jennings showed that strength in action.

A realist and a poet, Jennings was able to fuse these two traits

Fires Were Started: Humphrey Jennings' masterpiece of wartime film making dramatically highlights the tensions and dangers of civil defense during the London blitz.

in his masterpiece, *Fires Were Started*. Like so many British nonfiction films, its subject is deceptively simple: a typically dangerous day during the London Blitz for a unit of the National Fire Service. Jennings did not impose dramatic situations or caricatures upon this situation (as Dickinson did in *Next of Kin*), nor did he attempt to make heroes out of dedicated men doing their work. Rather, he established the individuality of the men who formed the unit and then followed them through their activities, from the routine maintaining of equipment to the unpredictable fighting of a warehouse blaze. Jennings understood men at work, their easy informality, their conviviality, their singing, and their anticipation. There is an excellent sequence showing the men at leisure while they wait for the alarms to sound; they sing, dance, play pool, tease each other, hardly aware that a dangerous and even deadly fire awaits them, as it does almost every night. The fire itself, shot under actual conditions, is never as exciting as it should be to support the first half of the film. The scene of fire fighting is long, tedious, and curiously devoid of the drama that one might expect, but, on the other hand, it is also just another fire to these men, just another opportunity to help in the defense of London. The nighttime photography is excellent, but the music fails to complement the action, as it does so perfectly in the first half of the film. It is only in the conclusion, with a fireman's funeral attended by his buddies, cross-cut with shots of the ammunition ship which he helped to save, that we understand the importance of the firemen's work. If it weren't for the unsatisfying lack of tension between the two parts of the film—the preparation and the fire—and for the lack of dramatic intensity in the fire sequences themselves, *Fires Were Started* would be an almost perfect film. As it is, it remains more than praise of the dedicated men and women of the Fire Service, for it is a particularly imaginative treatment of a thoroughly prosaic subject; like *Night Mail,* it will live as a work of art, long after the "Postal Special" and the wartime defense effort are memories.

Throughout the war, Jennings made films that stressed the strength and courage of the English people. Joining *London Can Take It, Listen to Britain,* and *Fires Were Started* were *The Silent Village* (1943), *The True Story of Lili Marlene* (1944), and *Defeated People* (1946). *The Silent Village,* a reenactment similar in

The Silent Village: A group of frightened children represents the need for vigilant defense in this harrowing re-enactment of what might have happened if British soil were occupied by enemy troops.

some ways to the "it can't happen here" format of Peter Watkins' later *The War Game* (1966), is essentially a fiction film with a propaganda intent. Made in the Welsh mining town of Cwmgiedd to honor the victims of Nazi attack on the Czechoslovakian mining town of Lidice, this film presents a lyrical view of quiet village life interrupted by Nazi occupation. The village resistance is shown in strikes, acts of sabotage, and rebel attacks on occupation soldiers. Although much of the dialogue is in Welsh, the people's reactions come through the language barrier. This film does more than draw parallels in its attempt at reinforcing the horror of war at home by contrasting it to the horrors abroad. It depicts in cruel terms what the British would experience if the Nazis were to occupy their land. It is a mythical analog and a real warning, meant to strengthen morale and sharpen consciousness of the need for total defense against the enemy. The American film *Fellow Americans* (1942) is somewhat similar in intent, but less effective in its attempt to relate the attack on Pearl Harbor to an attack on American homes. *A Diary for Timothy* (1946) takes the form of a story told to a new-born baby, recounting the sacrifices and struggles of the British people, but stressing his luck in being born after the worst of the war was over. The film ends with a challenge to Timothy and others of his generation: "Are you going to let this happen again?" Blurred in focus and development, its emotion and directness make up for its uncertainty. The commentary, written by E. M. Forster, is far too sad and sentimental to serve the purpose of the film, although it is beautifully read by John Gielgud.

In England, as in America, the resources of the feature studios were made available for the war effort. Production and distribution facilities, men and machines, all joined to support the work of the Crown Film Unit and the Ministry of Information. As in America, also, feature film directors contributed to the development of the wartime documentary, adding not only their artistry, but also their sense of dramatic realism. Among them were Carol Reed with *The Way Ahead* (1943), Anthony Asquith with *Freedom Radio* (1942), Charles Frend with *The Foreman Went to France* (1942), Frank Launder and Sidney Gilliat with *Millions Like Us* (1943), and Thorold Dickinson with *Next of Kin* (1942).

Setting aside his experiments with color and animation, Len

A Diary for Timothy: This single shot does more than the complete film by Humphrey Jennings to show the conditions in which wartime children could expect to grow up.

Lye compiled *Cameramen at War* (1944), a brief history of the work of top cameramen in combat. The film shows the highly specialized activities of these experts, and introduces many of them, but it is memorable for a shot of D. W. Griffith in the trenches of World War I. As a film, it bears about as much resemblance to the style of Lye's characteristic films as Frank Capra's war films bear to the distinctive style of his comedies. The war effort was, obviously, of primary importance. The lasting record of the work of these combat cameramen is preserved in the films compiled from the footage they gathered on various fighting fronts. Such films as *Wavell's 30,000* (1942), *Tunisian Victory* (1943), and *Desert Victory* (1943) are full-length campaign films, similar to the shorter American films such as *Report from the Aleutians, The Battle of San Pietro,* and *The Liberation of Rome.* The best of these British films is *Desert Victory,* an account of the victory over Rommel's troops by General Montgomery's army at El Alamein. This graphic document brings the reality of war home to the civilian audience. It sketches the geographical and military background of this major turning point in the allied efforts against the Nazis, and depicts the physical hardships and obstacles that proved a more formidable threat than Rommel's German-Italian army. *Desert Victory* is complete, incisive, and lucid in its handling of combat footage, some of it captured from the Germans in their retreat. Combat is shown at a terrifyingly close range, and the shots of nighttime artillery attack are spectacular. Like such later American films as *With the Marines at Tarawa* and *To the Shores of Iwo Jima, Desert Victory* captures the immediate strategy of battle in contrast to the lives of the individual fighting men from the general in command to the infantrymen in a trench. The narration here is much less strident than that of the American combat films, and, for the most part, the sound is directly recorded on the scene.

Another film compiled not from combat footage, but from that dealing with a problem aggravated by war is Paul Rotha's *World of Plenty* (1943). A diffuse film dealing with food and nutrition, it attempts to educate viewers on such matters as equable food distribution, food imports and exports, subsidies to farmers, the Lend-Lease Plan, and the overall duty of the British government to ensure the nation's health. It deals with wartime shortages, postwar

World of Plenty: Scavenging through garbage cans, a family represents the poverty and famine that come in the wake of war. Photograph courtesy The Museum of Modern Art Film Stills Archive.

food production, and means which will be taken to prevent the famine and pestilence that followed World War I. Finally, it focuses on science as the answer to devastated farmlands, and advocates a world food plan based on man's right to be free from hunger. *World of Plenty* is an extremely ambitious film, but in its overall attempt to cover this vast subject, it loses focus and direction. To maintain the viewer's attention on a complex problem and to hearten him with hopeful postwar plans, Rotha uses many unique elements, some of them evident in his earlier *New Worlds for Old*. There is a ponderous "voice-of-god" narration challenged by a colloquial American voice. There are graphics and diagrams, also challenged by the American. There is an American visitor to London interviewing British housewives on the ration system. And overall there is a slick and somewhat superficial desire to make irreversible common sense out of a worldwide paradox of plenty existing side by side with poverty. Undoubtedly this film was also intended to show British citizens that rationing was an equal problem in America and that they would have a voice in postwar planning and prosperity. If *World of Plenty* is not wholly effective in its presentation, it is a superb example of how much shape and style could be given to footage shot at different times and places. With *Desert Victory* and *Listen to Britain,* it was influential on Frank Capra's "Why We Fight" series.

The British wartime films constitute an extraordinary achievement in the development of nonfiction film. Nearly all of them are achievements in film *as* film, reflecting the ten years of experimentation and development in nonfiction film that preceded the war. With a degree of emotion that is still effective and always moving, these films are an eloquent record of British unity, patriotism, and humanity in time of peril.

American War Films

The American motion picture industry, including Hollywood professionals and independent documentary film makers, joined together in a massive effort to keep America informed of its role and responsibility in World War II. Impressed by the Nazi and British film programs, American military and civilian authorities agreed that film could inform the predominantly isolationist people of America of how, where, when, and why they were fighting. They had to understand the significance of combat in places they had never heard of before; they had to understand the reasons behind rationing, twenty-four-hour industrial production, victory gardens, and the War Department telegrams announcing the deaths of their brothers and sons and fathers. Generally, these films were shown to the men in service and to the workers in industrial plants, but many were released to the commercial theaters. American wartime film production falls into several distinct categories: military training films; propaganda films for domestic use; propaganda films about America for overseas use; action and combat footage shaped into propaganda films for military and domestic use. Many films overlap these categories.[17]

The earliest example of a wartime documentary that defies specific categorization is Louis de Rochemont's *The Ramparts We Watch* (1940). A "March of Time" production, this is a daring and successful attempt to counter the feelings of American isolation before World War II. Unlike other "March of Time" films, it is thorough in its historical explanation of the American role in World War I, and it is direct in its attempt to relate that struggle to World War II. The film is both a fictional reenactment and a compilation of newsreel footage, and while its sense of small-town America is somewhat trite, its overall picture of the American mind before World War II is convincing and accurate. In contrast to *War Comes to America,* it is immensely more appealing in its dramatic narrative, and it makes brilliant use of typical patriotic and popular war songs. Clearly sentimental, it also appeals to a sense of justice and democracy. It is set apart from the other slick "March of Time" films by its feature length, by its tempered narration, and by Lothar Wolff's skillful editing of newsreel footage, Nazi propaganda films, and reenactment footage. Ambitious as it is broad, general as it is specific, *The Ramparts We Watch* is superseded only by the "Why We Fight" series in its attempt to inform Americans about the war.

Military Training Films

Training films accompanied the soldier through every step from his induction, orientation, and training, to off-duty activities, demobilization, and even preparation for his postwar life. He was shown how to dress, how to keep himself and his gun clean, how to avoid disease, and how to salute his superior officers. The outstanding example of films produced primarily for the education and training of men in the armed forces is the "Why We Fight" series, American war documentary at its best. But there are many other films, showing the wide range of topics with which soldiers and their superiors had to be familiar. A good example is *Know Your Ally, Britain* (1944), first in the "Know Your Allies–Know Your Enemies" series. The British projected themselves in *Listen to Britain* (1942), a film very popular in the United States; *Know Your Ally, Britain* was America's attempt to understand and project British character and culture. It is a tough, simple film, stressing America's roots in England's past, similarities, rather than differences, and unity in the war effort. Through the use of homely figures of speech, athletic metaphors and analogies, and an unfortunately condescending use of stereotypes, the film succeeds in creating a lively impression of the British people. Its main strength is its refutation of Hitler's anti-British propaganda; and although it perpetuates certain silly stereotypes about English life, it is scrupulously fair in trying to understand the truth behind these stereotypes. In human terms, it is an interesting and effective film.

Another film with an honest intent, but also with an unfortunate use of stereotypes that diminishes its force, is *The Negro Soldier* (1944). Meant to instill pride in the role which blacks have played in the nation's defense since Revolutionary War days, the film also shows prominent blacks in sports, the arts, and professional life. It stresses the anti-Negro aspects of Nazi and Japanese propaganda, but it totally overlooks the segregation in the United States armed forces. The only integrated scenes of military life depict a church service and an officer's training course. There is, in fact, no direct reference to segregation; we see it, indirectly, though, but not intentionally, as a typical soldier's experiences are depicted (through a letter read by his mother). We see him going through enlistment, training, and combat in a segregated company. This is unfortunate, for the same film efforts that were made to acquaint fighting men with their allies and enemies might have been directed toward acquainting them also with their mistreated and misunderstood black fellow soldiers. It is not enough, however, that the film depicts segregation without attempting to correct such an injustice; it uses shuffling jazz rhythms and a musical comedy ending that is as offensive as it is destructive to the whole intent of the film. In a final montage, utilizing four images on the split screen, we see black soldiers marching to a jazzy march version of "Joshua Fought the Battle of Jericho." A curious conclusion for a film which begins with the serious fact that the first to die in the Boston Massacre was a Negro patriot.

As the war in Europe drew to a close, with victory over Germany and Italy, homesick troops looked forward to returning to the United States. To boost their morale, but also to prepare them for the inevitability of their transfer to the Pacific front, Frank Capra made *Two Down, One to Go* (1945), a sophisticated use of psychology on film. But more important in Capra's significant work for the war effort is his memorable "Why We Fight" series. Historically balanced, persuasively and dramatically presented, these films did more than any other to answer the doubts in people's minds. They are remarkable pieces of propaganda, made by film experts who had studied and restudied the best of the Nazi and British films. Equally important, they are good films, mostly compilations from many sources, but lucid and fresh in their handling of facts. The "Why We Fight" films filled a very important gap in America's effort to understand and justify the war. For civilian and fighting man alike, they explained government policy and diplomacy during the decade preceding the war, and stirred emotions through their continual emphasis on Nazi brutality. Looking back on these films, Capra wrote,

> . . . the WHY WE FIGHT series became our official, definitive answer to: What was the government policy during the dire decade 1931–1941? For whenever State, the White House or Congress was unable, or un-

willing, to tell us what our government's policy had been (and this happened often) I followed General Marshall's advice: "In those cases make your own best estimate, and see if they don't agree with you later." By extrapolation, the film series was also accepted as the official policy of our allies. . . . Thus it can be truly said that the WHY WE FIGHT films not only stated, but, in many instances, actually created and nailed down American and world pre-war policy. No, I won't say it. Yes, I will say it. I was the first "Voice of America."[18]

There are seven films in the series: *Prelude to War* (1943), *The Nazis Strike* (1943), *Divide and Conquer* (1943), *The Battle of Britain* (1943), *The Battle of China* (1944), *The Battle of Russia* (1944), and *War Comes to America* (1945). They were made basically in historical order, stressing the rise of Nazi aggression, the major battles of the war, and, finally, the impact of all the prewar and war activities on American public opinion. The final film, *War Comes to America,* is similar to the "March of Time" production *The Ramparts We Watch* (1940) in its cross-section view of isolationist America reluctant to enter another world war. Capra's film is a very persuasive piece of propaganda showing American values and the great shift in public opinion which led to our entrance into the war, while the Louis de Rochemont film is a dramatic reenactment which traces American reaction before World War I, helping people to see the similarities between that period and the period prior to World War II.

Prelude to War, the first of the series, is also the most patriotic and aggressively prowar of the films. Its purpose is to answer the "Why We Fight" question, and it proceeds toward this goal by contrasting the "free world" with the "slave world." The opening focus is on slavery, on German regimentation, on Japanese militaristic opportunism, on organizations of "Fascist stooges led by dictators." The film documents terrorist executions, the destruction of churches and synagogues, brainwashing, and the indoctrination of children. In a brilliant montage of goose-stepping Nazi soldiers, the film makes its strongest point about regimentation. In his treatment of the free world, Capra stressed freedom of the press, of worship, of education, and of elections. But he was tough in charges of alleged United States isolationism and lack of support for the League of Nations. His overall logic is simple—"It's their world or

Prelude to War: The "Why We Fight" series heavily stressed the indoctrination tactics of enemy countries; here, an Italian child is shown learning the fascist salute. Photograph courtesy The Museum of Modern Art Film Stills Archive.

ours"—and his persuasiveness is tough: "The chips are down." In its vigorous handling of an explosive question, this film sets the tone of the distinguished series to follow.

The Nazis Strike is a highly charged, emotionally told history of the "maniacal will," the "madness," and the "insane passion for conquest" of the Nazi leaders. It stresses their terrorist tactics and propaganda and explains their pincer strategy (an aspect fully detailed in *Divide and Conquer*). It is, perhaps, the most fervently anti-Nazi film in the series, and in its use of music ("Warsaw Concerto" and "Onward, Christian Soldiers") it creates a mood of moral righteousness that, despite its good intentions, detracts today from its effectiveness. But, again, subtlety and reserve are not the hallmarks of wartime propaganda.

Divide and Conquer records the high point of the Nazi Blitz and the low point of Nazi treachery, the period in which Belgium, Holland, Denmark, Norway, and France were invaded preparatory to the Blitz and planned invasion of Britain. The title refers to Hitler's method of using propaganda to confuse and ultimately conquer the little free countries. Methods such as sabotage, the fifth column, strikes, riots, and hate literature are depicted. The tone of the narration is remarkably factual, but it caters to its audience as it compares Hitler's lies and "efficiency" with the tactics of the gangster Dillinger. There is also heavy irony—a Capra specialty in these films—in the comments on the Low Countries' neutrality and the Nazi betrayal of the Dutch surrender in the bombing of Rotterdam and its civilian population. France is portrayed as disillusioned and cynical, mindful of her heavy World War I casualties, dismayed at the failure of the League of Nations, and weary of her own ideals. Such criticism is typical of the overall attitude the "Why We Fight" series takes toward hesitant countries, isolationism, and inaction by allies of the League of Nations. A well-organized film, clear, explanatory, persuasive in its use of charts, maps, and diagrams, *Divide and Conquer* is an especially hard-hitting attack on Nazi policies, "a new low in inhumanity."

Three films in the "Why We Fight" series are devoted to specific military campaigns. Of these, *The Battle of China* is the weakest, and *The Battle of Russia* the strongest. *The Battle of*

Divide and Conquer: Hitler reviews his troops as they prepare for their attack on France. Photograph courtesy The Museum of Modern Art Film Stills Archive.

Britain is a picture of Britain at its lowest point, after the defeat at Dunkirk and during the blitz of London and Coventry: "Hitler could kill them, but damned if he would lick them." As with the other films, there is a stirring use of martial music to excellent purpose and effect; here, for example, the familiar British "Land of Hope and Glory" and "British Grenadier" provide ironic musical comment on the fiery swastikas burning across the map of Europe.

In *The Battle of China,* the commentary is pro-China, but simple to the point of being corny. While the narration is, again, ironic, its tone of moral outrage lessens the impact of the film. Horribly graphic photographs of the wounded and killed do what the narration does not. As with *The Battle of Russia,* the film is a record in praise of the people's resistance against aggression, and, with the other films in the series, it uses colorful figures of speech to make its points. For example, the Burma Road brings the "blood plasma of supplies" and the Yangtze River is "China's sorrow." Ending with the assertion that "China's war is our war," this film, like the others, depicts the consequence of enemy aggression and the necessity of resistance and defense. And, with the others, it makes the indirect point that we fight over there so that we won't have to fight here at home.

The Battle of Russia is a tough, fast, informative film. As usual, an assemblage, with some staged or reenacted scenes, and almost one-half hour longer than the other films, it is a thorough coverage of the depth and breadth of the massive Nazi attack on Russia. The cross-sectional view of Russia's natural and human resources is far too long and far less exciting than similar sequences in *War Comes to America,* the last film in the series. But with the other films, it is hard hitting, heavily ironic, and full of praise for the strength and determination of the Russian people in their fight against the Nazis: "Generals may win campaigns, but people win wars." Capra and his staff were successful, in these films, in their use of music native to the countries whose plight they were portraying; here, there is a colorful use of many types of Russian music from choral songs, to folk ballads, to themes from great classical works. More analytical than the other films, *The Battle of Russia* discusses individual reasons for the final Nazi failure in Russia. More dramatic than the other films, it reaches its climax in the Siege of Leningrad and a final, unforgettable shot of a captured German soldier trudging across the ice in a pair of makeshift paper shoes, an ironic comment on the so-called invincible Nazi juggernaut. And with the other films in the series, it concludes with the ringing of the Liberty Bell and a superimposed "V" for victory.

War Comes to America begins with the usual explanation that it is a War Department film, compiled from authentic newsreels, official films from the United Nations, and captured enemy film, and that, when necessary, for the purposes of clarity, reenactments have been made. It is concerned with the great shift in public opinion in the decade before the war, tracing the gradual shift from isolationism to support of America's entrance into the war. A careful film, it makes several important background points. First, it shows the American fight for freedom from Jamestown, through the westward movement, through the immigration movement which built the country, through World War I. Second, it emphasizes the attributes of the American people, and shows them to be hard working, inventive, enterprising, educated, sports and pleasure loving. But, more important, it stresses Americans as a free people who believe in the future, in the liberty and dignity of man and peace; people who hate war, but who will fight to preserve freedom. Third, it asks "Is the war necessary?" and answers that world events make it so. To appeal to the average soldier in the audience, it parallels his childhood and adolescent years with actual world events, from the Depression through the Neutrality Act through the Japanese-Chinese conflict to the Munich Pact. It utilizes figures from the Gallup Poll (referred to as an expression of "we the people") to substantiate the rising war sympathy among Americans and footage from the Nazi rally in Madison Square Garden to demonstrate the closeness of a war that some might have thought was limited to foreign shores. As the war effort builds, we see a cross-section of all men who joined up ("This is the Army, Mr. Jones" on the sound track), Hitler's invasion of Europe ("The Last Time I Saw Paris"), and the bombing of Pearl Harbor. It skillfully combines public opinion polls, official testimony, and historical fact and reference in its method; its chief feature is its comprehensive picture

The Battle of Russia: Four captured Nazi officers in a Russian prison camp are imperious reminders of the enemy's strength. Photograph courtesy The Museum of Modern Art Film Stills Archive.

of the diversity of American life. Perhaps the most carefully documented answer to the overall question "Why We Fight," *War Comes to America* is a dramatic, fast-moving, patriotic, and ultimately convincing film.

The "Why We Fight" series is persuasive, dramatic, and forceful in its presentation of known facts; and sophisticated, especially, in its use of sound, narration, music, and speech. These films are masterful in their compilation of many kinds of film footage, a brilliant triumph of form over content. The narration is tough and ironic, wholly American in its rhythms, figures of speech, and attitude toward the enemy. Psychologically insightful, these films never admit the possibility of an American defeat; instead, they make a beast out of Hitler and heroes out of the ordinary citizens who were his victims. The American fighting man is encouraged to persist, to believe in the moral necessity of his job, and to have faith in the simple, underlying principle on which these complex films were made: the rights to freedom, to justice, and to happiness are undeniable, worth the fight, and within grasp. The films suggest that Americans need strength and determination to prevail against the enemy. These are strong films determined to help men win. The "Why We Fight" series is not only the best group of films to come out of the war, but also the best film record of the reasons behind that war, the most dramatic account of the battles in it, and the most eloquent tribute to the civilian and military men and women who fought and died in it.

On a totally different level, but one of the most instructive and successful of the films made by the Army exclusively for the armed forces, was the biweekly, twenty-minute newsreel series *The Army-Navy Screen Magazine*. These short films were designed to accommodate audience requests, and, therefore, were quite flexible and informal in their presentation of material. Folksy, humorous, optimistic, they were produced to give information and to build morale. For example, when a man wrote that he wanted to see a picture of his home town, he usually got it. Another soldier sent in lyrics of his own composition, asking without much hope that it be set to music and that the Army get "some dame to sing it. I'd faint!" Shortly thereafter, the song was recorded and filmed; the commentator remarked, "Here you are soldier, go ahead and faint."[19] This diverse screen miscellany included cartoons (Private Snafu); quick, factual instructions on various subjects; and more serious reports (such as J. Edgar Hoover's narration of Nazi espionage in the United States). But above all, they were the G.I.'s own films, and carried a lesser degree of government propaganda and a stronger degree of entertainment than other wartime films.

During the war effort, thousands of films were produced for training purposes. Some of these are sophisticated lessons in navigation, and others are basic instruction in how to survive on the desert. Among the more imaginative are the animated color films made by Walt Disney Studios for the U.S. Navy. Bright, colorful, and clear, they turn the complexities of meteorology and navigation into fun.

Incentive Films

Although it is difficult to make clear distinctions between films produced for domestic propaganda purposes and those produced for incentive purposes, there is a group of films which seems more clearly intended to boost the morale and, therefore, the production levels of industrial workers than to appeal to the average civilian. These films range from the whimsical *Out of the Frying Pan into the Firing Line* (1944), a Walt Disney-Minnie Mouse collaboration on the saving of fat scraps, to the serious *The Story of Big Ben* (1944), a tribute to shipyard workers. *Road to Victory* (1944) features Bing Crosby and Frank Sinatra in an effort to sell war bonds, while *America's Hidden Weapon* (1944), similar to Britain's *They Also Serve,* documents the work of farmers and victory gardeners in supplying the nation's increased agricultural needs during wartime. *How Good Is a Gun?* (1944) is designed to compliment and motivate munitions workers, the same kind of defense workers pictured in *War Town* (1943), a brisk, straightforward presentation of the problems in a typical Alabama town overcrowded with defense workers and their families.

Combat Films

While many professional film makers were busy producing overseas propaganda about America, scores of combat cameramen were overseas gathering direct photographic records of the war. Often working under the worst conditions, under live fire with men dying around them, they preserved a record that is immediately shocking in its ability to bring the war home to civilians.[20]

In an effort to relate the soldiers of World War II to those who have protected America since the wars of revolution in the eighteenth century, Garson Kanin made *Ring of Steel* (1942), a brief film narrated by Spencer Tracy. Also designed to instill a sense of history and a realization of the present conflict is Kanin's *Fellow Americans* (1942), an emotional and often impassioned challenge to vigilance. Through a self-consciously poetic narration, spoken by James Stewart, the film relates the bombing of Pearl Harbor as if it had happened to four typical American cities. The bombs fell, but "no one heard, no one saw," the idea being that direct attacks on troops abroad are also indirect attacks on people at home. As with many war films, the use of music is very effective; here, American patriotic themes are used in crescendo to drown out the sounds of warfare. But although they try, neither of these films brings the immediacy of combat home to civilian audiences.

Among the first war films to provide a picture of American troops in action were *War Department Report* (1943) and Darryl F. Zanuck's *At the Front in North Africa* (1943). Samuel Spewack's *The World at War* (1943), a compilation film somewhat in the "Why We Fight" genre, provides historical background to America's entry into combat. But the first really professional film to give Americans a close look at their troops in action was John Huston's *Report from the Aleutians* (1943). In color, rarely used for combat films, this is an intelligent information film which details the activities and missions of an isolated bomber squadron. For the most part, it was made away from the immediate scenes of combat, a factor which obviously influenced its excellent color photography and careful organization. There is a characteristic

Huston toughness in conception, direction, and narration that sets it apart from some of its contemporaries, and which reserves for it, as for William Wyler's *Memphis Belle* (1944), a special place in the effort to bring the war home to civilians. John Ford's *Battle of Midway* (1942) is a sentimental tribute to actual pilots, but it is so badly photographed and edited that one never knows who is shooting at whom. The color photography does not compensate for the trite narration—"The Battle of Midway is over; our frontyard is safe"—read by Jane Darwell, Henry Fonda, Donald Crisp, and a "voice of god." The use of such songs as "Red River Valley," "Anchors Aweigh," and "Onward, Christian Soldiers" is, perhaps, valid in Ford's attempt to bring his feeling for America to a nonfiction film, but it does little to enhance a film that is awkwardly conceived, badly edited, and embarrassingly folksy.

As the war progressed, techniques in combat photography, planning of combat films, and organization and narrative improved, not only with experience, but also with the gradual influence of certain theatrical elements brought to the films by their makers, many of whom were top Hollywood names. *Report from the Aleutians* and *Memphis Belle* are early distinguished films reflecting these influences; however, *AAF Report* (1944), *Attack: The Battle for New Britain* (1944), and *The Liberation of Rome* (1944) are exciting, but routine combat films. Huston's *The Battle of San Pietro* (1944), one of the most distinguished films to come out of World War II, is, like his other war films, an informative, and moving, human document. The film uses diagrams to explain the military strategy behind the long battle in the Italian mountains, and the faces of the people involved reveal the brutal impact of war. There is direct footage of soldiers being shot and killed, of bodies being placed in unlabeled white sacks, of townspeople returning to a devastated mountain village.[22] And through these harrowing sequences, we are never allowed to forget the importance of the foot soldier, the tenacity of the townspeople, and, remarkably enough for a propaganda film, the Allied doubts about success over the Nazis. Made in the heat of fire, the photography includes, with the films that were to come from the Pacific front, some of the best footage from the war. In all of Huston's war films, there is a deep

The Battle of San Pietro: Carrying a homemade coffin on her head, a woman flees the destroyed village. Photograph courtesy The Museum of Modern Art Film Stills Archive.

pacifism, and this accounts for the continual editing and reediting which War Department officials required for his work. *The Battle of San Pietro* did not appear until after 1945, a year after it was made, because it offended officials in Washington; *Let There Be Light* (1945) was never released, probably because it is one of the most moving antiwar statements ever put on film. But neither of these films is directly or intentionally a "pacifist" film, for they reflect, with grim immediacy, the need for stopping the Nazis and the awful cost behind the politics of war. But it is not in rhetoric or in policy that war is justified or denounced; it is in the faces of little children returning to the bombed-out ruins of San Pietro and in the dazed and uncomprehending reactions of shell-shocked veterans (*Let There Be Light*) that the real story of war is told.

The films made in the latter part of the war in the Pacific reflect the extent to which photography, editing, and narration had progressed from the early records. Among these tense and professional combat films from the Pacific are *Brought to Action* (1944), *The Battle for the Marianas* (1944), and *Guam: I Saw It Happen* (1944). Two films which provide a well-prepared buildup to victory with intercut shots of the combat and the dead are *With the Marines at Tarawa* (1944) and *Fury in the Pacific* (1945). The former, in color, praises the Marines, while the latter is a more dramatic, and less ironic, overall picture of combat and casualty. No war film better captures the intensity of fighting in the Pacific than *To the Shores of Iwo Jima* (1945), a color compilation of footage by Navy, Marine, and Coast Guard combat cameramen. A full record of the complex invasion and capture of this strategic Japanese stronghold, the photography is so real that it seems almost as if the scenes had been restaged for Hollywood cameras. It is not a reenactment, but rather the product of the organized, efficient, and professional cameramen who recorded the action. At this point in the war, the battles were monumental, and the fighting was epic; in almost unreal color footage, this film documents those proportions.

Behind the scenes in combat were the day-to-day activities which supported the invasion and the attacks. Less a combat film than a theatrical record of these workings and their importance is *The Fighting Lady* (1945). The narration takes a tough attitude

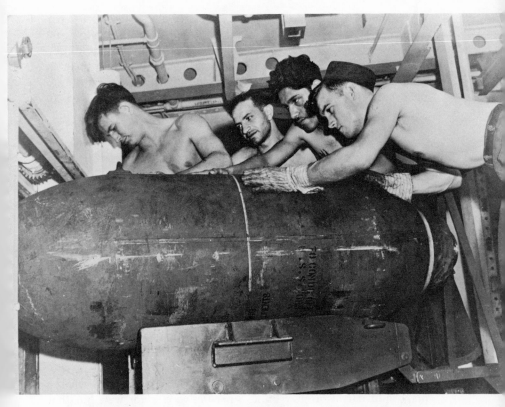

The Fighting Lady: Crewmen aboard "The Fighting Lady," named in honor of all U.S. aircraft carriers, prepare for the battle of the Philippine Sea. This Navy film combines a tribute to naval air power with a sentimental emphasis on the sailor and his duties. Photograph courtesy The Museum of Modern Art Film Stills Archive.

("Remember Pearl Harbor") as it relates the attack on Truk Island, the massive Japanese naval base, but it is also folksy and sentimental in its emphasis on the average sailor and his duties. With photography supervised by Edward Steichen, the film includes some spectacular color footage of combat, but it is essentially a propaganda film, for the civilians at home, recording the work of the aircraft carriers at sea.

Films on the Effects of War

Most wartime films were made during the war for specific military and civilian purposes, for training and for propaganda, and most of them depict, in one way or another, the effects of war on its participants. But there are films primarily concerned with the psychological, physical, and emotional results that preserve, sometimes forever, the horror of war. These films depict the casualties of the spirit, as well as those of stone; they document destruction and despair, poverty and disease, hopelessness and fear. They are the human documents, and because of that, they reflect the humanity that helps men endure in the face of opposition.

Frank Capra's "Why We Fight" films may explain the political and military reasons for war, but they do not explain the psychological and physical effect of war on soldiers. His graphs, charts, maps, and narration may build a persuasive case for war, but that kind of knowledge alone is not enough, for the destructiveness of war defies and transcends objective explanation; it can be viewed only in subjective human terms. The greatest films to come out of World War II—*Let There Be Light, The True Glory,* and *Le Retour*—record man's inhumanity to man, but they seek, also, to preserve his humanity.

John Huston's *Let There Be Light* (1945) is, ostensibly, a training film designed to convince the general public, especially employers, that soldiers suffering from neuropsychiatric damage can be rehabilitated and resume civilian life. The film has never been released, except for professional study, for various reasons, none of which seems particularly convincing in light of the massive problem which it does so much to help one to understand. But *Let There*

Be Light does more than "train" in the ways of psychiatric therapy; now, with the years and with a much more enlightened view of psychiatry, we look at the film as a record of war, not told in the numbers of rounds fired or enemy tanks captured, but in the numbers of soldiers reduced to uncontrollable weeping, to loss of memory, to loss of speech and muscle control, to loss of spirit.

The film opens in shadow; we see the stretchers being carried off ships and planes into hospitals. Huston reads the narration: "Here is human salvage—the final result of all that metal and mortar can do to violate human flesh." With a directness that only the concealed camera can record, we participate in actual interviews and hear the soldiers themselves tell of their hopelessness, their fears of death, their grief over lost buddies, their insomnia and nightmares. Balanced against the emotional impact of this footage is an intelligent explanation of mental illness and of the detailed therapy by which it is controlled and cured. Because of its technical vocabulary and disturbing realism, it is not an average layman's film. The primary purpose of the film is to show the techniques of psychiatrists as they attempt to locate the sources of illness; and in actual scenes, it depicts narcosynthesis, hypnosis, and group therapy. But it is not in these informational sequences that the film carries its power. It is in the unforgettably poignant moments before, during, and after therapy that the film's true message is conveyed. A soldier who has been mute finally cries out, "God, listen, I can talk; I can talk. Oh, god, listen." A soldier overcome with homesickness and nostalgia sobs when remembering a letter which contained a picture of his sweetheart at home. And a class of soldiers learns to play the guitar and strums "When I Grow Too Old to Dream." Theatrical, perhaps, but a moment of sentiment and realism that dramatically preserves a moment of life.

Let There Be Light suggests that happiness results from human relationships and from love, both of which give safety and security. In its implications, this means not only the security provided by professional therapy, but also, and more important, the security provided by understanding families, patient employers, and an enlightened public. William Wyler says it another way in his fiction film *The Best Years of Our Lives* (1946) when the amputee Harold Russell steps out of the cab on his first day home. In that moment are crystallized all his fears about a world which he hopes will understand what it has done to him. It is a subjective experience not easily conveyed, and if *Let There Be Light* ends a little too easily with a ceremony of discharge from the hospital, it does not create the impression that war-induced neuroses are easily treated.

As a documentary about war, *Let There Be Light* is without compare. It records the factual realities, and it reacts to them with moral vigor. It tells the truth, a sorry comment on its suppression by the government.[23] It shares with Huston's other war films—*Report from the Aleutians* and *The Battle of San Pietro*—the toughness of conviction and honesty of presentation that make them outstanding examples of the nonfiction art. *Let There Be Light* is a victim of an irony not intended by its title, and when men think about waging war, they should be required to see it.

On a larger scale, *The True Glory* (1945) stresses the common soldier and teamwork in a cross-section view of the Allied war effort from the Normandy invasion to the occupation of Germany. A joint British-American production, edited by Carol Reed and Garson Kanin, this compilation film relies on a beautifully edited mass of footage underscored by the voices of the men themselves, telling their own story. There is narration from all kinds of soldiers, low, high, young, old, white, black, American, British. General Eisenhower adds his own authoritative comments from time to time. In its use of sound, especially, *The True Glory* is a detailed account, in human terms, of war, and is not without its irony and its humor. The composite of pictures and episodes moves forward with a sense of strategy and progression, both in military and cinematic terms, but the ending seems abrupt and inconclusive. The war was not over, of course, when the Allied Forces entered Germany, and the meaning of the "true glory" is incomplete, although the following line is quoted from the English Book of Common Prayer in an attempt to explain it: "It is not the beginning but the continuing of the same, till it be thoroughly finished, which yieldeth the true glory."[24] From Eisenhower's narration, one would assume that it is the teamwork of a complex force of men. From the men's voices, it seems to be a miracle of cooperation and tenacity. From the overall film, it seems to be all of these, not victory itself, but the common pursuit of victory by men dedicated to peace and freedom. But what the film lacks in narrative focus, it more than compensates for in editing, rhythm, musical score, and overall impact.

But while the true glory of war lay in the victory for freedom, the truth of war lay in the hideous pits and ovens of Nazi concentration camps, in the unreal dust of Hiroshima and Nagasaki, in the wreckage beneath the waves of Pearl Harbor. These, too, are things we do not forget. For every smiling soldier on V-E Day, there was a mother waiting anxiously and in vain for a son that would never return; for every ship sunk at Pearl Harbor, there were hundreds of thousands of Japanese who, if not burned beyond any human recognition, were strange skeletons in a landscape that no one had ever imagined. The record of war is a record of victory and defeat, of man's humanity and inhumanity, of joy beyond belief, and of despair beyond imagination.

In the face of great catastrophe and human tragedy, the artist is often mute; in reflection, he finds that simplicity is the only technique by which to capture the magnitude of the events before him. Henri Cartier-Bresson is such an artist. His years of work as a still photographer proved to him the value of capturing not only the moment, but the meaning of the moment in the passing of time. Without text, his volumes of photographs relate, better than words, what it means to be alive. There are moments in the human experience which need no comment and no elaboration. And so, without much commentary (the narration is in French), his *Le Retour* (1946) stands as the most moving document of human agony and joy to come out of World War II. *Le Retour* is about the liberation of French prisoners from Nazi concentration camps, about their removal, half dead, on trucks, about their recovery in hospitals, and, finally, about their return to France and reunion with families and friends. It is a subtle film in its factual presentation of horror and happiness; neither of these extremes needs dramatic emphasis, and Cartier-Bresson relied on an almost static, almost still, camera to record them. The faces speak for themselves, and it is in the record of haunted eyes in sunken faces, in the tense, gripped hands of waiting relatives that this story is told. There is shape, flow, and rhythm to *Le Retour,* and there is music, sometimes too dramatic, but effective. As the ancient Greeks knew, art was needed to shape the tragedy of human life into a triumph of joy over despair.

The True Glory: American troops advance through the bombed ruins of Cologne; the shell of the famous cathedral is in the background. Photograph courtesy The Museum of Modern Art Film Stills Archive.

Cartier-Bresson knew, too, that the overwhelming emotion of great tragedy leads to the suspenseful catharsis of anticipation and joy. Through simple images, he recorded and preserved the triumph of life over death.

In the Pacific, the war came to an end with the dropping of the atomic bombs on Hiroshima and Nagasaki. Japanese cameramen recorded what they could of these devastating blows, but the film was confiscated by the U.S. Army and not declassified until twenty-five years later. And so the final statement about World War II was not released in any government film, but compiled from actual footage in *Hiroshima-Nagasaki: August, 1945* (1970). This stark and simple film is mainly a visual record of the physical and human destruction caused by the bombs, of cities reduced to ashes, of women with the patterns of their kimonos burned into their skin, of children brutally mutilated. The narration is by two voices: the poetic, simple comments of a Japanese woman victim, and the factual, but ironic comments of the American writer-editor, Paul Ronder. But it is a film record so horrible that neither the narration nor words here can describe it. *Hiroshima-Nagasaki* is a film about the ultimate: death. The voice of Robert Oppenheimer, one of the inventors of the bomb, repeats words from the *Bhagavad-Gita,* the Hindu book of devotion, to describe the weapon: "Now I am become death, the destroyer of worlds." The film closes with a statement against the testing of nuclear weapons. It makes no direct accusations against those who developed and dropped the bombs, and it makes no overly emotional comments on the victims. It is not a factual film, for the facts are too awesome, too horrible, to be treated objectively. But this film is a remarkable first step in helping us to understand the meaning of war.

NOTES

1 For an account of the shift in production from peace to war, see J. Mc-Donald, "Film and War Propaganda," *Public Opinion Quarterly* (Sept. 4, 1940), pp. 519–22; and (March 5, 1940), pp. 127–29.

2 Richard Griffith, "The Use of Films by the U.S. Armed Services," in Paul Rotha, *Documentary Film* (New York, Hastings House, 1952), p. 345. For a record of British production, see *The Factual Film* (London, Oxford University Press, 1947).

3 See: Alex Greenberg and Malvin Wald, "Report to the Stockholders," *Hollywood Quarterly*, 1, No. 4, pp. 410–15; and *Movie Lot to Beachhead*, ed. by editors of *Look* (Garden City, Long Island, New York, 1945).

4 "Seeing Terrible Records of War," *The Nation*, 160 (May 24, 1945), p. 342.

5 D. W. Gallez, "Patterns in Wartime Documentaries," *Film Quarterly*, 10 (Winter 1955), pp. 125–35.

6 Ezra Goodman, "Fact Films to the Front," *American Cinematographer*, 25, No. 2 (Feb. 1945), p. 47.

7 Griffith, p. 344.

8 Most of the factual information in this section on German propaganda films is derived from Siegfried Kracauer, *From Caligari to Hitler* (Princeton New Jersey, Princeton University Press, 1947), especially pp. 275–307. This later work incorporates the material in Kracauer's earlier short study: *Propaganda and the Nazi War Film* (New York, Museum of Modern Art Film Library, 1942). A more recent, and more general study is David Stewart Hull, *Film in the Third Reich* (Berkeley, California, University of California Press, 1969).

9 They capitalized on the fact that war correspondents were in danger and died in the pursuit of their material, an approach opposite to that shown in the British *Cameramen at War*.

10 For information on the showing of such films to Germans, see these articles by Robert Joseph in *Arts and Architecture*: "Films for Nazi Prisoners of War," 62 (May 1945), p. 16; "Film Program for Germany," 62 (July 1945), p. 16; and "Germans See Their Concentration Camps," 63 (Sept. 1946), p. 14.

11 See Chapter Five.

12 In Holland, Sweden, Denmark, and Norway, there was little film making during the war of direct relevance to the conflict.

13 For full information on the development of the E.M.B., G.P.O., and Crown film units, see *The Factual Film* (London, Oxford University Press, 1947).

14 See H. D. Waley, "British Documentaries and the War Effort," *Public Opinion Quarterly*, 6, No. 4 (Dec. 1942), pp. 604–09.

15 The Crown Film Unit cooperated with the Colonial Film Unit, so that films from the dominions were available in England and abroad. From Canada came *Wings of Youth*, from South Africa *Africa Marches*, from India *India Marches*, and from Australia *Forty Thousand Horsemen*.

16 J. Devine, "British Wartime Shorts," *Public Opinion Quarterly*, 5 (June 1941), pp. 306–07.

17 Films made by the OWI, essentially for overseas screening, are discussed in Chapter Eight.

18 *The Name Above the Title* (New York, The Macmillan Company, 1971), pp. 336–37.

[19] Griffith, p. 352.

[20] See Herb A. Lightman, "Shooting Production under Fire," *American Cinematographer*, 26, No. 9 (Sept. 1945), pp. 296–97ff.

[21] Griffith, pp. 355–56.

[22] Those white sacks of casualties have been censored out in the present version now available from various Army posts, but the sequence is preserved in the print available from the Museum of Modern Art.

[23] About its suppression by the War Department, James Agee wrote, "I don't know what is necessary to reverse this disgraceful decision, but if dynamite is required, then dynamite is indicated."—*Agee on Film* (Boston, Beacon Press, 1958), p. 200.

[24] This quotation appears in the closing credits, but is missing from some prints.

CHAPTER 8

Nonfiction Film in Transition: 1940–1950

If it is possible, for purposes of discussion and distinction, to separate nonfiction film production during the 1940's into two broad
categories—those films whose subject is World War II and those
films whose subject is not—then a clear line of development and
transition will be visible between those films made before the war,
those made during the war but not directly concerned with it, and
those films made after the peace was achieved. Since "war films"
were the subject of the previous chapter, this chapter will be concerned, as far as is possible (since war is too massive a social
phenomenon *not* to affect all modes of thought and expression),
with those films made in England and America during the 1940's
that are concerned primarily with nonmilitary subjects.

At the beginning of World War II, the nonfiction film movement was only ten years old in England, and even younger and less
organized in America, but, nonetheless, in both countries its developments and achievements more than outweighed its short life. In
England, a distinct school had evolved and matured, primarily in
the G.P.O. Film Unit; in America, the opposite occurred, with a
number of important individual film makers producing independen-
dently, although often with government support, films of high
quality and influence. As we have seen, the British documentary
film movement was founded on a principle which combined aesthetics and practical politics. The film makers who joined it had
abundant opportunities to experiment and to protest, to educate

and to influence, and to help improve the social conditions of their time. While their politics were often subordinate to the larger and more general concerns of their sponsor—the British government—this did not lessen their social consciousness or their determination to make films with a direct involvement in specific problems. In fact, this system of sponsorship resulted in a free creative climate of such proportions that it has been unequaled by any other similar film program since, with the possible exception of the output of the National Film Board of Canada in the 1950's. But in America during the 1940's, nonfiction film production unrelated to war was not spurred by anything like the momentum and continuity which carried the British movement from the 1930's into the 1940's. While film makers such as Pare Lorentz and Willard Van Dyke found themselves busy with the requirements of war film production, there was little to replace the production units of the armed forces once the war was over. Further, it is an ironic fact that the freedom which fostered American nonfiction film production before the war was its obstacle after the war. As soon as the conflict ended, people turned their attention to the pleasures of peace, and they wanted Hollywood movies, not socially conscious documentary films.

England

In the 1930's, England pioneered the documentary film and led the way for its future development; in the 1940's, English film makers continued to adapt the form to the needs of the moment. While part of their efforts was devoted to the production of films related to the war, as we have seen, another part was occupied with films for commercial and institutional sponsors. The old foundations, however, were being challenged. Producers such as Grierson and Cavalcanti had proved that film could be adapted for the education of the masses. They found drama and excitement in commonplace topics, and they did not have to compromise their aesthetics with the realities of their practical obligations. However, the base of sponsorship needed broadening; the G.P.O. and the various adventuresome industrial organizations which produced films during the 1930's had brought the documentary film—and the discussions which attended its birth and accompanied its development—to a point at which the underlying tension between aesthetic ideals and educational realities was threatening to fragment the relatively young movement. Major issues of great social importance had been tackled, and the solutions to major problems had been suggested. A great deal of useful information had been supplied, and a great many people had been influenced. Reform, action, and results were the keynotes of the movement. But as the movement grew, it became apparent that the expenses of film making required a kind of sponsorship that would allow both for the creative development of individual film makers and for the dissemination of the sponsors' particular ideas. Such an ideal situation was not always possible, of course, as Flaherty discovered in the United States with *The Land;* his later success with the unprecedented financing of *Louisiana Story* was a luxury that few film makers ever experienced. The danger, then, for those who wished to continue in the rapidly maturing documentary form was the possibility that unenlightened commercial organizations would use films only for their advertising possibilities and not, in the larger and more idealistic sense, as Grierson had envisioned. Fortunately, the tradition of government-sponsored film making continued in England through the 1940's, so that many film makers were engaged in the production and distribution of quality documentary films. At the same time, many commercial and industrial organizations were persuaded to use documentary films, and while their system of distribution could not equal the government's, they supported many imaginative and effective films. Films such as *The Harvest Shall Come* (1942) and *When We Build Again* (1945) are a reminder that commercial organizations can support and benefit from films of social significance as well as those with purely commercial intent. The Imperial Chemical Industries sponsored *The Harvest Shall Come,* a film about the refertilization of depleted soil; by focusing on the problems of individual farmers, on the necessity for an expanded agricultural effort, and on the challenge of the postwar future, this far-sighted treatment of a major social problem undoubtedly sold as many chemical fertilizers as any direct advertising campaign, and with a definite educational achievement as well.

A by-product of the mainstream documentary development—

which, as before, tended to produce films of less than feature length—was the appearance of the documentary-related feature film. While these films were fictionally based, their nonfiction approach was such that they provided added evidence of the vitality and immediacy of the nonfiction film. As we have seen, the fiction and nonfiction film have not developed exclusively of one another. Flaherty found it desirable to enhance fact with fiction in *Nanook of the North,* and films such as Harry Watt's *The Saving of Bill Blewitt* (1936), Pare Lorentz' *The Fight for Life* (1940), Ivens' *Power and the Land* (1940), and Flaherty's *Louisiana Story* (1948) are all essentially nonfiction films, but they are immeasurably enhanced by the imaginative fictional elements in their conception and narration. In each of these films, as in countless others, the need to dramatize and humanize certain subjects is clear. The same is true of many war films where the abstract concerns of battle are made more specific through the concentration on the activities of a specific individual or, more often, a specific and identifiable group; films such as the British *Squadron 992,* or the American *Fighting Lady* helped to bring the massive and global war effort into personal focus. In Britain, though, more than in America, the commercial film industry adapted the documentary and nonfiction approach successfully to a number of feature films which were directly concerned with the war effort. Representative of these films (which often featured popular star actors) are Thorold Dickinson's *The Next of Kin* (1942), dealing with the subject of security, Sidney Gilliatt's and Frank Launder's *Millions like Us* (1943), a cross-sectional incentive film stressing the need for the cooperation of all citizens—especially women—in the war effort, and a similar film by Carol Reed, *The Way Ahead* (1944), late but nonetheless humorous and effective in its depiction of a cross-section of men as they were before and after their conscription into the armed services.

Like their predecessors in the 1930's, the British documentaries of the 1940's were professional and accomplished achievements in the film art. Their treatment of social problems was, if anything, more direct and more incisive than in the earlier films, and they tended to have a longer running time than the earlier films. While an average length is thirty minutes, many prewar films were forty-five minutes and even one hour in length. They were different also from the earlier films in their extensive use of written dialogue, studio sets, professional actors (in addition to the actual people of the situation being filmed), diagrams, and multivoice narration. In short, the British documentary film makers continued to be professional in their handling of subject, brilliant in their photography and editing, experimental in their treatment especially of sound, and unrestrained by earlier notions of realism and length. Above all, their films preserved the essential British characteristics of understatement, thoroughness, clarity, and humor.

Two films by director John Eldridge provide an example of the somewhat narrow scope of British documentaries in the early days of World War II. Both were produced by the Ministry of Information, and both feature commentary written by Dylan Thomas. The first, and the shorter of the two films, *New Towns for Old* (1942), is an information film on city planning, but in eight minutes it can provide only a simple and unfortunately superficial question-answer narration regarding a subject that was so expertly handled in the earlier American film *The City* (1939) and in the later British film *When We Build Again* (1945). The Eldridge-Thomas collaboration *Our Country* (1944) is far more successful in its presentation of wartime Britain for overseas audiences. Similar to the American *War Comes to America* (1945), *Our Country* aims at presenting a cross-section of cultural and social patterns. However, it is overly sentimental (a pardonable fault of nationalistic films) and often superficial, and with the exception of a sequence in which a munitions plant worker expresses her relief at surviving a nighttime bombing raid, there is little sense of the personal emotions and values of the British people that come through so solidly in such films as *They Also Serve* and *Listen to Britain*. From the activity of London to the comparative quiet of a Welsh town, we see the spectrum of Britain through the eyes of a wandering British seaman, but what remains in the film is Thomas' memorable commentary, a lyrical tribute to the strength and determination of the British people.

In the tradition of Ivens' *Power and the Land* and Humphrey Jennings' *Spring Offensive* is Max Anderson's *The Harvest Shall Come* (1942). Produced by Basil Wright for the Imperial Chemical

Industries, this film is far-sighted in its realization that the world's depleted soil must be made fertile for a hungry world. Essentially a history of post-Victorian farmers, it reviews the problems incurred by the shift from an agricultural to an industrial economy and uses actors in its semifictional approach to the "neglected and forgotten" farm workers. While it is neither as dramatic nor as challenging as *The Plow That Broke the Plains* or *The Land,* it is an effective variation on the same theme. Its cautious, but hopeful ending—"This time it's got to be different"—characterizes the understatement of the film.

Paul Rotha was also interested in the land and its resources, but not exclusively in agriculture. *World of Plenty* (1943), *Land of Promise* (1945), and *The World Is Rich* (1947) are all concerned with the related wartime problems of agriculture, food, and starvation, while *A City Speaks* (1946) deals with postwar rebuilding.[1] *Land of Promise* is an ambitious, comprehensive, and almost wholly successful feature-length documentary "argument about our houses and homes." Based on the idea that a house is not always a home, it criticizes the British government's handling of housing problems between the first and second world wars. Hard-hitting and challenging, it is much more ambitious than *The City,* for example, but ultimately less successful than that film in its plea for uniform planning. The reasons are evident in the film's technique. If anything can be said of the many films written and directed by Paul Rotha, it is that they are too ambitious in their technical approach to be wholly satisfactory. Rotha favors the well-organized film; here there are three parts: homes as they were, as they are, and as they might be. Predictable and neat as such organization may be, it is hardly imaginative, even though this particular film is beautifully paced and edited. Eager to further the development of the modern documentary film, Rotha combines several incompatible techniques. *Land of Promise* uses a question-answer narration, a skeptical man-on-the-street narrator (actor John Mills), in addition to other narrative voices, and diagrams for explanation and clarification. Detailed in explanation, graphic and convincing in argument, and almost militant in intent, the sheer variety of these technical devices tends to blur the film's focus on the need for urban planning. *Land of Promise* is a fascinating example of all that can be done with the documentary approach; unfortunately, all of it should not have been done in one film.

Similar to *Land of Promise* in its use of multivoice narration and diagrams is Rotha's *The World Is Rich,* an ironically titled film about the massive problem of hunger after World War II. Essentially a compilation film, it shares some of the same footage that comprises *The Pale Horseman* (1946), but it lacks the impact achieved by the editing of that film. After the war, Rotha turned his attention to purely civilian matters in *A City Speaks* (1947), a full-length film of the processes of local government in Manchester, England. An aggressive but pleasant public relations film, sponsored by the Manchester Corporation, it recounts the history of this important manufacturing center. It carefully explains local elections and government; while it takes an optimistic and idealistic view of bureaucratic democracy, it does not shirk from showing realistically the "rotten leftovers of yesterday" in the city's slums. This is a sponsored film with just enough sense of responsibility to make its social consciousness acceptable. Sometimes superficial in approach and presentation, it is more effective as a spirited challenge to the future than as a record of the present. *A City Speaks* demonstrates that professional skill, technical virtuosity, and comprehensiveness do not necessarily make an effective documentary film when genuine commitment to social problems is absent.

In the mid-1940's the commercially sponsored film resumed its important role in British documentary production. Few institutions or corporations are enlightened enough to devote their interest, imagination, or funds to films involving social problems or human relationships, but those that do have made possible such films as Flaherty's *Nanook of the North* and *Louisiana Story,* the Van Dyke-Steiner *The City,* and Basil Wright's *Song of Ceylon.* Both *The Harvest Shall Come* and *Land of Promise* are commercially sponsored films, but they are surpassed by a group of films made following the war.

Sponsored by Cadbury Brothers, the chocolate manufacturers, Ralph Bond's *When We Build Again* (1945) is an excellent documentary on urban planning in the tradition of *Housing Problems* and *The City.* Like *Housing Problems,* it incorporates interviews with people in their own houses, but unlike the earlier film, it makes strong points in favor of the integrated planning of new cities. Like *The City*, it emphasizes the advantages of light, quiet, and open spaces. The film begins with a commentary written and spoken in part by Dylan Thomas: "When we build again, we must build for people." A good example of the problem-solution film, *When We Build Again* integrates visual image, commentary, and music in a persuasive and pleasant social documentary.

A film which might have been sponsored by an organization representing the coal industry, but which was, instead, produced by the Crown Film Unit of the Central Office of Information, is Humphrey Jennings' *The Cumberland Story* (1947). Ironically, it exhibits the faults that might be expected in a commercially sponsored film, and lacks the virtues that generally characterize a social documentary produced by the government. It is, for these reasons, unique and worthy of study. *The Cumberland Story* deals with the reorganization, reactivation, and redevelopment of an outdated coal-mining operation in a depressed area. Narrated by the new manager of the mines, a well-intentioned and progressive individual who counters fear and resistance among the villagers, the film takes a dogged and predictable approach to the resolution of these problems. While Jennings' view is straightforward and comprehensive, incorporating some excellent dramatic reenactment, this film lacks the humanity of his earlier *Fires Were Started*. The British Film Institute chose it as the outstanding documentary of the year, a questionable distinction for a film that promises so much more than it provides. Nonetheless, it is an interesting variation of the most persistent theme in British documentary: the importance of the individual worker in the industrial environment.

Other postwar films sponsored by commercial organizations include two films by Ralph Keene: *Cyprus Is an Island* (1945) and *String of Beads* (1947), a travel-information film for the International Tea Bureau which, for some unexplainable reason, presents the lush beauty of Ceylon in black-and-white photography; and two films by John Eldridge: *Three Dawns to Sydney* (1948), a fragmented tribute to air power made for the British Overseas Airways Corporation, and *Waverly Steps* (1949). Made for the

Scottish Office, and intended as a film to promote interest in and travel to Edinburgh, *Waverly Steps* owes something to the "city symphony" tradition in its attempt to capture the diverse cultural interests of the Scottish capital. While it pictures the sights and sounds of Edinburgh and shows the cordial reception given to a non-English-speaking Danish visitor, *Waverly Steps* makes up in warmth what it lacks in the mysterious emotional mood of the earlier continental city symphonies such as *Rien que les Heures, Berlin,* and *Gamla Stan.* It is remarkable for its avoidance of clichés (only once do we hear bagpipes), for its imaginative and rhythmic editing, and for its use of the moving camera. More about actual people in the city (as in Arne Sucksdorff's *People in the City*) than the patterns of a city (Ruttmann's *Berlin*), this is, nonetheless, more distinguished than the conventional travel film.

The Cumberland Story is an example of what can happen when a government agency sponsors a film of essentially commercial interest and fails to do justice to the subject matter. Terry Bishop's *Daybreak in Udi* (1949), made by the Crown Film Unit for the Colonial Office, is a film about Nigerian social development, and illustrates what can go wrong when government policy takes precedence over subject matter. The situation depicted by the film is the construction of a maternity hospital in the jungle, and the problem is seen through the eyes of the British officer for the district. Unfortunately and, no doubt, unintentionally, the film reflects an imperialist attitude that is particularly offensive, for, on one hand, the officer encourages the preservation of tradition and, on the other, the use of a sort of persuasive logic that ignores ancient native feelings. In contrast to the natives, who are shown to be reasonable and intelligent, the officer seems officious and unnecessarily paternalistic. The problems of minority-opposition superstition are formidable, and these are well presented, but solved so glibly as to make a strong case against the necessity of any British assistance or supervision. In short, it is a film that ignores all of Grierson's teachings about the balance of presentation and propaganda, and ultimately, a film that betrays its sponsor.

The editorial magazine film, begun in America with the "March of Time" series, was less influential in England, although in Canada the "World in Action" series (1940–46) was a distinguished contribution to this hybrid field. The English "Wealth of the World" series was concerned with various natural and industrial resources. *Transport* (1950) is an example of the approach taken in a discussion of the British railway system. Recounting the history of railways, coaches, buses, and heavy trucking, the film neglects any thoughtful consideration of union problems in its overall emphasis on the efficiency of the socialized transport system. Similar to the "March of Time," its superficial presentation sacrifices accuracy and depth. At the end of the decade, the nonfiction approach continued to influence fiction film making in such full-length feature films as Phil Leacock's *Life in Her Hands* (1950), on the training of nurses, and *Out of True* (1950), on mental hospitals.

By 1940, documentary film was firmly established in England as a major creative movement, sponsored both by the government and by nongovernment organizations. Technical experimentation resulted in significant achievements, and the film makers used sophisticated and imaginative approaches to complex social problems. During the 1940's, development continued, but the achievements were uneven, in contrast to the consistent quality of production in the 1930's. There were fewer films, of course, due to the war effort, and while these tended to be more ambitious in scope and in length, few of them equal the memorable films of the previous decade. One part of the problem was the uncertainty of sponsorship, and another was a lack of focused leadership; these factors are reflected in the quality and quantity of production.[2] It was not until the 1951 Festival of Britain provided commissions for several outstanding productions that the strength of the British documentary movement was to be seen again. If the 1930's are the high point of the British movement, and the 1940's a period of transition, then the 1950's mark the revitalization of the one form of film making that Britain can truly call its own.

The United States

During the 1940's, the development of nonfiction films unrelated to war was complicated by several factors, not the least of which were loose organization among the major film makers, inadequate financing, lack of government interest—a factor both intrinsic to the American government's attitude toward the arts and its massive support of specific war films—and a general confusion regarding the status of the form itself. As before, the confusion stemmed from the "art or propaganda" question. In England, as Richard Griffith writes, "Grierson was building his successful British documentary movement on a principle of compromise between the interests of adult education on the one hand and the interests of big business and big government on the other."[3] But there was no one with Grierson's tenacity in America, at least no one able to unite film makers as diverse, for example, as Lorentz, Van Dyke, Strand, and Hurwitz into one production group.[4] Willard Van Dyke summarizes one of the problems:

> As a documentarist, I have always been slightly envious, however, of the artist who makes his personal statement without compromise. Films cost money, and to travel to underdeveloped places with camera and crew is beyond the resources of most film-makers. No matter how much one would wish to make an impassioned film plea for justice in the Congo, for instance, the direct experience of finding the appropriate images on the spot and transferring them to film is out of the question without substantial financial support from someone. And if such aid is forthcoming, it will be from sources that have a stake in the kind of film that is to be made. You have to be lucky to have a sponsor whose goal is the same as yours.[5]

Much of the effort of American documentary film makers during the 1940's was directed toward producing films for the Office of War Information. These films were designed primarily to project the American way of life to audiences abroad. Shown both to military and civilian groups, these OWI films marked the high point in U.S. propaganda films, and furthered the continuing development of quality nonfiction films. Involved in this effort were such prominent documentary film makers as Alexander Hammid, Irving Jacoby, Boris Kaufman, Irving Lerner, Lawrence Madison, Sidney Meyers, and Willard Van Dyke. Their films are marked by unabashed patriotism, and sometimes by an oversimplified and almost antiseptic portrait of America, but they are, nonetheless, films of feeling and, at times, films of simple beauty. They stress traditional, small-town America, avoid major urban problems, and emphasize the American values for which people were fighting. If they are romantic, they are so with a purpose; propaganda does not always paint realistic pictures. Some of these films are humorous (*The Autobiography of a Jeep*, 1943) or educational (*The Grain That Built a Hemisphere*, 1943) or instructional (*Water: Friend or Enemy*, 1943). But, for the most part, the OWI films are concerned with American values and life as it had been, life as it was, and life as the film makers hoped it would be in the future, after the war.

Viewing these films, a foreign audience would get this impression: America is a country of small towns, quiet church-going citizens, and lazy leisure-time activities. Such an impression is given in Josef von Sternberg's *The Town* (1944), a short account of the cultural and architectural traditions Americans inherited from Europe. More effective in its attempt to depict America's ability to absorb foreign immigrants is *The Cummington Story* (1945), a beautiful and moving evocation of the American Dream. With genuine sensitivity for American and foreigner alike, this lovely film captures all that is best in a small New England town, and, by implication, in the country. The story concerns four foreign families who leave the turmoil in Europe for a new life; when they arrive in Cummington, townspeople are cool, even aloof; eventually, the minister, who narrates the film, helps them all to understand their self-consciousness and, in time, to build mutual confidence and respect. *The Cummington Story* is a sentimental view, enhanced by Aaron Copland's music, but it remains a true and intimate variation on the "melting-pot" theme.

Willard Van Dyke's *Northwest U.S.A.* (1944) is more folksy than *The Cummington Story*, but also more factual; it depicts the Northwest as a trade crossroads for over-the-pole flights and documents the building of the Grand Coulee Dam, especially the role it played in supplying power to World War II industries. Depicting another region of the United States, Alexander Hammid's *The Valley of the Tennessee* (1944) takes a straightforward look at the TVA project, but is careless in its attempt to minimize the complex cultural and political obstacles to the project. While the film emphasizes the development of people through the development of natural resources, it does not give proper emphasis to the communal aspects of the project. Hammid's *A Better Tomorrow* (1945) is even more superficial in its view of the New York City school system. Filmed in a high school, it pays primary attention to the new aspects of progressive education, and only minimal attention to bad schools, racial problems, and teaching deficiencies. This is American war propaganda at its low point, for it is as unfair to its subject as it is to the country, and by avoiding the present, it distorts the future. In a completely different vein, Jules Bucher's *The Window Cleaner* (1945) provides a brief "day-in-the-life" account of a Manhattan window cleaner. The film takes a realistic and independent attitude, the underlying thought being that the window cleaner is as much a part of the American scene as the skyscraper. This simple subject is saved by a whimsical jazz score and a tough, plucky commentary spoken by the window cleaner himself.

While some of the OWI films concentrated on regional values, towns and places, and projects such as the TVA, others were concerned with wholly American institutions and the people who run them. Henwar Rodakiewicz's *Capital Story* (1945) recounts the work of the U.S. Department of Health, and John Houseman's *Tuesday in November* (1945) explains the American electoral system. Alexander Hammid's *Library of Congress* (1945) presents a lively picture of the library's work in preservation, education, and service to the academic and lay communities. Willard Van Dyke's *San Francisco: 1945* (1945) records the drafting and approval of the United Nations charter at its founding conference. The film, at first, appears to be reedited newsreel footage, but it soon becomes clear that the use of the camera and the tone of the narration accomplish more than factual coverage of this historical event. They emphasize that the world's hopes in the United Nations were based on its intention to prevent future wars. Alexander Hammid's *Toscanini: Hymn of the Nations* (1945) is unlike these other OWI films, for it concentrates almost wholly on presenting a sensitive portrait of maestro Arturo Toscanini conducting a radio broadcast of Verdi's "Hymn of the Nations," programmed in celebration of Mussolini's fall and the liberation of Italy. Reportedly the most famous and most popular of the OWI overseas films, this is not only a rare photographic record of Toscanini at work, but also a master-piece of planning, camera work, and sound editing. More than just a film about music, it conveys the color and power of Verdi's patriotic score through masterful photography of the faces of the performers and their conductor.

It is difficult to assess the effectiveness of OWI films overseas, but it is relatively easy to evaluate them as products of the film art. First, they concentrate on unpretentious, sentimental, and romantic pictures of America. Second, they tend to overlook the faults and concentrate on the virtues, especially when those virtues are part of the hope for the postwar future. Third, they were produced, written, and directed by the men who had already established the quality reputation of American nonfiction film, and, therefore, they are almost always first-rate examples of photography, editing, and musical scoring. Finally, within the limited content of war propa-ganda for overseas purposes, they can be excused for what they leave out, only because what they leave in is so good.

In addition to making films under OWI sponsorship, many of these same film makers continued to create nonfiction films for commercial and institutional organizations. In 1944, Van Dyke and Ben Maddow made *The Bridge* for the Foreign Policy Association. This low-key film assesses the effects of World War II on the trade and transportation problems of South America, and is as much an affirmation of the power and efficiency of air transport as it is an analysis of foreign blockades, surplus stocks, widespread disease, and other massive social problems. The film's narration is too general to give real meaning to the significance of air transport; this narrative vagueness also detracts from the effectiveness of Van Dyke's *Journey into Medicine* (1947), produced by Irving Jacoby for the State Department. Van Dyke and Jacoby also collaborated on *The Photographer* (1948), a film visit with famed still-photographer Edward Weston. Notable for its intimacy, this film is flawed by narration that detracts from the beauty of its photography. Jacoby's *The Pale Horseman* (1946), a film about postwar relief and re-habilitation work, is a brilliant compilation film. Marking a depar-ture from his earlier work, Jacoby wrote a sincere and gentle narration to offset the grim reality of the scenes of famine, pesti-

lence, and epidemic disease. It details the work of the United
Nations Relief and Rehabilitation Administration, and of the
members of the Allied armies, in their efforts to relocate people,
stop epidemics, and provide shelter. But its value does not lie in its
presentation of fact, but rather in its moving picture of human
suffering; one does not soon forget the sight of a child sitting on a
pile of rubble, shaking so pitifully that he is unable to accept the
food being offered by a soldier.

After the war, Hollywood suffered several major setbacks that
were to affect not only the course of motion picture history, but also
the development of the film art. Box-office income fell, costs rose,
studio-owned theater chains were dissolved by court order, and
television invaded American homes. The production of feature-
length fiction films decreased, as audiences enjoyed the new excitement of television in their living rooms. Distribution arrangements
were confused and tangled by the new ownership of theaters, and
the nonfiction film—always popular, but never of primary importance to the viewing public—suffered accordingly. As we have seen,
the production of nonfiction films during the 1940's depended
almost solely on sponsorship by the government, and while these
films—for the OWI and for the USIS—employed many directors,
writers, cameramen, and technicians, they did not support them all
or constitute a movement. A film which distinguished itself as an
important contribution to American nonfiction film making and
which, along with Flaherty's *Louisiana Story* (1948), promised new
hope for the commercially distributed, feature-length nonfiction
film was Sidney Meyers' *The Quiet One* (1949).

Like *Louisiana Story*, *The Quiet One* concerns the private
world of a boy. But the young black boy of Meyers' film does not
have the freedom of a boat and water, nor does he have animals to
play with and forests to explore. The product of a broken and
unhappy home, he is courageously trying to find himself in a
remarkable school established for such youngsters. Like Flaherty,
Meyers presents the odyssey of a boy in search of himself, in search
of meanings for a world which he does not yet understand. And,
like Flaherty, he allows the film to move at the boy's pace and
rhythm, but while the young Louisiana boy's day was filled with

The Quiet One: Before leaving for the Wiltwych School, Donald sits pensively on a Harlem sidewalk. Photograph courtesy The Museum of Modern Art Film Stills Archives.

activity and wonder in the natural world around him, this boy's world is marked by unbearable boredom, isolation, and frustration in the slums of Harlem. The first half of the film shows and explains the experiences which bring Donald to the Wiltwych School, while the second half, narrated by the school's doctor, details his experiences there.

The Quiet One emphasizes Donald's courage and determination in overcoming his reticence and refusal to communicate; the film is not an advertisement for the school, but rather shows it only as the environment in which Donald can find the security to take the first steps in healing himself. The problem is never treated simply, as is best seen in the sequence in which Donald runs away from Wiltwych. At one point, trapped against a cliff by a passing train, his whole life flashes before him in one awful memory. At that point, he decides to return to school, to continue his education and his recovery. *The Quiet One* makes no compromises with Donald; he is a child, but not a child actor, and his performance is unaffected and memorable. Like Flaherty, Meyers had the patience and ability to capture the spontaneity of children on film. The commentary, written by James Agee, is gentle and factual and serves to unify the film's content and visual style. It is the rare and untypical commentary, informative without being didactic, illuminating without being strident, poetic without self-conscious lyricism, and, above all, understanding.[6]

Canada

In 1938 the Canadian government asked John Grierson to make proposals for the organization, coordination, and distribution of nonfiction film making in that country. As a result of his report, the National Film Board of Canada was formed in 1939 with Grierson as its first Commissioner, a post he held until 1945.[7] He drafted many of his former colleagues from the G.P.O. Film Unit and encouraged prominent film makers from other countries to help in the effort. The National Film Board began production and distribution on a massive scale, and created as many as three hundred films by the end of the war.[8] Grierson's approach to

Canadian film making was an extension of his work in England, with the primary emphasis on massive public information and education. For this purpose, two major series of films were produced: "Canada Carries On" and "World in Action." The first was devoted to Canadian activities and achievements, while the latter included films on world affairs, and owes something to the style of the American "March of Time" series. These films were screened monthly in theaters, mobile units, schools, and factories, and reached an audience of millions. NFB production was varied, ranging from the whimsical animated films of Norman McLaren to the outstanding "Mental Mechanisms" series, including *The Feeling of Rejection* (1947), *The Feeling of Hostility* (1948), *Overdependency* (1949), and *The Feeling of Depression* (1950). These special-interest films widened the nonfiction film audience and influenced American production of films concerned with psychological and psychiatric matters.

The success of the NFB during the 1940's can be measured by the extent of government support and by the enthusiastic audience reception for the numbers of films produced. If it was too highly organized and too much restrained by the necessity of spreading government information, it was, nonetheless, the force which made Canada a major contributor to the world nonfiction film market in later years.[9] In the 1950's and 1960's, Canadian nonfiction films proved to be the major influence on the Americans and the British working in the same field.[10]

* * *

Both in England and in America, the decade between 1940 and 1950 was a crucial one for the development of nonfiction film making. The major factor underscoring this development was World War II. The war occupied the time and talents of many film makers who might otherwise have been engaged in the production of their own films. The war directly and indirectly affected the entertainment as well as the economy of the world, so that the desire for, and response to, nonfiction films fluctuated with events. However, the war increased immeasurably the possibilities for the uses of nonfiction film and provided many advances in the technical aspects of production. The postwar years were uncertain ones for sponsors, for producers, for directors, and for the audience. Yet these were not fallow years, for they occasioned the development of a stronger and more independent system of production and distribution, the creation of the National Film Board of Canada, and the film program of UNESCO, and, most important, provided the foundation for the extensive nonfiction film experiments in the 1950's and 1960's.

NOTES

1 See Chapter Seven for a discussion of *World of Plenty*.

2 For a debate on the quality of postwar nonfiction film see Winifred Holmes, "What's Wrong with Documentary?" *Sight and Sound*, 16, No. 65 (Spring 1948), pp. 44–45; and John Grierson, "Prospect for Documentary: What Is Wrong and Why," *Sight and Sound*, 17, No. 66 (Summer 1948), pp. 55–59.

3 Richard Griffith, "Post-War American Documentaries," *Penguin Film Review*, No. 8 (1949), p. 92.

4 Griffith gives considerable credit to Mary Losey for her pioneering efforts with the Association of Documentary Film Producers between 1939–42.

5 Willard Van Dyke, in "Foreword" in Sheldon Renan, *An Introduction to the American Underground Film* (New York, E. P. Dutton & Company, Inc., 1967), p. 6.

6 *In the Street* (1952), directed and photographed by Helen Levitt, Janice Loeb, and James Agee—and incorporating much footage intended for, but not used in, *The Quiet One*, is available from the Museum of Modern Art Circulating Film Library; its primary use is as a study film.

7 For details, see John Grierson, *Grierson on Documentary*, ed. Forsyth Hardy (London, Faber and Faber, Ltd., 1966), pp. 25–28.

8 See *Presenting NFB of Canada* (Ottawa, National Film Board, 1949).

9 See Basil Wright, "Documentary: Flesh, Fowl, Or . . . ?" *Sight and Sound*, 19, No. 1 (March 1950), pp. 43–48.

10 With his belief in documentary film as a force for internationalism, it was only natural that John Grierson should become the founding force behind the film-making program of UNESCO. In 1947 he accepted a post as that organization's Director of Mass Communications and Public Information, creating a division which provided a link between documentary film producers all over the world and which furnished advice on the production and use of educational films. See John Grierson, "Production Unit Planned: Mass Media to Be Used for Peace," *UNESCO Courier* (Feb. 1948), p. 3.

CHAPTER 9

Old Traditions and
New Directions: 1950–1960

Both in spirit and in quality, the nonfiction film hit its low point in the late 1940's and early 1950's. Factors which continued to inhibit production included a lack of broad sponsorship and financial support, uncertain distribution, and an unpredictable audience. At the same time, however, there were two major factors that would give new life to the moribund movement: television and the beginnings of "direct cinema." The role which television has played in the history of the nonfiction film since the end of the war cannot be overemphasized, but it should not be overpraised. Television supplied the two basic elements which characterized the early English documentary movement: a group dedicated to a common journalistic aim working in a creative atmosphere, and, equally important, sustained sponsorship. But it also had inherent limitations and obstacles and did not prove to be the right medium for all film makers. The beginnings of direct cinema in England were less auspicious and certainly less organized than the productions for television, but it became immediately clear that the nonfiction film was taking an exciting new approach to the treatment of reality. When directors like Lindsay Anderson, Karel Reisz, and Tony Richardson began their careers with unpretentious, short, and curiously vital film records of the everyday life around them, the British tradition got a much-needed boost, and the nonfiction movement around the world reaped the benefits. The films that were made neither for television nor with the concept of direct cinema tended to be traditional, often feature length and in color, and produced for theatrical showing. But, in short, the 1950's continued to be years of transition from an older school to a younger one, years of experimentation with television and the new portable equipment, and years of cautious anticipation for the future of nonfiction film. The results of these years can be seen in the 1960's with the dynamic rebirth and revolution of all forms of film making.

England

If anything, the 1950's were better years for British film makers than they were for the Americans. Not only was the British movement better staffed and suited to continue its limited film-making activities, but several major public events gave impetus to expanded production. Appearing early in the decade were the "Wealth of the World" series, produced by the Pathé Documentary Unit in association with Film Centre, and Paul Dickson's *The Undefeated* (1950), a study of the rehabilitation of war casualties. In its restraint and humanity, Dickson's film recalls John Huston's *Let There Be Light* and his own brilliant film *David* (1951). The Festival of Britain, celebrating the one hundredth anniversary of Queen Victoria's Crystal Palace Exhibition, did for nonfiction film in the 1950's what the 1967 Montreal Expo did for it some years later. By providing film makers with commissions, with theaters, and with large audiences, these international exhibitions focused attention on the creative excitement of the medium and on its superior ability to tell an informative story in an imaginative way. Among the Festival of Britain films were *The Waters of Time, Forward a Century,* and *David.* Basil Wright's and Bill Launder's *The Waters of Time* (1951) is a film of the Thames River, of the locks and docks of London's waterway. It is in the G.P.O. tradition of explaining a process with the direct dialogue of men at work, but it is a slow and tedious portrayal, hindered even more by a pretentious poetic narration which attempts to look back and to capture the color of the Thames in Elizabethan times. *The Waters of Time* tries to make poetry out of a prosaic subject, but unlike Lorentz' *The*

River, it does not succeed. Napier Bell's *Forward a Century* (1951) records the hundred years' growth since the Crystal Palace Exhibition, and suggests that the challenge for Britain now is not industrial progress, as it was then, but human progress. Based on still photographs and engravings, and told by a narrator and a voice representing Queen Victoria, the film reviews Britain's past industrial strength, but claims that the British prefer humanity to imperialism and progress. The pictures are brought alive by an imaginative mix of sound effects, narration, and music. The idealism and superficiality of the film are more than overshadowed by political reality, and while the old photographs are interesting, the film lacks conviction and challenge, clear focus and direction. The parallel exhibitions provide a good structural framework, but this idea is not developed with any meaningful insight into British economy and culture. Like *The Waters of Time, Forward a Century* is a commemorative film, too happy with its subject to be honest about it.

It is Paul Dickson's *David* (1951), made through the British Film Institute for the Welsh Committee of the Festival of Britain, that demonstrates the continuing vitality of British nonfiction film making. The film tells the story of an elderly caretaker of a Welsh school, its students, and his bid for the first prize in the Eisteddfod, the Welsh national competition of poetry and singing. The sad and lovely story is true, but the approach is more dramatic and fictional than the conventional documentary allows; one is reminded of Flaherty. The film is notable for its use of real people of the Welsh village of Ammanford, for their complete lack of self-consciousness, and for its warmth of presentation of customs and tradition. *David* is filled with national pride and a reverence for tradition that sets it far apart and high above its contemporaries. This is a film of uncommon beauty, and while David wins second prize for his epic poem, this seems less important than the young boy's friendship with and love for the old man. Its emotional strength is formidable, its impact memorable. Like the old man himself, it is not a film to be forgotten; like Lindsay Anderson's *Every Day Except Christmas* (1957), it proved that films of genuine human warmth and beauty still had a place among all the tributes to transportation systems, oil resources, and conquests of nature.

David: Paul Dickson's lovely film tells the story of an elderly and lonely Welshman; here, through a flashback, we see him as a smiling bridegroom, several years before the death of his son and the melancholy events of his later years.

Basil Wright's *World Without End* (1953) is a UNESCO film and demonstrates one of the major problems of making films for that world organization: presenting a massive social problem of a country without offending its political sensibilities. Wright's problem here was to contrast the problems and the progress of peoples in Mexico and Thailand who were emerging from traditional methods into more enlightened approaches toward agriculture, health, sanitation, and education. Faced on one hand with appalling conditions and, on the other, with a desire to educate without offending, Wright steered a careful course and succeeded. He took the "land of contrasts" approach without the obsequious narration of the traditional travel film, and by combining native music, beautiful soft photography, and an intelligent, informative narration, he showed both problems and solutions. Another problem faced by film makers working for the United Nations is the question of language. If films are for an international audience, they should be narrated in English or French; if they are for a specific country, they should be in the language of the country. Sometimes they are for both audiences and separate narrative tracks must be prepared; when this occurs, of course, the relationship between the pictures and the sound must be flexible enough to allow for language differences. But this did not seem to present too much of a problem for the makers of *World Without End* (Paul Rotha directed the Mexican sequences, while Wright directed those in Thailand), and it succeeds in an area marked by obstacles to clear, imaginative film making. Another notable British film is Robin Carruthers' *They Planted a Stone* (1953), a succinct account of the harnessing of the Nile River for hydroelectric power and industrial growth.

The year 1953 in England was marked by two events of major historical importance: the Coronation of Queen Elizabeth II and the conquest of Mount Everest by Edmund Hillary and Sherpa Tenzing. Remarkably enough, both events took place within four days. Although several newsreel-type narratives of the Coronation (June 2, 1953) were filmed, the "official" record is preserved in Castleton Knight's color production *A Queen Is Crowned* (1953). The six hours of procession, pageantry, and ceremony are captured in ninety minutes of footage taken from superbly advantageous camera positions. Solemn and sentimental, splendid and stately, this seems to be a complete record, but the editing lacks the pace and rhythm that would have built anticipation and excitement for the appearance of the young Queen. Christopher Fry's narration is factual and informational at times, and poetic and reverent at others; it is spoken by Laurence Olivier in a combination of excited and hushed tones. The film serves more as a historical record of a nation's crowning moment, than as an investigation of the meaning and function of monarchy. Sixteen years later the British were to make two films about monarchy that would prove to be as analytical and insightful as they were entertaining: *A Prince for Wales* (1969) and *Royal Family* (1969). Both films are thoughtful studies of the function of a constitutional monarchy within a democratic political system.

The 1950's witnessed the climbing of the world's highest mountains; first, Annapurna, in 1950, recorded on film in *Annapurna* (1953), and, second, Mount Everest. *Annapurna* is an uneven film, combining reenactment with actual footage shot on the ascent; like *The Conquest of Everest*, it is beautiful and striking, but essentially unmoving. The problem was to give human drama to a scientific expedition that lacked the human suffering which made an earlier similar record—Ponting's *Ninety Degrees South* (1933)—such a memorable film. *The Conquest of Everest* (1953), a film by Thomas Stobart and George Lowe, presents a straightforward account of the efficient preparations for the expedition. But when they present the events of the expedition itself, they rely on the ominous background sound of falling snow and ice, of heavy breathing, and of an occasional avalanche to add some drama to what is, otherwise, a highly scientific and carefully planned effort. There is a series of anticlimactic sequences that make the crest seem impossible to reach, and an unfortunate confusion in narration as to who was actually leading the expedition. But there is no confusion, and plenty of excitement, when Hillary and Tenzing finally record the historic pictures of their conquest of the highest mountain peak in the world. Although the summit was actually reached on May 29, the news was announced as "the crowning glory" of the Coronation on June 2.

Mountains were not the only aspects of nature that were

conquered and filmed during the 1950's. No listing would be complete without reference to *Kon Tiki* (1951), *The Sea Around Us* (1953), *African Lion* (1955), and the first of Jacques-Yves Cousteau's brilliant underwater films, *Silent World* (1956). In this category, too, are Walt Disney's nature films.

With the exception of some of the documentaries made for the BBC television service, the Grierson tradition in documentary film making was rapidly disappearing in England. But the older tradition did not die, and surely is not dead today; it is too important, too flexible, and too good for an early death. Like all continuing forms, however, it requires adaptation to meet the times. An example of one of the ways in which the older tradition of film making was adapted is Thorold Dickinson's *Power Among Men* (1958), made in color and black-and-white for the U.N. Film Services. A film about the work of UNRRA, it is, like Dickinson's *Next of Kin* (1942), a blend of the fictional and the nonfictional approaches, although it does not use professional actors (it is narrated by actor Laurence Harvey). Like a Rotha documentary, it is neatly divided into four parts, corresponding to efforts in four geographical areas, and is based on the general theme, "Men build, men destroy." But if it were not for U.N. sponsorship, and for the inherent limitations of films produced for that organization, *Power Among Men* might have been an interesting film; as it is, it is but a weak reminder of the strong tradition out of which it came.

Films like *Power Among Men* contribute to the mistaken notion that nonfiction films—and, especially, "documentary films"— are synonymous with dullness, with information, with travelogues. Such reactions obscure, of course, the achievements of Grierson, Flaherty, Cavalcanti, Jennings, Lorentz, and others. The nonfiction film, and the documentary film in particular, needed, once again, to be free enough to capture the humanity and lyricism of life. The Free Cinema Group gave it this chance in 1956.

Writing in *Sequence,* Lindsay Anderson defined his own approach as well as that of the English Free Cinema Group: "The first duty of the artist is not to interpret, nor to propagandize but to create."[1] He was dissatisfied with the current course of the documentary approach, and felt that its realism and authenticity were proving to be obstacles. Anderson argued that the documentary film approach inhibited a film maker from imposing his own ideas on his raw material and that the sociological base of the Grierson approach was no longer applicable in a complex world.[2] This is not to say that Anderson was unimpressed by the great tradition of documentary film making, for he has acknowledged his debt to Humphrey Jennings, and Jennings' influence is readily apparent in such Anderson films as *Every Day Except Christmas*.[3] It is a feeling for people, not social issues, that Anderson admired in the work of Jennings, Flaherty (whose *Louisiana Story* he praised), and John Ford. In Ford's films, he saw a feeling for individual values and for rooted tradition that proved to be a major influence on his approach to the culture of his own country. With his contemporaries, Karel Reisz and Tony Richardson, Anderson began his career in nonfiction films and went on to make distinguished fiction films. Not coincidentally, this pattern has been repeated by some major French directors, although not by the Americans. But the few years that the members of the Free Cinema Group were to devote to nonfiction film changed its course of development and proved a significant influence on the "direct cinema" (or *cinéma vérité*) approach.

Lindsay Anderson's early films are conventional, sponsored industrial documentaries: *Meet the Pioneers* (1948), *Idlers That Work* (1949), and *Three Installations* (1952). The first indications of his later style are apparent in *Wakefield Express* (1952), but it was not until *Thursday's Children* that he found the mode of expression that culminated with *Every Day Except Christmas*.

Thursday's Children (1953), written and directed by Guy Brenton and Lindsay Anderson, forms an important link between the traditional British documentary film and the direct cinema of the 1960's. Traditional in subject matter, it concerns the Royal School for the Deaf in Margate, England; contemporary in approach, it achieves an extraordinary degree of intimacy—in both camera and sound work—in its observation and explanation of the teaching of the deaf. Furthermore, the approach is unsentimental as it details the painstaking process by which a deaf child is taught to read lips, to read print, and to speak. The film is optimistic at times, but never at the expense of the subject matter. It stands comparison with Sidney Meyers' *The Quiet One* or Allan King's

Warrendale in its concern with a special school, but, unlike those films, it does not portray emotional problems (which must exist), nor does it investigate the family backgrounds of the youngsters. This is an isolated school, where children live together with others sharing the same handicap; when their homes are mentioned, they are discussed only in terms of friendly letters and parcels of goodies. However, the school situation is similar in that it relies on a communal spirit to reinforce the awareness and the concentration needed to overcome the handicap. The lyrical commentary is beautifully spoken by Richard Burton; the words emphasize the silent world of those who cannot hear them. For Anderson, people are not alone, no matter how different they may be. From the quiet world of *Thursday's Children,* to the bizarre world of *O Dreamland,* to the flower-fresh, nighttime world of *Every Day Except Christmas,* Anderson sees the unique man, but he also celebrates mankind.

Anderson's *Thursday's Children* represents a distinguished achievement in the field of nonfiction film reporting, but his other 1953 film, *O Dreamland,* had more influence on the Free Cinema Group. *O Dreamland* (1953) is a satiric, but heavy-handed comment on a popular English amusement park. As a picture of a tawdry place, it is conventionally ironic and is, for the most part, an elementary exercise in film making. It had an influence on a whole group of film makers precisely because it dared to criticize the tasteless ways in which the British working classes spend their leisure time, but it steers a careful course between outright criticism of the people and outright criticism of the proprietors of the park. It is interesting to note that Anderson's *Every Day Except Christmas* concerns the very same working people who might spend their Saturdays and Sundays at Dreamland; when these people are working, Anderson seems unaware of class distinctions. The theme of class is a major one in his fiction films *This Sporting Life* (1963) and *If . . .* (1968). But *O Dreamland* was more a diversion for Anderson than an indication of the direction in which his films were to move. Its influence, however, was considerable.

Following Anderson's lead, Karel Reisz and Tony Richardson took their nonfiction cameras into a London jazz club to observe the working classes at a different kind of play. *Momma Don't Allow* (1955) shows a genuine feeling for British popular culture in the mid-1950's, but seems more interesting as a record of clothes, hairstyles, and music, than as a film. Like so many experimental films, it never finds the answers to the questions it pursues. Similar in approach, but even closer to the direct cinema of the 1960's, is *Nice Time* (1957), a film by Claude Goretta and Alain Tanner. Observing London's Piccadilly Circus with the same fascination that inspires so many American students to film Times Square at night, Goretta and Tanner turn their cameras at random on the catalog of various pleasures. As in *O Dreamland,* they make ironic comment with music on the crowds waiting for fun. It is overdone, and overlong, but it freshens one's visual sense of a familiar location. Anderson supervised the editing of Lorenza Mazzetti's *Together* (1955), a well-intentioned but unsuccessful film about the lonely, isolated lives of two deaf-mutes. Although Mazzetti clearly understands the extent to which the "outside" world can persecute handicapped people, she indulges in an overly dramatic conclusion —of the accidental death of one of the boys—that distorts the focus of the film. If she had been more influenced by *Thursday's Children* than by John Steinbeck's *Of Mice and Men,* she might have created a statement that would have helped us better to understand the meaning of silence; instead, she makes a despairing "life-goes-on" statement that, however much it may reflect the angry British culture of the 1950's, is notable for its lack of staying power. Daniel Paris' music does, however, distinguish the different worlds of those who can and cannot hear.

The year 1956 was the turning point for British nonfiction film. In February, the first Free Cinema program was screened at the National Film Theatre; it included the films discussed above, as well as French films by Franju, Truffaut, and Chabrol, and the American film *On the Bowery.* On the stage, it was the year of John Osborne's *Look Back in Anger,* and in the streets, mods, rockers, and teddy boys captured the imagination, not only of film makers but also of playwrights and, of course, of the new rock music groups. An important step in the development of the sociological film is Karel Reisz' *We Are the Lambeth Boys* (1959), a serious attempt to understand working-class youth in nonstereotyped terms. What all of these film makers achieved was not so much the films themselves, but rather a spirit of free and uninhibited inquiry. The films are important, especially for their experimental and inventive handling of sound, but even more for their place in the development of the live, direct cinema which was to follow. They foreshadowed a new kind of film making that questioned conventional film symbolism, pioneered new methods of sound recording, and encouraged the development of lightweight equipment that allowed the cameraman to move as he wanted.

In his program notes for *Every Day Except Christmas* (1957), Lindsay Anderson made this idealistic statement of his film principles: "I want to make people—ordinary people, not just Top People—feel their dignity and their importance, so that they can act from these principles. Only on such principles can confident and healthy action be based."[4] This lyrical film is in the British tradition of clear explanation, excellent photography, and imaginative sound; in addition, it restores a sense of appreciation for the commonplace that had been missing since Humphrey Jennings' wartime films. Here, with unqualified joy, Anderson celebrates the simple virtues of the ordinary working man in London's Covent Garden, the central market for fruit, flowers, and vegetables. His film offers a thorough, interesting, light observation of the typical activity which goes on behind the scenes of this vast market. But it is in its charm, in its narration, and in its delightful musical score that *Every Day Except Christmas* becomes a gentle tribute to the ordinary people who work at uncomplicated tasks.

Anderson is concerned not only with the work activity of these people, but also with their jaunty, friendly relations with one another, their devotion to neat, careful handling of perishable produce and flowers, and their pleasure in serving their customers. Not unlike Grierson's insistence on the nobility of the craftsman, Anderson finds dignity in the work of Alice, the last of the famous women porters. Watching her, we feel a whole age come to life on the screen. From the days when "Victoria was Queen, and every gentleman wore a buttonhole," to the present, when elderly street-corner flower sellers come in the later morning to buy the bargains, Anderson pictures more than a genuine bit of London's commerce; he gives us the people behind the tradition. His camera and sound equipment capture and celebrate life; in the direct cinema way, the sound is often not synchronous with the picture, and provides

Every Day Except Christmas: Alice, the last of the famous women porters at London's Covent Garden, reminds us of an era that is all but forgotten in Lindsay Anderson's beautiful study of ordinary people in ordinary jobs.

contrapuntal comment on the activity we see. But long after we forget the new film technique, we remember the faces—"Alice and George and Bill and Sid and Alan and George and Derek and Bill and all the others . . ." to whom the film is dedicated. Like Flaherty's *Nanook* and Jennings' *Fires Were Started,* and so many other films, Anderson's *Every Day Except Christmas* finds beauty in the ordinary, and creates art out of the unexpected raw materials of reality.

British nonfiction film making between 1950 and 1957 consisted of a varied, inconsistent list of productions by a fragmented, unallied group of film makers. Not until 1956, and the organization of the short-lived Free Cinema Group, was it to feel any real commitment and vitality. There are exceptions, of course—*David* and maybe *World Without End*—but the short list provides few memorable titles. Even though they argue to the contrary, Anderson and Reisz were really the forerunners of the contemporary direct cinema and they must be given the credit for reviving the tradition of outstanding British nonfiction film making.

American Films

In America, the situation was, if anything, even less productive and exciting than in England. With the exception of a few films—notably *On the Bowery* and *All My Babies*—this period marked the beginning of the outstanding television documentary coverage that stems from Edward R. Murrow's and Fred W. Friendly's "See It Now" series. Producers, film makers, and audiences turned their attention to television, rather than to the independent nonfiction film. The first American experiments in direct cinema began with Richard Leacock's work for the "Omnibus" television program, but it was not until Leacock's *Primary* (1960) that American film makers took the new approach seriously.

A keen and insightful social consciousness has been the distinguishing characteristic of American nonfiction film makers from Flaherty to Lorentz to Van Dyke to Leacock, so it is not surprising to find that the few significant American films of the 1950's were those dealing with health, hospitals, alcoholism, and the environment. Whether photographed directly or reenacted, the emphasis was on matters of social, scientific, and economic importance. Certainly, the immediacy of television and its ability to make instantaneous reports aided the cause of the prepared, edited film documentary; in addition, the developing prominence of the so-called art house called attention to foreign films and to films *as* art. While there was little production sponsored by commercial institutions or by the government, the field of independent production was sufficient to support some notable work.[5]

In England, as in some European countries, it is a natural progression for a film maker to begin his carreer with nonfiction films—with documentaries, newsreels, travel films, advertising films —and if he is successful, to progress to fiction films; directors such as Lindsay Anderson, Karel Reisz, Alain Resnais, and Michelangelo Antonioni, among many others, have made similar progress in their careers. In America, however, the two fields of film making tend to remain exclusive of one another, with little interchange between them. A notable exception, of course, occurred during World War II, when such major directors as William Wyler, John Huston, Frank Capra, Fred Zinnemann, Anatole Litvak, and John Ford made films of every type and description for the government. Aside from this war effort, it is a rare occurrence when a "Hollywood" director makes a nonfiction film. For this reason, Fred Zinnemann's *Benjy* is worthy of attention.

Benjy (1951) tells the story of a crippled boy; of his parents, who cannot understand his condition; and of the work done by the Los Angeles Orthopedic Hospital in correcting his condition and his parents' attitude. Using professional actors and scripted dialogue, Zinnemann's treatment moves briskly toward a predictable conclusion; in between are moments of genuine human emotion conveyed by some child actors. Ironically, Zinnemann and his production staff were too professional, and overpowered this simple subject with their approach. *Benjy* seems a forerunner of television hospital serials. The extent to which handicapped children are capable of conveying an immediate sense of their own problems is better seen in Lindsay Anderson's and Guy Brenton's *Thursday's Children*.

The sponsored nonfiction film in the United States has never been a significant form, although there have been many successful productions in the field of sponsored educational documentaries. Robert Flaherty's *Louisiana Story* (1948), produced with the support of Standard Oil, was critically and commercially successful, but did not stimulate increased production of sponsored nonfiction films. The name of George Stoney, however, stands out for his distinguished and prodigious contributions. Since 1950, Stoney has produced and directed over forty films, many of them on the subjects of physical and mental health care. Like Pare Lorentz, Stoney often formulated his nonfiction films within a fictional framework, but also like Lorentz, Stoney controlled the dramatic conflict, so that it did not overshadow the resolution of the problem at hand. Stoney's best film is *All My Babies* (1952), and represents a breakthrough not only in its careful approach to the training of Negro midwives in Georgia, but also in its direct photography of an actual childbirth. Like Lorentz' *Fight for Life, All My Babies* begins with a class in which midwives (not doctors) are admonished for the death of a baby in a recent case. But unlike the opening of *Fight for Life,* the midwife system is already in operation, and it is only necessary to review the fundamentals with the participating women as the film expands to document each step. Lorentz relied on a careful script and tight conflict to bring drama to his treatment of the theme, but Stoney worked within a much looser framework. His film depicts fear and ignorance, proper cleanliness, and safe and successful childbirth with such simplicity that the overall effect is much stronger than that of Lorentz' careful, professional treatment. This is not to say that Stoney's film is careless or unprofessional, for it is obviously made with great care and especially noteworthy editing. The sound recording is not direct, in most scenes, but the mix of Negro spirituals and gentle narration by the midwife, Miss Mary, provides an effective complement to the straightforward photography, most of it shot in actual cabins and houses of the people involved. Like Lorentz, Stoney contrasts a home that is dirty, unprepared, and full of fear with a home that is physically and psychologically ready to handle both pre- and post-natal care, as well as the childbirth itself. The scene of childbirth is directly and unflinchingly photographed, in detail and in close-up, providing a dramatic climax to the film's instructional value. All the tense conflict and high-contrast photography of *Fight for Life* are little, compared with this scene that is literally and visually bursting with life. *All My Babies* presents a sentimental, easy solution to the very real problem of infant mortality in depressed and underprivileged areas, and it might easily be criticized for its approach; but it was made for instructional purposes and it now teaches an audience far beyond the relatively small group for which it was intended.

Before 1956, when Allan King made *Skid Row* and Lionel Rogosin released *On the Bowery*, no nonfiction film maker had ever taken an in-depth look at alcoholism.[6] Although a number of nonfiction films had made frontal attacks on such major social problems as inadequate housing, bad hospitals, poor nutrition, and weak schools, none had really concentrated on the sustained suffering of the alcoholics' world. In 1945, Hollywood made a daring break with the melodramatic *The Lost Weekend*, but, aside from that, the subject was taboo. In the 1960's the massive problems of alcoholism and drug addiction demanded the attention of nonfiction film makers (Pennebaker's *David*, a film about Synanon, for example), but to Rogosin must go the credit for opening this crucial subject and for influencing the direct cinema that followed. Like Flaherty with *Nanook of the North*, Rogosin tells the story from the inside, and, like Flaherty, he tells it with keen observation and deep compassion. Also like Flaherty, he was able to go into the open with his portable equipment, to record the sights and sounds of a world that his audience knew mostly by superstition and stereotype. Rogosin presents the world of the so-called "Bowery Bum," a world of inaction and indolence, and while a certain staged quality of the film reveals some of the standard clichés about Skid Row, the film is a remarkably direct one. Rogosin's vision is of a world caught in a cycle of despair. Men drink, fall down, are arrested and released; they drink again and are rehabilitated by evangelist missions; they drink again and fall down. They will do anything for a fellow drunk, but they will also do anything *to* him if it means another bottle. The "hero" of this film is Ray, who is both victor and victim in this jungle of isolated, unloved men and women. He cannot sleep on a flophouse floor, goes out in the night for a drink, is hustled by an alcoholic woman, gets beaten up and robbed. While there is some hope, based on companionship, the old men around him are philopsophical and resolute in their acceptance of fate. At the end of the film, Ray leaves, but we are told "He'll be back." If not Ray, someone like him will enter this world of one day's work, of pawnshops, of nights spent in doorways. There is a morning wake-up sequence in *On the Bowery* that is a nightmare vision straight from hell: men in every conceivable state of drunkenness and filth, shaking and shuddering as they awaken and face the new day from filthy gutters and backstreet doorways. In another sequence, Rogosin's camera captures a Bowery evangelist as he reveals his own hypocrisy. Here Rogosin shows the extent to which direct cinema can capture the truth, and foreshadows the candor of Pennebaker's picture of Bob Dylan in *Dont Look Back* (1966), Richard Cawston's portrait of Billy Graham, *I'm Going to Ask You to Get Up Out of Your Seat* (1966), and the Maysles' *Salesman* (1969). Before *On the Bowery*, film makers had taken candid looks at depressed areas, but few, if any, of them had focused for an entire film on a problem for which there were no easy solutions.

American nonfiction film making since World War II has been characterized by social conviction, sincerity, and high standards of production skill. Yet aside from the few examples set by *The Quiet One, All My Babies, On the Bowery,* and a handful of other titles, American production has not reached the quality established and maintained by British film makers before and after the war. American film makers have generally failed to awaken and involve large audiences in the great issues of our time, but they have moved in the direction of a more personal, more direct film, one concerned with the individual problems that mirror national ones. The nonfiction tradition was founded partially on a concern for social problems, and with many distinguished exceptions, it often related to human beings as members of a group rather than as individuals. But films dealing with specific individuals—artists, for example—are noticeably weak in their attempts to capture the essence of life on film. The many films dealing with art and artists in the 1950's tend to exploit the subject for a cinematic purpose quite different from the spirit of the works themselves. The list of film titles concerned with artists, the creative process, and art works is long and potentially exciting, but most of these films fail as they explore abstract works with childlike innocence (*Works of Calder*), foster idol worship with dramatic accounts of artists' lives (*The Titan*), or mistake the relationship between art and reality (*Le Mystère Picasso*).[7]

Canada

Since its founding in 1939, the National Film Board of Canada has served as a model production unit within a central government information program. While American—and, to some extent, British—film makers were searching for the right mode of expression following World War II, Canadian nonfiction film makers knew that the approach lay in films which focused directly and individually on human beings, their patterns and problems in living. Canadian production during the 1950's is varied and distinctive, reaching from such unique films as *City of Gold* to the experiments by the Canadian Broadcasting Corporation which culminated in the 1960's with such films as Allan King's *Warrendale* (1966).[8]

Distinguished achievements from Canada include the improbably titled *Paul Tomkowicz: Street Railway Switchman* (1954), *Lonely Boy* (1962), and *City of Gold* (1957). The creative collaboration of Tom Daly, Colin Low, and Wolf Koenig, *City of Gold* is a thoroughly enchanting, completely surprising, and delightfully original film about the late nineteenth-century gold rush to the Yukon. In what seems to be a conventional beginning, the narration recounts the old days of Dawson City and memories from the narrator's youth, set against motion pictures of the city as it was when the film was made. From that point, the film breaks from this conventional film approach to history in its use of still photographs. With a huge collection of glass plate photographs, the film makers illustrate the spectacular drawing power of the gold. We see the overnight transformation of Dawson City from a tiny mining village to a city that is, at once, rough but sophisticated, full of saloons and whores, but free of violence. Beneath the factual history and the wonderfully arranged photographs is a spoken narration of genuine feeling and simplicity. While it lacks the dynamic rhythm of the narration in *The River* or the poetic intensity of that in *Night Mail* or the charming directness of that in *Every Day Except Christmas*, it is nonetheless as memorable as the literary values of those films. Its tone is full of wonder, nostalgia, and sentiment, but it is also curiously analytical, dispassionately objective, and refreshingly free of pretentious psychological interpretation. Pierre Berton speaks it with such perfection that he demonstrates (as does Richard Burton in his narration of *Thursday's Children*) the necessity of matching certain voices to certain visual images. *City of Gold* is a film that one might easily overlook, but to see it is a rare and wonderful experience. *City of Gold* is a pioneer in the use of still photographs in a motion picture to illuminate a historical moment; its influence can be seen in countless television nonfiction films, for it represents a new approach to the established compilation film.

Television

In the late 1920's and early 1930's, John Grierson's policies, predictions, and principles seemed to be just words; while some of his ideas were transformed into film production units and into actual films, many of the things Grierson proposed for the documentary and nonfiction film were misunderstood, unrealized, or simply disregarded. But in the 1950's, Grierson's words seemed even more prophetic than, perhaps, even he had imagined. The failing quality and decreased quantity of film production was a result of many factors—lack of sponsorship, of distribution, of audience interest, and of qualified film makers—but it also resulted from a failure to understand the medium of nonfiction film. In his excellent study, *Documentary in American Television*, A. William Bluem comments on a central factor influencing this decline after World War II:

> The intent to persuade and influence, to involve great audiences, to make exciting the great issues and causes of our time, lost its force with the end of violence; and by the time the crises of the world loomed large once more, television had arrived and was ready to assume this documentary responsibility.[9]

The Hollywood motion picture business was damaged more by television than by any other single factor,[10] but television also became the single most important boost to the nonfiction film since the war. In 1955, Paul Rotha and others seriously questioned the role that nonfiction film was to play in television production and programming,[11] but by the early 1960's, it became apparent that television played a major role in helping nonfiction film makers to survive the postwar years.[12]

Bluem sees the television documentary (and he consistently uses the term *documentary*) as the product of two influences: the radio documentary programs of the 1930's and the general nonfiction film tradition. The first television documentaries were essentially journalistic with their on-the-spot newsreel coverage. The first documentary approach to achieve distinction was evident in the "See It Now" series, begun by Edward R. Murrow and Fred W. Friendly in 1951. These two newscasters were the most influential in the development of television documentary during the 1950's, although their allegiances seemed always to be first to the word and second to the image. Their backgrounds in radio broadcasting, journalism, and public affairs made this literary approach to film only natural, and it was not until the 1960's that the truly creative possibilities of television documentary as *film art* were explored by men who were film makers first and reporters second. While there are far too many television documentaries of distinction to receive comment here,[13] a few names must be mentioned. "See It Now" was canceled as a series in 1958, and was replaced in 1959 by a new approach, "CBS Reports." In 1960, NBC introduced "White Paper," a series of documentary news programs created by Irving Gitlin, and at ABC the "Close Up!" series marked a breakthrough in television documentary as it proved to be the first series designed to fulfill the creative possibilities of the television medium. During the 1960's television provided many film makers with the opportunity to experiment with the direct cinema approach. Under the general direction of Robert Drew, film makers such as Richard Leacock, Gregory Shuker, Hope Ryden, and James Lipscomb formulated new approaches toward nonfiction film for television.

Bluem indicates three approaches to the making of television documentary: the compilation approach, the biographical approach (often utilizing compilation techniques in addition to dramatic structure), and the dramatic approach to interpreting actuality. The compilation approach is one of the most familiar, and is certainly remembered in the CBS series, "The Twentieth Century" (1957–64) and in Henry Salomon's series "Victory at Sea" (1952–53). The biographical approach is less easy to identify than the compilation, for so many films incorporate biography in varying degrees, but it is notable in the historical biographies of "Project XX" (1954–62), "The Twentieth Century," "The World of ————" series, "The Story of ————" series, and the "Biography" series by David Wolper. The dramatic approach to television documentary is evident in countless films, from those that recorded inherently dramatic events to those that imposed a dramatic framework upon events. Among the noteworthy attempts in this field are "Circle Theatre" (1950–55), Robert Drew's "Living Camera," which included the tense account of Paul Crump's fight to avoid execution, *The Chair* (1962), and William Jersey's *Manhattan Battleground* in the NBC "Creative Projects" series. "Omnibus" provided brilliant examples of the screen magazine form, and combined all three of these approaches into a fascinating, urbane series of programs that seemed culturally ahead of the medium.

The television documentary has one distinctive advantage over its counterpart made for theatrical showing: immediate, simultaneous screening over television networks to millions of viewers. There are certain limitations in making films for television, but these do not impose serious creative restrictions. The advantage that a mass audience can be reached in their homes at no admission cost to them cannot be denied. Most of these television documentaries are "programs" or "specials," rather than films that stand on their own; of course, some of them are regarded as individual film efforts and are still distributed, screened, and studied as such.[14] For twenty years, television has taken the nonfiction film audiences out of the commercial theaters and kept them in their homes, but it has provided them with such a rich and varied series of films, and has enriched the art—through the experiments with direct cinema, as just one example—that its impact has proven to be more than commercial. And while television might not succeed in fusing the Flaherty and the Grierson approaches to nonfiction film making, as Bluem suggests,[15] it does provide vast opportunities to inform, to educate, and to entertain, not only with regular programming, but also with sincere, serious, creative nonfiction film production.

NOTES

[1] "Angles of Approach," No. 2 (Winter 1947), p. 5.

[2] Elizabeth Sussex, *Lindsay Anderson* (London, Studio Vista, Ltd., 1969), pp. 12–14.

[3] For Anderson's prose tribute to Jennings, see Lindsay Anderson, "Only Connect: Some Aspects of the Work of Humphrey Jennings," *Sight and Sound*, 23, No. 4 (Apr.–June 1954), pp. 181–86.

[4] Sussex, p. 33.

[5] A glance at the documentary films nominated for the Academy Awards between 1950 and 1960 reveals some memorable, if not altogether important, titles; see Appendix B.

[6] Basil Wright, "On the Bowery," *Sight and Sound*, 26, No. 2 (Autumn 1956), p. 98.

[7] Two articles on the art film are (1) John Read, "The Film on Art as Documentary," *Film Culture*, 3, No. 3 (13), (Oct. 1957) pp. 6–7; and (2) John Berger, "Clouzot as Delilah," *Sight and Sound*, 27, No. 4 (Spring 1958), pp. 196–97.

[8] Two retrospective articles on the NFB are (1) Peter Harcourt, "The Innocent Eye," *Sight and Sound*, 34, No. 10 (Winter 1964–65), pp. 19–23; and (2) Howard Junker, "The National Film Board of Canada: After a Quarter Century," *Film Quarterly*, 23, No. 2 (Winter 1964–65), pp. 22–29.

[9] (New York, Hastings House, 1965), p. 59.

[10] Gerald Mast, *A Short History of the Movies* (New York, Pegasus, 1971), pp. 315ff.

[11] Paul Rotha, "Television and the Future of Documentary," *Film Quarterly*, 9 (Summer 1955), pp. 366–73.

[12] Burton Benjamin, "The Documentary Heritage," *Television Quarterly*, 1, No. 1 (Feb. 1962), pp. 29–34.

[13] Those interested in the subject should consult Bluem's study.

[14] Because some of the most distinctive of these films are now in general circulation, they are discussed, not as television programs, but as films representing the direct cinema method, in the following chapter.

[15] Bluem, pp. 241–45.

CHAPTER 10

The New Nonfiction Film: 1960–1970

There was such a resurgence of creative activity and production in the nonfiction film during the 1960's that the term *rebirth* is not an exaggeration. Television had brought the nonfiction approach into the homes of millions of Americans, enriching ordinary news programs, significant "specials," and documentary series such as "See It Now," "CBS Reports," and "The Twentieth Century." As audiences responded at home to nonfiction film coverage of important historical and current events and topics, they also showed a willingness to leave their homes for theatrical showings of distinctive nonfiction films. The feature-length nonfiction film belongs more to the late 1960's and early 1970's than to the early years of the decade, but there is no doubt that television prepared audiences for it by making them more aware of the world around them, more visually literate, and more conscious of the power of film to interpret the world. Additional factors contributing to the renewed interest and heightened activity in nonfiction film making are those technical developments in equipment that allowed film makers even greater mobility and freedom than before. Each year brings new developments in portable, lightweight equipment, and much of the credit must go to those who developed the equipment used by television film crews. Especially significant is the new sound recording equipment which made possible greater realism in journalistic reporting and created one of the major breakthroughs in the development of direct cinema: direct, synchronized sound.

The list of important, influential, and distinguished nonfiction films produced since 1960 is long; it includes films about war, about ordinary people, about environmental problems, films in the Grierson manner of social documentaries, and films in the Flaherty tradition; it includes films made for educational and commercial organizations, for theatrical showing, for television, and for the New York and Montreal World's Fairs. In addition, it includes films made by the National Film Board of Canada, by the U.S. Information Agency, by documentary film groups in Chicago and Puerto Rico, to name but two such local efforts, and by the major research and philanthropic foundations. In short, the list is long, covering a range of subjects and reflecting a variety of approaches that synthesize all that has gone before and point the way to all that will undoubtedly characterize the future development of nonfiction film. A brief listing of memorable American and British titles might include the following: *Operation Abolition* (1960); *The Black Fox,* and *The Exiles* (1961); *Nine from Little Rock,* and *The School at Rincon Santo* (1963); *Point of Order!, The Bus, Four Days in November, To Be Alive!, The Captive,* and *The March* (1964); *Rush to Judgment,* and *JFK: Years of Lightning, Day of Drums* (1967). But such a listing is unreliable, because it is incomplete; for instance, it does not include such major television productions as *Harvest of Shame,* and *The Children Were Watching* (1960), and *A Time for Burning* (1966), to name but a few. Nor does it include such hybrid, but unique films as *The Olive Trees of Justice* (1961), *The Sky Above, The Mud Below* (1962), *To Die in Madrid* (1965), *The War Game* and *Endless Summer* (1966), *Portrait of Jason* (1967), *No Vietnamese Ever Called Me Nigger* (1968), and *The Queen* and *Medium Cool* (1969), and *Interviews With My Lai Veterans* (1970). Even if these titles were added, the listing still would not be complete.

The obvious, but simple conclusion to draw from this brief listing is that its variety precludes categorization. There are some films about war, some about social institutions, some about people, and some which cover all three of these topics, as well as some which cover completely different ones. At such a close proximity in time, it is impossible to talk about whether or not any of them establishes new traditions, but it is possible to chart the continuing development of certain established traditions. And at such a close proximity, it is difficult to separate the distinguished from the distinctive, the memorable from the momentary. What does emerge, however, from this indistinct situation helps to clarify it. The three most significant areas of nonfiction film making during the 1960's were in television, in the U.S. Information Agency, and in the approach known as *cinéma vérité*, direct cinema, or as the Maysles brothers prefer to call it, nonfiction film.[1]

The New Nonfiction Film

The "new" nonfiction film seems to pose as many problems in terminology as it presents approaches and techniques. Whatever one calls it, the new approach represents a decisive stage in the development of modern nonfiction film making. The French film maker Edgar Morin was influenced by Dziga Vertov's silent Kino-Pravda films, and used the term *cinéma vérité* ("film truth"), although others, Mario Ruspoli among them, insisted that *cinéma direct* was more appropriate.[2] Whatever the term, the basic desire was the same: to use lightweight equipment in an informal attempt to break down the barriers between film maker and subject, to oversimplify procedure to get at the whole truth and nothing but the truth, and to catch events while they are happening, rather than to question events that have happened in the past. The technical characteristics of the new approach are simple: impromptu interviews, hand-held cameras, direct sound recording, and conscious informality.

But if there are problems with terminology, there are larger problems with the implications of these terms, implications which make the distinctions between *nonfiction* and *fiction* seem even simpler than they are. For instance, if direct cinema is "direct," can we assume that other films (fictional films, presumably) are "indirect"? If so, what does *indirect* mean? Does it mean that the films were produced with a script, with actors, with definite intentions? Does it mean that these considerations deflect the true nature of the film art into something that is indistinct and even indefensible? Does it suggest, on an even more important level, that *indirect* is synonymous with *untrue*, while direct cinema is somehow "true"? A. William Bluem tries to clarify the matter when he suggests that direct cinema "assumes at the outset that the camera is the only real reporter and must not be subservient to script, to preconceived thematic statement, to plotted narrative, to someone's idea of a story—to anything, in fact, but the chronological unfolding of events."[3] Such a comment seems the answer to some of the questions posed by the problem until we remember that film is an art, and that art presupposes an intrusion by the artist upon his subject matter. No artist merely records phenomena, as we know; as Andy Warhol has shown, even the simplest "home movie" reflects the attitude of the man behind the camera, and in that attitude is the foundation of the creative process. The film art is so highly complicated, so directly and indirectly affected by theories of time and space, by principles of editing, by types of film, by lenses, by weight of equipment, by finances, by dozens of factors, that anything like the kind of film making suggested by Bluem is more hypothetical than possible. And while it is possible to make a film based on the "chronological unfolding of events," it is in the presentation and interpretation of those events that the process of photography (an art in itself) becomes the art of film.

Both Jonas Mekas, the critic, and David Maysles, the film maker, agree that *nonfiction film* is a better term to apply to the new form. However, they use *nonfiction film* as a parallel to Truman Capote's paradoxical concept of the *nonfiction novel,* which, however successful it has proved to be in practice, is a term more notable for its contradictory quality than for its clarity as definition. Nonetheless, it is useful to examine the parallels which David Maysles finds between these films and Capote's fiction; he writes,

> Truman Capote's book [*In Cold Blood*] is the closest thing to our own work we have come across. What we [David and Albert Maysles] are doing is in direct parallel in motion picture form to what Capote is doing in the literary form. . . . He, for instance, is very conscious of intruding upon his subject, of making any kind of intrusion. That's

why he doesn't take notes. The same way that we try to build our equipment. We try to gain a certain kind of rapport, some relationship with the subject, as Capote does. To establish this relationship, we have perfected a camera that doesn't make any noise. It helps us get that type of spontaneity, of rapport, without someone being self-conscious because of the equipment.[4]

But inherent in the art of film making is the process of selection: the selection of subject, of crew, of images (photography and editing), and of distribution. And what all these theories about direct cinema neglect to discuss is the importance of selecting the subject. It is easy enough to insist on objectivity once the subject has been chosen, but if the subject is inherently dull, devoid of the "spiritual energy" which D. A. Pennebaker insists is at the heart of these films, then the film will be dull. No amount of lighting, camera work, sound recording, editing, or music will erase that fact. Flaherty knew it and proved it with *Nanook,* but not with *Moana;* Pennebaker proved it with *Dont Look Back,* but not with *Jane;* the Maysles proved it with *Salesman,* but not with *Showman.* There are times, of course, when the subject matter presents problems; Leacock's *Happy Mother's Day* objectively records the impact made by the Fisher quintuplets on Aberdeen, South Dakota, but the film's viewpoint is more concerned with the effect than with the cause. One wonders if the facts speak for themselves or if Leacock cannot hide his distaste for the crass people he is filming. An almost perfect example of direct cinema, *Happy Mother's Day* forces us to question whether the "point of view" is the film maker's or ours. Again, with Leacock's *A Stravinsky Portrait,* we wonder if the composer was really a witty, charming gentleman, as well as a musical genius, or if it was the film maker's admiration for him that resulted in this particular selection of images about him. Do the Maysles have a kind of admiration for the con-artistry of Paul Brennan in *Salesman,* or do they merely give him enough footage to indict himself? With the best of direct cinema, the possible answers are many; with the worst, we are reminded that when the artist loses control over any aspect of his art, he loses control over all of it.

What, then, is the new nonfiction film? It is an attempt to capture a carefully selected aspect of reality as directly as possible, with a minimum of obstacles between the film maker and his sub-ject; to this end, it is unscripted, unrehearsed (although internal evidence in many films indicates some preparation), and relatively unlimited as to where the persons in the film may move, what they may say, and where they may say it. The camera work is intimate, often giving the viewer the immediate sense that he is "there"; the sound recording is direct, and often clouded by pickup of back-ground noise that lends even more reality; and the editing tends to be continuous, rather than discontinuous, striving for a chronologi-cal, rather than dramatic, presentation of events. Its pioneers in-clude Lindsay Anderson, Karel Reisz, and Guy Brenton in England; Wolf Koenig, Roman Kroiter, Pierre Perrault, Allan King, and Michel Brault in Canada; and Jean Rouch, Edgar Morin, Mario Ruspoli, Chris Marker, and Georges Rouquier in France. However, the most important pioneers in developing and influencing the direction of the new nonfiction film have been American film makers (and, here, *film makers* must be broad enough to include producers, directors, cameramen, sound-record-ing engineers, editors, and musicians, for many of the distinguished American films have been group efforts, rather than films signed by any single director); a list of these pioneers includes Richard Leacock, D. A. Pennebaker, Robert Drew, Gregory Shuker, Albert and David Maysles, Charlotte Zwerin, William C. Jersey, and Frederick Wiseman. They have influenced the course of nonfiction film making as significantly as John Grierson and his colleagues in the 1930's; they have encouraged others to join them, and they have developed such an audience for their work that, in the late 1960's and early 1970's, big names at the box office were feature-length nonfiction films such as *Dont Look Back, Monterey Pop, A Married Couple, Salesman, Warrendale, Woodstock, Gimme Shelter,* and *Blue Water, White Death.*

Richard Leacock

It is impossible, in some instances, to separate the work of Richard Leacock from that of his contemporaries, for "his" films are

often collaborative efforts; but it is clear that he has had a paramount influence on the development of American nonfiction film
since the early 1950's. Leacock began his career as Flaherty's
cameraman on *Louisiana Story,* moved through assignments for the
U.S. government, for the "Omnibus" television series, for the "Living Camera" series sponsored by Time-Life, Inc., to films sponsored
by a variety of commercial and institutional organizations, and,
finally, to films produced for theatrical audiences. He has served as
director, producer, photographer, and/or "filmaker" (a title used
by Leacock and Pennebaker) on almost forty films, ranging from
the short, but exciting pioneer films for "Omnibus" to the full-
length *Monterey Pop,* the first of the films to cover rock festivals.[5]

Leacock's first film for "Omnibus" was *Toby and the Tall Corn*
(1954), an entertaining look at the "uninhibited theater" provided
by one of the last touring tent shows in America. The tent show is
Toby's and the "tall corn" refers to his brand of humor. Leacock's
approach here established a major approach to film making with its
focus on a subject that might otherwise escape notice, with its direct
sound recording, and with its analytical, insightful narration. Although British film makers in the 1930's were the first to record the
reactions of workers to their own jobs, Leacock here photographed
Toby and his actors commenting *directly* on their work as they
prepare for and do it. The narration, written and spoken by Russell
Lynes, who also appears in the film as the reporter, provides a
direct, inquisitive look into an indigenous tradition of show business in middle America. We see Toby and his troupe arrive in
town, set up their tent, and place advertisements; we see them
applying makeup in their dressing rooms, and acting their corny
vaudeville and down-home drama on the stage; and we see them in
their less exciting capacities as ticket takers, ushers, program salesmen, and publicity promoters. We watch the audience of plainfolks,
farmers, housewives, and children as they laugh at the traditional
humor which Toby and his fellow actors provide. None of their
stage business is intrinsically worth recording, but, as a human-
interest story, *Toby and the Tall Corn* preserves the unique flavor
of its wholly American subject. Like Anderson's *Every Day Except
Christmas* or the Maysles' *Salesman,* it leaves us with the intense

and memorable experience of hearing ordinary people comment on their somewhat extraordinary jobs. For this first of his important films, Leacock chose his subject with care, and took a candid, penetrating look at a little-known aspect of society. Later he would capture lesser and greater people on film, but he shows here the achievement of maintaining a direct, intimate contact with his subject.

Happy Mother's Day (1963) concerns something that would probably only happen in the USA: the all-out reaction of a small town when a local mother of five gives birth to quintuplets. Because Leacock and Joyce Chopra, with whom he made the film, maintain such a balance between their amusement with the situation and their objectivity as film reporters, it is never clear whether or not their implicit judgments are more important than their direct reportage. They are amused, as we are, at the human comedy in the townspeople's display of a mixture of happiness, hypocrisy, commercial exploitation, and a desire to maintain the family's privacy and dignity.

Leacock's camera is ably focused on many delightful details: the sober discussion by the town's businessmen as they suggest ways to satisfy tourists and to protect the Fishers' privacy; the planning for a parade, commemorative souvenirs, and a testimonial luncheon; the refusal by the doctor who delivered the quints to join the parade. Perhaps most remarkable, though, is the manner in which the Fishers themselves are completely ignored, how their "privacy and dignity" are discussed at the same time city fathers are debating visiting hours, special viewing facilities, and other impositions. Through all of this, Mrs. Fisher displays a combination of bewilderment and calm, and her reaction seems somewhat like ours; she doesn't know whether to cry or to laugh.

Leacock's objectivity can be interpreted as being heavily ironic, for instance, at the conclusion when the narrator comments, "It was a typical day in Aberdeen, South Dakota." At other times, it is just the presence of his camera and microphone that provides all we need to know about the contradictions within American society. He doesn't have to tell us that we can be ridiculous, pretentious, and presumptuous; all he need do is record the moment when a woman community leader tells Mrs. Fisher about the flowers she is to wear at "her" luncheon and "her" parade. Leacock's look at "Quint City" (the film was originally titled *Quint City, U.S.A.*) is direct, but not impartial; for instance, he does not let us know if any townspeople opposed the hoopla. He does not achieve sufficient intimacy with the Fishers to reveal, except by inference, how they really feel about their new life, full of cameramen, reporters, and many thousands of dollars in prizes. And yet the Fishers appear to be warm, simple people, vitally concerned for the privacy of their children and able to make quick judgments based on their stern religious values. The real worth of the film is not in the irony of the title, or in the clinical precision of the photography and sound recording, but in the mirror that it holds up to society.

Separately and together, Leacock and Pennebaker have made several films about musicians, including Geza Anda, Van Cliburn, Susan Starr, Dave Lambert, Bob Dylan, and the performers at the Monterey Pop Festival. Certainly one of the most intimate and revealing films ever made about a musician is the Leacock-Rolf Liebermann production, *A Stravinsky Portrait* (1964). The challenge here was to make a film which would reveal both the man and his music, avoiding both the interview and the concert approaches. Leacock and Liebermann, who narrates and appears in the film, more than meet that challenge and provide the rare experience of watching a musical genius create, discuss, and conduct his work. *A Stravinsky Portrait* proves a major point about the new nonfiction film: it is the subject, not the treatment, that matters. No amount of camera work can create an interesting film about a dull person, but, on the other hand, an unimaginative film maker can make a dull film about a great person. The tedious films about Picasso reveal little about him; on the other hand, the fascinating film about Martha Graham, *A Dancer's World* (1957), overcomes obstacles of dance vocabulary to present that "spiritual energy" that Pennebaker insists is the reason for making direct films about people.

In this thoroughly intelligent film, Stravinsky is totally oblivious to the camera. Leacock did not approach his subject with awe, but rather with understanding and respect; he did not cater or condescend to his audience.[6] We see Stravinsky in intimate moments, at lunch with his wife and friends, in discussions with Robert Craft, Pierre Boulez, Christopher Isherwood, and Gerald Heard. We see him and George Balanchine plan a ballet scenario for a Stravinsky score; they are drinking vodka, and Stravinsky urges, "Take some more, let's be drunk!" We hear him explain his work: "The creative process is the fun and pleasure of doing it." But it is the gentle, impelling enthusiasm of the great composer that makes this film; charming in explanation, delightful in humor, with eyes sparkling, Stravinsky fills each frame with his presence. *A Stravinsky Portrait* is much more than a film *about* a great musician. Through the delicate intimacy of its camera work and sound recording, it is a portrait of the man, illuminating and illuminated by his personality and his work.

Leacock-Pennebaker

As "filmakers" (their own term), Leacock and Pennebaker teamed with Robert Drew and others to make the "Living Camera" series for Time-Life, Inc. The series of ten television films aimed at presenting a crucial day, week, or month in the lives of their famous and unknown subjects; it was described: "It's unscripted, it's unrehearsed . . . for the first time the camera is a man. It sees, it hears, it moves like a man. . . ."[7] This recalls Dziga Vertov, although the Russian didn't have sound; "Living Camera" was not the first to try, but it is an important step in bringing human insight to creative photography. Some of these films have a definite dramatic structure (*Eddie* and *The Chair*) which is not imposed upon the material, but comes from within it. Others (*Primary*, for example) are closer to journalistic reporting and rely more on the significance of people and events than on the shape and direction of circumstances.

Primary (1960) is a film by Richard Leacock, D. A. Pennebaker, Robert Drew, Al Maysles, and Terry Filgate. With the analytical approach of a political reporter, it follows the Democratic Party campaign in the 1960 Wisconsin primary election. The viewer has a sense of being there, of seeing the campaign through the eyes of the candidates, Hubert H. Humphrey and John F. Kennedy. In fact, the camera follows the two men so closely at times that it seems to be mounted on their shoulders. We see the endless handshaking, the speeches, the street-corner electioneering.

Within this intimate behind-the-scenes look at the machinery of political campaigns, there are the usual spectacle, the predictable verbal abstraction, and the silly hullabaloo. But there are also the unpredictable and memorable moments: Humphrey directing a rehearsal of his own television program; Jacqueline Kennedy fidgeting while she recites a Polish sentence she has learned for a gathering of a Polish political group; Kennedy waiting in the night for the final results of his two-to-one victory over Humphrey.

Primary comes as close to balanced, objective reporting as a film about politics can. The film makers leave everyone to judge for himself, and attach no labels through editing that might have distorted the words or actions of either side. There is no direct reaction to the outcome of the election, unless one wants to attach implications to the closing shot: the famous old Humphrey car going down the road, accompanied by the candidate's country-western campaign song. The sequences are well balanced between the two campaigns; the narration is impartial, and there is little of it in comparison to the amount of direct sound recording. The candidates act out their own scenarios and tell their own stories; the film makers are there to record and to reveal, not to interpret. This, however, was not always the position taken in films for the "Living Camera" series.

In *Eddie* (1960), Leacock, Pennebaker, Abbot Mills, Bill Ray, and Al Maysles turned their cameras on Eddie Sachs, the race driver. Two years in a row, Sachs was "on the pole," the prime position in the Indianapolis 500 (the film was originally titled *On the Pole*); and two years in a row, Eddie lost. The subject matter is interesting, but the film treatment of it might have been ordinary if the film makers hadn't cared so much for Eddie. They like him, and, because of this, we like him too; we are on his side not because he has lost, but because he wants so much to win. Unlike the underdogs in *Salesman,* Eddie is genuine about success. One really cares about him because the race is exciting and because his enthusiasm is sincere and believable.

Primary: Candidate John Kennedy being welcomed at a rally; Mrs. Kennedy is at his side. Photograph courtesy Leacock-Pennebaker, Inc.

The photography of *Eddie* was done primarily from fixed locations, not from cameras mounted on the cars, a technique typical of Hollywood films about racing, but this does not diminish the excitement of the racing footage. The sequence in which Eddie discusses his future is intercut with shots of crashes; he even prophetically forecasts his death in a crash, which occurred three years after the film was made. When he loses for the second year, because of a misunderstood and heartbreaking tire weakness, he does not lose faith: "I'll never give up because I keep doing better every year. I'll be a better man next year. I've got the determination to win. It's just a matter of time." Eddie Sachs never won the Indianapolis 500, but that is a small matter compared ₒo his dedication and determination to win. The film makers obviously have great affection for Eddie, and they reflect this in their comprehensive picture of him in all phases of his racing. They also show him in his more private moments, when he cries as "Back Home Again in Indiana" is sung before the big race, when he stoically discusses his near-victory with his wife.

Where the film makers were scrupulously objective in *Primary,* and unashamedly affectionate in *Eddie,* they were clearly partial in their film *The Chair* (1962). Part crime reporting, part courtroom drama, part human interest story, *The Chair* is about the last few days and hours in the life of Paul Crump, convicted of murder and sentenced to die in the Illinois electric chair. The film concentrates on the successful efforts of lawyers Louis Nizer and Donald Moore to convince the authorities that Crump has been rehabilitated during his years in prison and that his death sentence should be commuted to life imprisonment. There is structure to this tense film, but the drama is real.

The film makers—Leacock, Pennebaker, and Gregory Shuker—clearly favor the efforts of Nizer and Moore; since Moore was the principal lawyer (Nizer was brought in at the last minute to add his prestige to the appeal), the film stays closely with his activities—in his office, on the telephone, with his secretary and aides. He is a remarkable presence on the screen, at times apparently aware of the camera with his theatrical gestures, and at times oblivious to its presence, such as when he breaks down and cries after hearing that

The Chair: Attorney Donald Moore argues last-minute details before appearing in court in defense of Paul Crump. Photograph courtesy Leacock-Pennebaker, Inc.

the Catholic Archbishop of Chicago will issue a statement to aid his appeal; moments later, when he composes himself, he adds a comment that could only be spontaneous: "But I don't even believe in God!" But the partiality of the film does not stem from the film makers' own feelings; rather, it comes from the case itself. The prosecution bases its case upon outmoded, outdated, and irrelevant legal and moral principles. There is no real understanding of Paul Crump's case, and certainly no compassion or humanity. The prosecuting attorney makes his points on incomplete evidence, and calls witnesses who are his own worst enemies. The events tell us this, not the film makers. When the parole board recommends, and the Governor confirms, the commutation, the film makers do not comment; they do not express regret or happiness that Paul Crump has been imprisoned for life, instead of being executed or released, for, again, the events speak for themselves. In that memorable moment when Crump is questioned by reporters—with some cameramen calling "look up" and "speak out"—and is so overcome with the news that he cannot speak, the film has made its point. It does not have to remind us that life is better than death; although Crump will spend the remainder of his life behind bars, we are told that his years will be, as they have been, devoted to counseling young convicts about "going straight" once they are released.

The direct camera approach catches many fine moments in this tense struggle on Crump's behalf: the steel and concrete labyrinth of the Cook County Jail; his best friend, the warden, a tough, likable career cop; an interview with his editor to put the final touches on a novel that will be published after his scheduled execution; his mother, sitting small and quiet in the hearing room as men talk abstractions about whether her son should live or die; a witness for the prosecution, making fine points about sin and contrition. All of these are dramatic touches, to be sure, but the difference between *The Chair* and a conventional television courtroom drama is that all of the events were true, filmed directly, as they were happening. The photography is unobtrusive and intimate, and the sound recording makes very effective use of telephone conversations, random comments, the sounds of bells and clanking steel doors, and the direct testimony in the hearing room. We rarely hear Crump speak, but we are caught up in the central life-and-death struggle of this convicted man; we must remember that the man is real, not an actor, and that the struggle was not shaped by a playwright, but by the events themselves.

The Chair makes another point about the new nonfiction film, one that should answer any critics who think it is the biased interpretation of events by so-called liberal film makers. As we have noted, a dull subject generally makes a dull film; but, it can be said that a true subject does not necessarily make a true film. The Crump situation being what it was, the evidence consisting of what it did, the film makers could not have succeeded in making a case *for* the prosecution. They might have produced a film for a group favoring capital punishment, but they could not have produced a film that would have been acceptable to the millions of television viewers whose interest in justice was larger than their specific views for or against capital punishment. It should be noted here that the film takes its stand on the matter of rehabilitation, not on the merits of the capital punishment argument. The facts and the truth do not lie, so that to arrange the facts in a dramatic framework which accentuates their truth is not to alter them, or to express a particularly partial viewpoint, but, rather, to demonstrate the vitality and the power of the camera to record reality, not to interpret it.

D. A. Pennebaker

Producer, cameraman, director, distributor, Donn Alan Pennebaker is a film maker in his own right. Associated with Richard Leacock, the Maysles brothers, and others on many films, his name also appears on his own films, including *Opening in Moscow* (1959), *David* (1961), *Jane* (1962), *Lambert & Company* (1964), *Dont Look Back* (1966), *Monterey Pop* (1968), and *Original Cast Album: Company* (1971). While some of these productions, too, incorporate the creative efforts of his contemporaries, they reflect Pennebaker's determination to make films which reveal the "spiritual energy" of the people he chooses as subjects. Most often, these people are prominent in the arts, especially music, and the record that Pennebaker has preserved of their thoughts and activities is an important addition to the chronicle of performing arts and artists in the 1960's. His interest in the newer forms of music, especially rock, led to the critically and commercially successful *Monterey Pop*, the first of the big rock festival color films which include *Woodstock* and *Gimme Shelter*.

An early Pennebaker film, made with Gregory Shuker and Bill Ray, for Time-Life, Inc., and Drew Associates, shows in a limited way the kind of film Pennebaker would come to make in *Dont Look Back*. The film is *David* (1961) and documents the efforts of a young jazz musician to free himself of drug addiction; filmed at Synanon House in California, it is a "true story" but one which has been dramatically edited to focus on David and his decision, rather than on the controversial drug rehabilitation program. *David* utilizes direct autobiographical comment, narration, dialogue, conversation between group leaders, and actual footage of an encounter group to show the inside workings of Synanon. David recounts his past and present problems, and we see the tension which results from his sense of responsibility to his wife and child and to himself. *David* makes a strong statement for the "alternative" that Synanon presents to prison, addiction, or death, but its overall point of view is unclear. It does not remain impartial and is definitely on David's side, but its ending shots of a whirling carousel ironically suggest a circular pattern—Synanon as a revolving-door clinic—and add little to our understanding.

While it was difficult for Pennebaker to get inside David's personality, or, to put it correctly, to persuade David to reveal himself unselfconsciously to the camera, it should not have been difficult to persuade actress Jane Fonda. *Jane* (1962) was filmed when Miss Fonda was preparing for her Broadway debut in *The Fun Couple,* a play which critic Walter Kerr calls, during the course of the film, one of the five worst plays he has ever seen. But the trouble with *Jane* is Jane, not the play. She lacks the "spiritual energy" necessary to transform the reportage of this tedious backstage drama into a film which would reveal her own personality in addition to making a comment on the production. The film has a real and genuine feeling for show business. We get a good sense of

Dont Look Back: Bob Dylan riding on a train in a quiet moment between interviews and concerts during his tour of England. Photograph courtesy The Museum of Modern Art Film Stills Archive.

backstage conflict and of opening-night excitement; we see the rehearsals, the rewriting, the reviewer. But we are also aware of being on the outside, of not "being there" as it happens. The film takes a particularly distant attitude toward its principal subject, even though there are direct, candid moments in which she speaks directly to the camera about the pressures and problems of her role and her debut. Ironically, we can see her trying almost as hard to make this a good film as she is obviously trying to make her dreadful role into something more than it is. Still, the film is flat, and Fonda seems as if she is in a film about a film about a play. It is understandable that the actress can obscure the woman, and vice versa; here the problem is that neither emerges through the rather interesting framework of the film.

It is with *Dont Look Back* (1966) that Pennebaker found in Bob Dylan the perfect subject for his approach to film making. Dylan's fans argue that their idol "performed" in this film and "put on" the film makers; there are aspects of performance, aside from those filmed on stage, and Dylan seems conscious of them. In these moments, Dylan is acting for fans, for reporters, for associates, acting out their impression of him. But this is a minor criticism, for the film is an endlessly fascinating record of Dylan's 1965 tour of England, and it reveals the young singer who, several years later, would be acknowledged as an artist of genuine originality, virtuosity, and significance. Taking its title from a well-known Dylan song ("She's got everything she needs, she's an artist, she don't look back"), the film pictures Dylan in candid interviews with newsmen, in informal chats with teen-agers, in concert after concert, typing while Joan Baez sings her own kind of folk song; we see him arguing with hotel managers, dealing with his manager, Albert Grossman, and according a surprisingly polite reception to the delightful lady Sheriff in an English town. In short, we see the varied moods of a gifted artist.

From the evidence presented in the film, it is difficult to tell whether or not Dylan's behavior is a "put on" of the film. If it is, it is the artful act of a man who had not yet realized the extent to which he would capture, and would continue to hold, the minds of his generation. If it is not a put on, it is what we would have hoped for: a candid portrait of a brilliant poet and performer. The excitement of *Dont Look Back* comes from the tension which results from Dylan, as he is, and Dylan, as the press and his fans want him to be. In sequence after sequence, we see newsmen and reporters putting words into his mouth, trying to elicit answers that fit their preconceived notions of how a pop singer (which is how they regard him) should behave. The film is about the mass media and how they distort art and artists as much as it is about an artist and his art.

The photography is grainy, the lighting is often bad, and the sound recording is not what it might be, but *Dont Look Back* has what its technically proficient predecessors, *David* and *Jane*, lack. Dylan is not only interesting, but fascinating; his originality infuses every frame, from the opening sequence in which he holds up "idiot cards" printed with some of the words of his song "Subterranean Homesick Blues" (as Allen Ginsberg lurks strangely in the background) to his energetic arguing with just about everyone he confronts in the film. *Dont Look Back* is not for everyone; especially, it is not for those who confuse pop culture commercialism with genuine originality, for those who expect long-haired troubadors to be mindless leaders of screaming fans, for those who refuse to believe that someone under thirty can be great as well as successful. And it is the measure of Dylan's "performance" in this film that he never underestimates his audiences. Those who understand him understand this film; those who don't understand him will learn a lot from it.

The first of the big rock festival films was *Monterey Pop* (1968). Pennebaker avoids the lightweight propaganda that characterizes the later *Woodstock* and *Gimme Shelter;* he seems content to capture the artistry of the performers and the exuberance of the crowds. And at Monterey, the Hell's Angels stayed out of trouble. The film preserves some memorable performances by The Who, Jimi Hendrix, Otis Redding, Ravi Shankar, Janis Joplin, the Mamas and the Papas, and Simon and Garfunkel. Because Joplin, Redding and Hendrix are dead, *Monterey Pop* becomes a special artifact of our times, a reminder of pop music festivals before violence ended them in Altamont, before dope killed some of rock's major stars. Most of all, *Monterey Pop* is notable for excellent color photography, for footage which understands musicians at work, and for brilliant sound recording.[8]

Pennebaker never gets as close to his subjects as Leacock did to Stravinsky in *A Stravinsky Portrait* or the Maysles did to Paul Brennan in *Salesman*. But he does choose his subjects with an original sense of the potentialities of the new nonfiction film, and he reveals a particularly strong feeling for sound, for music, and for the personalities that make either or both. He has worked with Jean-Luc Godard and Norman Mailer on film-making projects; his latest film is *Original Cast Album: Company* (1971), marking the first time a film has been made of the recording session of a Broadway hit. It is a colorful, engrossing film.

Allan King

The Canadian film director Allan King has set himself apart from his contemporaries—Leacock, Pennebaker, Wiseman, and the Maysles brothers—by a film approach which stresses empathy with his subject matter rather than observation of it. He does not necessarily deal with topical social issues or events, and his films (especially *Warrendale* and *A Married Couple*) reflect a direct concern with individual humans and with interrelationships. Unlike his contemporaries, he does not record or reveal these people so much as he encourages the viewer's personal response to them. He says, "I am interested in getting into films in which we can expand our own ability to feel how it is for another person."[9] As influences on his work, King acknowledges the style of Flaherty, the naturalism of Rouquier's *Farrebique,* and the films of Jean Renoir, Jean Vigo, and Mark Donskoi (especially *The Childhood of Maxim Gorki*). His own particular style is evident in nearly twenty films, most of them made for the Canadian Broadcasting Corporation, including *Skid Row* (1956)—which appeared at the same time and covered the same subject as Rogosin's *On the Bowery—The Pemberton Valley* (1957), *Warrendale,* and *A Married Couple.*

That King's films elicit strong viewer response is, perhaps, best demonstrated by *Warrendale* (1966), King's controversial use of the direct cinema technique to record the therapy of emotionally disturbed young people. The film is not about the treatment so much as it is a "personal, selective record" of the experience; King communicates his involvement and, in so doing, makes criticism a particularly difficult task. The subject matter of *Warrendale* is ideal for the direct cinema approach; the children are vitally alive and their problems are an unavoidable part of our times. Warrendale, a center in Toronto, uses a therapy of "holding" instead of drugs and other conventional techniques. The children are encouraged to be violent so that they can be enveloped in the protective arms of a staff member. Their reactions to this therapy are as unpredictable as the emotional hysterics that result when their cook dies, but the overall intention seems to be a demonstration of trust and love. King's camera achieves an extraordinary intimacy in recording their violent reactions, their responses to the holding therapy, and their therapists and counselors; the sound recording, however, is generally poor, and detracts from the immediacy of the film.

Like the other new nonfiction films, *Warrendale* captures a situation so intensely that it becomes difficult to know where reality ends and film art begins. Indeed, these distinctions may even be irrelevant, as so much of the criticism of the direct cinema approach reveals. We often find ourselves agreeing or disagreeing with the subject matter of the film instead of analyzing and criticizing the technique. The new nonfiction film breaks down the traditional concepts of form and content; in fact, form and content become one, not something necessarily larger, but something definitely different from earlier films. *Warrendale* prompts many responses, ranging from pity to revulsion to fear to empathy. The private tragedies are so intense that one cannot remain detached from them, and yet the absence of information about this particular form of therapy raises many questions about its validity and effectiveness. Unlike *Dont Look Back* or *Salesman,* for example, *Warrendale* maintains such a tight control over the aesthetic distance between the film and the viewer that one is either absorbed or repelled. Some maintain that such films cannot be criticized in terms of art because they *are* reality, while others remind us that the films cannot be dealt with as pure reality since they are photographed, edited, and distributed as commercial films.[10] It is enough to say that the depth of one's interest determines the extent of one's appreciation, or lack of it; criticism is very much a personal matter, as far removed from the criteria which one applies to a film made on Grierson's principles as the new films themselves are.

Allan King has a keen, perceptive way of filming the unusual, and he has remarkable ability for penetrating situations that are both tender and violent and for emerging with extraordinary films. The propriety of that investigation, as we have seen, can be questioned, and King's *A Married Couple* (1969) raises questions of taste as *Warrendale* raised questions of censorship because some of the children's language was alleged to be obscene. The film is about the private life of a real couple, played by themselves, the "actuality drama" (King's term) of the marriage of Antoinette and Billy Edwards. One of the real problems presented by this film is that the Edwardses are really not very interesting people; perhaps, none of us would be any more or any less interesting if our day-to-day activities were photographed. Because the Edwardses were both actors at one time, they seem to be more aware of the camera than, by theory, they should be in such a film. They acknowledge the camera in both direct and indirect ways, as does Paul Brennan in *Salesman,* and they "act" in a "natural" way. They bring us into their lives, but they control our relationship (in the bedroom scenes, for instance) ; they seem concerned with satisfying our natural curiosity about their lives, but they also seem eager to give us a good show.

A Married Couple lacks imagination. The Edwardses lack the imagination to be themselves in front of the camera, and King lacks the imagination and intuition to shape his footage into something more than what exists. The Edwards' marriage is on the rocks and they try to find means to save it through the act of making a film. Perhaps *A Married Couple* will be of interest to viewers in such a predicament, but it fails to fulfill the promise of King's approach in *Warrendale.* King asks more than our interest in his subjects; he asks that we care about them. In so doing, he takes nonfiction film beyond the familiar expectations and probes new areas in which the audience becomes more than a spectator.

Warrendale: An apprehensive member of the Warrendale community considers an aspect of the controversial "holding" therapy. Photograph courtesy The Museum of Modern Art Film Stills Archive.

Frederick Wiseman

The new nonfiction film makers—Leacock, Pennebaker, King, and the Maysles brothers—have tended to focus directly on individuals. Unique among them is Frederick Wiseman, who chooses not to personalize one man, but rather to concentrate on one institution and, by that means, to comment on the men in it. Individual in his approach, Wiseman brings a strong, inquiring intelligence to these subjects, and his viewpoint is generally implicit in his choice of subject, his shooting of sequences, and his editing. Wiseman clearly dislikes institutions, especially big, bureaucratic ones, but he does not pretend to suggest alternatives. In each of his films, one sees the external nature of an institution; a man, or men, who reflects its policies; and a conflict between those who are in authority and those who are not. About this subject, Wiseman comments,

What I'm aiming at is a series on American institutions, using the word "institutions" to cover a series of activities that take place in a limited geographical area with a more or less consistent group of people being involved. I want to use film technology to have a look at places like high schools, hospitals, prisons, and police, which seem to be very fresh material for film; I want to get away from what I consider to be the typical documentary where you follow one charming person around or one Hollywood star around. I want to make films where the institutions will be the star but will also reflect larger issues in general society. In other words, the specific issues that I'm filming, such as institutional management, should be very relevant by analogy to some of the larger issues around us.[11]

Wiseman's films are very much in the direct cinema tradition, but he is skeptical about the larger claims made for the approach: "There's something terribly misleading about the idea that such films are Truth."[12] Defining his own approach, Wiseman says,

The way I try to make a documentary is that there's no separation between the audience watching the film and the events in the film. It's like the business of getting rid of the proscenium arch in the theater, and, by analogy, at least, narration is the proscenium arch because it immediately separates you from the experience you're going to see and hear, by telling you that it has nothing to do with you, or by telling you what to think about it.[13]

His films are superb examples of the quality that can be achieved with hand-held cameras and direct sound recording. The absence of narration brings them very close to an ideal situation in which explicit, objective film reporting is given implicit critical focus by the selection of details. They mark an important stage in the development of the new nonfiction film; in technique, they stand midway between films such as *Happy Mother's Day* and *Salesman*.

Despite what appear to be their outward intentions, Wiseman's films are curiously ambiguous. There is no narration to guide the viewer, and no music to set a mood; instead, there is a clear and direct concern with one subject: the uses and abuses of institutional power. The viewer must make up his own mind; if he is poor, the situation presented in *Hospital* might seem familiar, however deplorable; but if he is able to afford private health care, it might seem more than enough for the less fortunate. If he believes in the authoritative voice of the armed forces, then *Basic Training* will appeal to him, but if he is a young recruit, fresh from similar experiences, his reaction might be quite different. Wiseman says,

> My films are totally subjective. The objective-subjective argument is from my view, at least in film terms, a lot of nonsense. The films are my response to a certain experience. To the extent that people who are acknowledged experts . . . recognize similarities between what they find in my films and in their own work, that's all well and good. But what I want to avoid is any of the films being considered the definitive statement on the material or on the institution in question.[14]

For their directness, their incisive analysis, and their technical skill, Wiseman's films deserve a very special place among the achievements of the new nonfiction film. Like Grierson, Wiseman is fascinated with the internal operation of institutions, but instead of showing *how* they work, he tries to show *why* they don't.

Since 1964, Wiseman has made five films: *The Titicut Follies* (1967), a frightening look at a hospital for the criminally insane; *High School* (1968); *Law and Order* (1969), which concerns a big city police department; *Hospital* (1970); and *Basic Training* (1971), a film about the initiatory routines of the U.S. Army. With the exception of *The Titicut Follies,* which has been embroiled in legal disputes since its release, each film has been shown on tele-

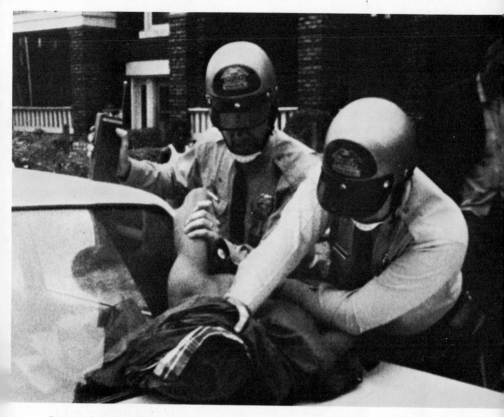

Law and Order: Two officers deal with a resisting hit-and-run offender in Frederick Wiseman's study of urban police methods. Photograph courtesy Zipporah Films.

vision. In 1967, *Titicut Follies* won documentary first prize at the Mannheim Film Festival, and both *Law and Order* and *Hospital* have been awarded Emmys by the Academy of Television Arts and Sciences.

The Titicut Follies (1967) echoes Peter Weiss' play *Marat/ Sade;* the Weiss play was fiction based on fact, but Wiseman's nonfiction film is only fact. The film is a disturbingly candid view of the Bridgewater State Hospital in Massachusetts, so disturbing that it triggered a bitter legislative hearing, considerable political controversy, and a court censorship case. The film's title derives from a public benefit put on by the inmates and guards of this mental hospital; they called it "Titicut Follies" (after the Indian name for the Bridgewater area) and scenes from this sad "entertainment" open and close the film. But the film's real concern is not the follies of the evening, but the foolish, degrading and almost inhuman treatment of patients in this state prison for the criminally insane. Undoubtedly, the discomfort felt by the lay audience must have been shared by the Massachusetts legislators and the institution's supervisors, for they charged Wiseman with violating the rights of patients and with breach of contract; the film was banned in Massachusetts, although it was shown at the 1967 New York Film Festival.

Titicut Follies is a horrifying film about a modern-day Bedlam that many viewers would have thought had been outlawed. Unlike Anatole Litvak's pioneering fiction film on this subject, *The Snake Pit* (1948), it does not need a dramatic structure to give intensity to the horrors; they are there and need only to be filmed. *Titicut Follies* exposes more about us than it does about Bridgewater. It shows how supposedly rational and professional men demean and cheapen the quality of life; how they mistreat and humiliate the sick and incompetent; and how they betray the expectations of therapy and rehabilitation. Its sensational elements—naked inmates, a masturbating man, brutal treatment by guards, and unfeeling prison boards—are shocking and, at times, sickening. The psychiatrists seem more interested in inmates' descriptions of sexual behavior than in ways in which they can help them, diagnose their problems, and prevent their unnecessary deaths (as they fail to do once in this film). As seen through Wiseman's lens, the inmates of Bridgewater become victims—almost prisoners—of an insidious institution that mocks and betrays its purpose.

Wiseman relies primarily on visual images to present the Bridgewater story; there is no narration or commentary to tell us what we are seeing or how we should feel. Indeed, in this as in Wiseman's other films, the visual always provides its own kind of narration. The subjects of his films do all the talking that, in combination with the picture, is necessary to provide us with the materials for response. *Titicut Follies,* like *Warrendale,* raises serious issues which affect viewer response. One's interest will determine his involvement in these and other films which go beyond the common experience and expectation of subject matter. In his review of *Titicut Follies,* Arthur Knight asked, "But, inevitably, it must raise the ethical question: Where does the truth stop and common decency begin?"[15] Wiseman reveals to us the ugly truth that institutions such as Bridgewater were built to hide; if we had more films with the truth and honesty of *Titicut Follies,* we might not have to ask such a question.

High School (1968) was filmed at Philadelphia's North East High School, an urban school with an almost all-white student body occupying a functionally modern campus. On the outside, it would appear to be a "model" school, and to parents and administrators it probably is; but to Wiseman, looking at it from the inside, it is something very different. With characteristic thoroughness, Wiseman takes us through a wide, comprehensive range of curricular and extracurricular activities. We do more than observe them; because of his remarkably intimate camera work, we participate in these activities, from academic to vocational and physical-training classes, from parent-principal conferences to conflicts between gym coaches and students, from sex-education and hygiene classes to rehearsals for fashion shows. This list only suggests the range of people and places that Wiseman's camera records; he is rigorously thorough and manages to be flexible enough so that we see things from the viewpoint of the students, the teachers, the parents, and the film maker himself.

A common theme links the many incidents in the film: the

rigid, mechanical nature of authority in this self-contained society. Principals, counselors, and coaches all follow a code of discipline that allows little tolerance of individual behavior. Time and time again, we see intelligent, curious students meeting obstacles of unthinking authority. Some classrooms seem like irrelevant vacuums: an older teacher presents an uninspired reading of "Casey at the Bat," assuming that it is an unforgettable masterpiece. Another, younger teacher is much more successful in her use of a Simon and Garfunkel recording to teach poetry and poetic devices. But for every dedicated and creative teacher, there seems to be one whose knowledge, and, therefore, whose advice, is based on rigid forms. Memorable among student-teacher confrontations is a session in which a counselor insists that a girl attend college, even though the girl has determined that she wants to attend a training school for beauticians, and a scene in which a gym instructor refuses to grant a boy's version of an incident. To make his account complete, Wiseman continually intercuts with reminders of aspects of the school that are somewhat more admirable: generally mature and intelligent lectures on sex, for instance. But these lectures are given by a local doctor, and when we later hear the principal instructing students on the question of "style" (i.e., conformity) in dress for the senior prom, or eavesdrop on a political discussion in the faculty cafeteria, we know the prevailing tenor of thought in the administration and faculty.

As the film progresses, one wonders how Wiseman will end it. Piling one example on top of another often has the reverse of the intended effect, and Wiseman seems to have known this. The best sequence in the film was, ironically and luckily, the very last to be shot, and it was unplanned and unexpected. It provides a climax to the film that could not have been invented. At a faculty meeting a teacher is reading to her colleagues a letter from a former student; the young man, stationed in Vietnam, is writing to express his appreciation for the school, the system in which he was an "average or sub-average student." Because he is on the eve of combat duty, he decides to make the school the beneficiary of his $10,000 Army insurance in the event that he is killed. The teacher concludes her reading of this poignant letter, and says, in effect, that it proves that the school is doing the right thing. The film opens with shots of the school's factorylike buildings—low, functional, and undistinguished —and it closes with a testimonial from one of the products of this educational assembly line. The most depressing aspect of the school system is crystallized by this letter; it does not teach its students to question, to challenge, or to think, so that when this congratulatory message arrives, it merely serves to confirm the existence of an institution which, ironically, is dedicated to the education of free and independent minds.

Wiseman's third film, *Hospital* (1969), is perhaps his best to date. On the outside, the film's subject is the social aspect of medicine, but at its heart is the flow of human suffering through a vast health-care facility. The film was made at New York's Metropolitan Hospital, and covers many services, from the emergency, receiving, and operating rooms, to the wards, clinics, and supporting social services. It can be argued that no routine cases are presented, that we see only the dramatic ones; for instance, we do not see any children or any maternity cases, nor do we see the long waiting lines that the obviously overcrowded conditions must necessitate. But this is a minor fault compared to what we do see.

Hospital is not a television soap opera drama about urban medical problems. Here we see the real thing: a mistreated child for whom the hospital has difficulty finding a bed; a psychotic homosexual pleading for help; a confused alcoholic; a heroin addict; a terrified young man suffering from a bad mescaline trip, screaming "I don't want to die" as he vomits out his guts. We see many black and Puerto Rican patients in this public hospital, and in addition to the routine heart attacks and other diseases, there is a blood-soaked knife-fight victim, a woman who has been shunted back and forth from one hospital to another (the attendant comments "It don't make sense"), and a gripping sequence in which a terrified woman tries to talk to her dying mother. But the memorable thing about *Hospital* is not the human suffering, for it is what one properly expects in such an institution; we remember the staff's faith in reason, order, efficiency, and sincere, dedicated care. Unlike the high school teachers and administrators, they are free to respond to each patient with a variety of medical and psychological tools.

There are times, of course, when the bureaucracies of the welfare system make a mockery of intelligent medical care—especially when a psychiatrist pleads on the telephone with a welfare-office clerk to obtain some aid for the young homosexual—but, for the most part, we are aware of an overworked group of doctors, nurses, and orderlies who project considerable humanity despite their surroundings. Of course, there are moments when we see people out of touch with one another, as, for instance, when a priest in the hospital chapel delivers his sermon in English to what appears to be a congregation made up entirely of Spanish-speaking people. And the exterminator who appears several times in the film, spraying the walls and trash receptacles, is a fact of life that says more about cleanliness than all the white robes, rubber gloves, and scrubbed hands can possibly say. These and other small moments deepen the texture of Wiseman's picture—grim medical school lectures, a boy in a wheelchair forgotten in a hallway—but the important thing is that this hospital and its staff are at least in touch with the patients. This hospital is a functioning institution, not a moribund one.

It might be argued that *Hospital* is not typical of Wiseman's best work, for the simple reason that it is not as critical as his other films. But his intention seems to be incisive sociological analysis rather than direct criticism. A weak institution is its own best critic, although it makes this criticism indirectly as it unintentionally reveals its weaknesses. The hospital is merely stronger than the high school, not perfect by any means, just more able to cope with its sizable and particular problems. *Hospital* is an unpleasant picture of a massive social ill—inadequate health care for the urban poor—but it is determined in its presentation, unflinching in its realism, and consistently intelligent in its viewpoint.

Wiseman's most recent film, *Basic Training* (1971), seems to be almost a culmination of his concern with institutions. It is about the U.S. Army and shows and says everything that the films of world War II did not and could not. The institution is founded on tradition; it is inflexible; at times, it is remarkably sad and, at others, unexpectedly funny. It is photographed and edited with great ease and skill. *Basic Training* presents a world in which a white recruit's family thinks the Army will make a "man" out of him, the same

Basic Training: Recruits learn hand-to-hand combat in Frederick Wiseman's full-length, in-depth study of U.S. army training. Photograph courtesy Zipporah Films.

world in which a young black recruit wants to be put in the base jail because he is "tired of people." It is a world in which guns are called "weapons," not guns, in which "killing" is called "self-defense," not killing. *Basic Training* both confirms and challenges the viewer's ideas about the Army. Like all of Wiseman's films, it is a complex and unforgettable experience.

Frederick Wiseman's films are more consciously and more rigorously sociological in their focus than the films of his contemporaries, and they are more consistently expressive of one man's vision of society than are the films of Leacock, Pennebaker, or the Maysles. Yet, Wiseman joins his contemporaries in his direct, intimate use of the camera and of sound-recording equipment, in his tightly controlled editing, and in his choice of original and compelling subject matter. While he does not use narration or music, he seems vitally concerned with the power of film to communicate, and he uses visual images intelligently both in his direction of the photography and in his editing of the footage. His concern is societal, not individual, but his independence and his control over his films give them a greater degree of critical focus than the more objective reportage of the other film makers whose approach he uses and adapts. Trained as a lawyer, Wiseman understands injustice with the same intuitiveness that Leacock and Pennebaker understand creativity; he captures institutional eccentricities with the same sensitivity that the Maysles record individual ones. If his approach is a limited one, it is limited only to an insight into and an understanding of American society, and it yields films of unquestionable value and merit in helping us to understand that society.

Albert and David Maysles

Albert and David Maysles are unique as film makers, not because they are brothers working together, but because they bring to their films a combination of originality, intelligence, and theatricality that is unparalleled in nonfiction film making today. They seek out the unusually gifted, eccentric, and compelling individual; they are interested in revealing character, not in social comment. They make what they call "nonfiction films," following Truman

Capote's concept of the nonfiction novel, and they hope to give the viewer the feeling of what it is like to be involved in the incidents they film. Luckily, they have been "there" with some of the most interesting people in the world before their camera, and their sensitivity to these people—the well known and the unknown—is extraordinary.

The Maysles entered film making in 1956; they worked as a team, individually on their own projects, and with Leacock, Pennebaker, and others in the Time-Life, Inc., projects, such as *Primary* and *Yanqui No!* In 1962, they formed their own film production company, and since that time they have made *Showman; What's Happening! The Beatles in the U.S.A.; With Love from Truman— A Visit with Truman Capote; Meet Marlon Brando; Salesman;* and *Gimme Shelter.* For these films, the Maysles have developed their own special photographic and sound-recording equipment.[16]

The Maysles' first film was *Showman* (1963), a candid and informal portrait of Joseph E. Levine, the film producer-distributor. Despite its poor editing (especially in the early sequences) and its lack of continuity, *Showman* succeeds in giving the viewer a sense of Levine's daily activity, but not much of an impression of the man himself; but, then, the activity may be the man, and the man, the activity. But it is the film's spontaneous enthusiasm for its subject that compensates for its faults. Levine was just too self-conscious, too uncomfortable, to behave naturally in front of the camera (the way, say, that the lawyer Donald Moore behaved naturally in Leacock-Pennebaker's *The Chair*). Nevertheless, the memorable moments in the film involve him completely: telling stories about his youth at a reunion of old neighborhood buddies (as a boy, Levine sold pieces of broken cake that a bakery discarded and claims he didn't know what it was to be cold until a friend mentioned it), screaming at David Susskind about art and public taste, and taking the Oscar for his production *Two Women* to Sophia Loren in Rome (and calling her "Sophie"). Levine is clearly larger than life, but more human than the stereotyped picture of a movie mogul that one expects. For one thing, he is not really a producer; Levine is a shrewd businessman who buys the rights to, and distributes what he hopes will be major films. For another, at the time *Showman* was made, he was just too much in awe of his success, of his contacts with people like Sophia Loren, to be pompous or domineering. While we get a rather detached picture of Levine, the sense of "being there" is both enhanced and thwarted by the constant presence of assistants, reporters, and crowds in general. There are few moments of direct character revelation, although there are those previously mentioned brilliant moments that indirectly reveal the man. At the end of the film, Levine comments that the work leading to his success has been "tiresome," but aside from that, we see little but a confirmation of the tenement-to-riches myth. The problem with this film is clearly Levine's (he has prohibited its exhibition), not the Maysles'; their inability to get as close as we would like to their subject is not characteristic of their second film.

The Maysles' second film, *What's Happening! The Beatles in the U.S.A.* (1964), begins with the arrival of The Beatles in New York, and records the Beatlemania that accompanied the group on its initial visit to the United States. Here The Beatles are short-haired, seemingly shy, and thoroughly overwhelmed by their reception. They do little but mug and clown in front of the cameras, suggesting the hijinx of *A Hard Day's Night,* the movie they were later to make. The Maysles' film is not an interpretative document, but rather an objective record which communicates the sheer fun that The Beatles had off stage. Moreover, their infectious personalities and sense of humor provide genuine insights into their tremendous audience appeal and later success. The film suggests comparisons with *Dont Look Back,* for we see The Beatles, as we saw Bob Dylan: on stage and off, with their manager, putting on reporters, and disarming their fans. The irony of the Maysles' approach in *Showman* also characterizes their later *Meet Marlon Brando* (1965), but their approach is affectionate in this hour-long romp with The Beatles.

Affection for their subject is also the keynote of the Maysles' *With Love from Truman—A Visit with Truman Capote* (1966). Here, in a synthesis of journalistic reporting and direct cinema, they provide a close-up picture of the novelist discussing his work with an interviewer from *Newsweek* magazine. We see Capote in many moods and in many places, telling how he wrote *In Cold Blood,* showing New York to friends he made while writing the "nonfiction novel," recounting delightful anecdotes, and talking candidly and intimately of his affection for the two convicted murderers that are at the center of his masterpiece of crime reporting. For the most part, Capote is unconscious of the presence of the camera; when he is conscious of it, he adds delightful little theatrical touches, such as when he mixes drinks in his summer house. The main concern of this film is to present a picture of the man from whom the Maysles adapted the approach to film making which characterizes their later and more mature work. *With Love from Truman* is a fairly conventional filmed interview with a thoroughly unconventional man; from Capote, the Maysles learned the ways in which fictional techniques can be used to shape the reporting of actual events. Their success with adapting his approach to film can be seen in *Salesman*.

The titles credit *Salesman* (1969) as being a film by the Maysles brothers and Charlotte Zwerin, their editor. This reflects more than the work Miss Zwerin contributed to the film; it is an acknowledgment of the importance of editing to the new nonfiction film. Many significant nonfiction films before *Salesman* owe much to their editors; one recalls Helen Van Dongen's work for Joris Ivens and Robert Flaherty. Since the films of the Maysles brothers and their contemporaries are shot without a formal script, following the events as they occur, it becomes the responsibility of the editor, working with the film maker, to give shape and movement to the footage. Commenting on this relationship, Zwerin says,

> One of the really important contributions of an editor in a *vérité* film arises from the fact that he only sees what is on the screen. The cameraman will tell you that a great deal of what he gets in shooting depends on his relationship to the subject, but whatever is happening between himself and the person he's shooting distorts the event for the cameraman; he can't see the scene in perspective. But the editor has the advantage of knowing that something either *is* or *is not* conveyed on the screen. His immediate reaction isn't blunted by any personal knowledge. . . . I think this removal from the scene [the filming of *Salesman*] helped my judgment and helped me to understand more clearly what the viewer would feel.[17]

Salesman is clearly a film about which the Maysles felt deeply, and the scenes with Paul Brennan, especially, reveal an underlying tension between their affection for him and their desire to remain objective in their filming. It is to Zwerin's credit that this tension is both controlled and communicated to the viewer.

Al Maysles believes that unobtrusive, lightweight equipment of his own design allows him to get closer to his subject than he would otherwise be able to if he were working with ordinary equipment, and he has found that most individuals are considerably less self-conscious in front of a camera than might be expected. While this does not seem to be supported by *Showman,* it is abundantly clear in *Salesman.* The film is an extraordinary achievement in nonfiction film making, for it gives dramatic shape and structure to the words and actions of real people, and in such a way that the viewer has the definite feeling of "being there." There does not appear to be any cinematic equivalent of the proscenium arch between us and the four salesmen, and their words and actions—most of all, their words—are so close to what we would expect that we have the feeling that they are reading lines in a script. But that is the paradox and the achievement of the new nonfiction film, as well as the special hallmark of *Salesman.* It brings us to that thin and wonderful region between fact and fiction, turning upside down what we might expect and, at the same time, confirming what we knew was there all along.

At the outset, the subject of *Salesman*—the door-to-door activities of Bible salesmen—seems special, even precious, the sort of thing that Tennessee Williams might make into a play, but hardly the subject for a full-length objective film.[18] And it is to this skepticism that the film is addressed, for at its heart is the central conflict between material and spiritual values. Here, the salesmen realize that their task is not so much to sell printed books, as it is to get a customer to examine his faith. In that split second between faith and doubt (the books cost dearly), the sale is usually made. *Salesman* follows four representatives of the Mid-American Bible Company in their selling territories of Boston and Florida: Paul Brennan, known as "The Badger"; Charles McDevitt, "The Gipper"; James Baker, "The Rabbit"; and Raymond Martos, "The Bull." Because of his gift of gab and his sales pitch ("This is not the Irish blarney, it comes right from the heart") and his outward personality, Paul is the focus of the film. He inevitably brings to mind Willy Loman from Arthur Miller's *Death of a Salesman,* for like Willy, he is losing touch, sales, and self-confidence, and is a sympathetic character. The aspect that separates him from his partners, though, is none of these characteristics, although they are very important; Paul is a natural actor, unaware of the camera, able to spin yarns, to reminisce, to laugh at adversity. Like another fictional counterpart, Harry Hickey in Eugene O'Neill's *The Iceman Cometh,* he represents more than just a salesman fallen on hard times. He is caught in an existential dilemma, trapped between the meaninglessness of his job and the dictates of his heart. He would be interesting if he were selling heavy machinery, or shoes, or insurance, but he is selling the Bible. Even though it is just another commodity to him (he carefully avoids religious talk), he works up a sales pitch that is a combination of hard-sell phrases and a certain moral imperative that helps him to break down the resistance of customers. Paul is pathetic when persuading a poor customer that she needs an expensive Bible in her home: ". . . it's the only thing that I know that you secure in a lifetime that doesn't depreciate. A car after three years is worth nothing. A Bible like that is really something that will really build up a heritage in the home." But all of this is just sales talk, for it really doesn't make any difference to Paul. His one claim to freedom is that he avoided joining the police force, as his father wanted him to, and avoided the routine and the inevitable pension that followed. But he is not so sure now, and in the last scene of the film, he is in a motel room, packing his things to move on to a new territory. His partners are in the room with him, and half to them, half to himself, he says,

> That's life. (*In Irish accent.*) Yeah, join the fahrce and get a pinshun. No sire, boss. Mary, she works for the telephone. She's got a lot of stocks. They're hardworkin', hardworking people. Hardworking . . . Yup . . . yup . . . Charlie's been working in the police fahrce now. The boy, he retires, he gets a pinshun. (*His voice catches as he contains his tears.*) He's all set for life. (*Framed in the doorway, fear in his eyes, he stares nowhere . . .*) [19]

Salesman is about Paul, about loneliness, about people's need for expensive books to confirm a faith that a strange salesman can talk

Salesman: In the final scene of this remarkable film, Paul Brennan is framed in a moment of self-revelation that underscores his anxiety about the future. Photograph Maysles Films, Inc.

them into, about the guilt they feel when they don't want the book or can't afford it, about American society and its values. It is not a pretentious film, nor a particularly deep one. Its surface shimmers with unforgettable people, houses, and comments. At times, some of them seem too "real" to be real: the Irish mother and daughter in Boston; the vice-president of the company that publishes the Bible, Melbourne I. Feltman, Ph.D., the "world's greatest salesman of the world's best seller"; the elderly widow whom Paul persuades into buying a Bible ("Well, I don't know how many years I have to read the Bible"); and the married couple straight out of a satire on American living customs, he in his undershirt, she with her hair in curlers, the hi-fi playing a heavily orchestral version of The Beatles' "Yesterday." All of these moments, and many more, make *Salesman* a sociological document to be treasured. Against this fabric, we see Paul, conning, joking, laughing, doubting, cursing. Paul and the other people mirror each other. He sells a Bible that costs $49.95 and can be paid for by one of three plans: "Cash, C.O.D., and also they have a little Catholic Honor Plan. Which plan would be the best for you, the A, B, or C?" It is a perfect example of *Salesman*'s masterful nonfiction film reporting that we don't know whether this representative bit of Paul's wit is a joke on him, on his customers, or on us.

Salesman is notable for its superb photography and sound recording, for its ability to sustain nonfiction reporting in a full-length film, and for its direct, penetrating look at an American institution—the door-to-door salesman. It is distinguished by its originality, by its intelligent handling of its subject matter, and by its fidelity to truth. And it will be remembered for many things, including the Maysles-Zwerin achievement of understanding and respecting the line between fiction and fact.

A glance at the list of important, successful nonfiction films of the 1960's and early 1970's indicates the importance of the new folk and new rock music: *Dont Look Back, Monterey Pop, Woodstock,* and *Gimme Shelter.* The latter two films—about rock festivals at Woodstock, New York, and at Altamont, California—represent polarities, not only in the festivals themselves and their significance to the so-called counterculture, but also in the approaches the film makers take to them. Michael Wadleigh's *Woodstock* (1970) is a lavish, lyrical poem to the green and grassy splendors of a pastoral event. Claimed to be a state-of-mind, as well as a weekend of fun, the Woodstock festival was unique and, in many ways, unreal; *Woodstock* captures the vast scale of this unreality. *Gimme Shelter* (1970), by the Maysles Brothers and Charlotte Zwerin, is a tight, jolting account of the violent rock concert held in 1969 in the burned-out hills of California. *Woodstock* is a film about love, music, and fun; *Gimme Shelter* records hate, music, and horror. *Woodstock* features more than a dozen top performers and groups; *Gimme Shelter* features Mick Jagger and the Rolling Stones. *Woodstock* marks the beginning of what might have been a period of youth, love, and peace—at least as it seemed to the performers and the mammoth audience; *Gimme Shelter* marks the abrupt end of that spirit, with the motorcycles of the Hell's Angels for a chorus and a murder for a climax. They are fascinating films in themselves, as films; moreover, they represent the opposite extremes of the new nonfiction film. Neither could have been made at an earlier time, for each is dependent upon the immediacy of a historical event, but *Woodstock* is a subjective record—a traditional nonfiction film— while *Gimme Shelter,* with *Salesman* and Wiseman's *High School* and *Basic Training,* comes as close to pure nonfiction film as any film has.

Confronted with the masses at Woodstock, not to mention the difficulties presented in filming varied performing acts outside with little chance to set up equipment, Michael Wadleigh must have felt something like Leni Riefenstahl when she was asked to film the Olympics; however, Riefenstahl had abundant time to prepare, while Wadleigh reportedly had only a few days. Nonetheless, his film, like *Olympia,* is a notable triumph of control over a sea of footage. From many hours of film, Wadleigh and his editors have shaped a three-hour film that is rarely boring and always alive. *Woodstock* can be considered a factual film—almost a newsreel of an historic event—as well as a documentary film, one that takes a predetermined and consistent attitude toward the events it records. The view is light-hearted and positive, and Wadleigh found people and things which strengthened his overall attempt to show that some 400,000 people can come together for fun, without violence. Outsiders and townspeople are interviewed, but they are generally so predictable in their responses that they have little or no effect on the main idea behind the film. Essentially, the festival speaks, or sings, for itself, and the film can or could do little more to further its effect or detract from it.

Woodstock is often humorous, for much of the Woodstock activity seems to have been fun. At times, the film tends slightly toward the boring—it could have been a monumentally boring panorama, however—but its pacing is calculated to prevent this from being a problem, and the lineup of performers and groups is such that even stationary camera setups cannot really detract from their quality. At least five different camera positions did little to relieve the monotony of some segments of the film. Arranged in episodes which, apparently, but not importantly, followed the order of the performances, the film devotes a fairly equal amount of time to each performer. What surprises, though, is the uneven quality of much of this footage. The episode featuring Joan Baez has a studio quality to it, for it is very clear and fine, much like her singing. The episode featuring Richie Havens is vital and alive and throbs with the intensity of his music, while Jimi Hendrix is often out of frame and curiously ineffective in his closing appearance; his screen presence here should be compared with his performance in *Monterey Pop*. Much of the footage was shot at night performances, and it is good; that which shows the onstage activity is interesting, and, above all, the sound, when heard under ideal theater conditions, is stereophonic and brilliant.

The content of the film fluctuates between the onstage activity and the offstage movement and reaction of the crowd, including their listening, pot smoking, swimming, sleeping, talking, dancing, practicing yoga. From time to time, the film juxtaposes images of really far-out human activity with images of a bewildered child or dog. Wadleigh frequently uses an image that is split into two or three sections and a variety of optical effects to keep the large canvas moving. Mirror images and other effects are imaginative accompaniments to the music.

Wadleigh's keen social consciousness is obvious in his earlier film *No Vietnamese Ever Called Me Nigger,* but in *Woodstock* he is a reporter, not a commentator. The larger moral and legal questions raised by the Rolling Stones' performance at Altamont are not relevant here, and *Woodstock* remains as a colorful, pastoral record of a real spirit in an unreal moment of time.

Several months after Woodstock, some 300,000 people gathered at the other side of the United States, in the bone-dry hills of northern California for a free concert by Mick Jagger and the Rolling Stones. The setting was the Altamont Speedway, and it was everything that Woodstock was not; if Woodstock was grass, then Altamont was speed. Where Woodstock was sunshine, flowers, and freedom in the woods and lakes, Altamont was the cold, dry night of California, explosive motorcycle engines, and the life-style of the Hell's Angels. Where Woodstock was almost unreal in its quality of tranquil participation in music and sharing, Altamont was a selfish display of self-indulgent and mean-looking people. Clearly Altamont ended what Woodstock began, and the proceedings were anything but pleasant. That a green revolution should begin in a peaceful eastern valley, spread across the nation in the course of less than a year, and end in a dry western gulch is almost too neat, too apocalyptic, and beyond the dreams of any novelist or film maker. However, two films survive to record, to document, and to capture—if, unfortunately, *not* to analyze—the phenomenon. Each is a valuable document, although *Gimme Shelter* seems less concerned than *Woodstock* with directly appealing to the box office. The roadshow ticket prices of *Woodstock* and the fact that the film was expected to recoup the large losses of the festival gave its glossiness and size a different dimension. The directness and power of *Gimme Shelter,* the less-than-circus size nature of its release, and the stunning, almost numbing effect on its audience are vital factors in the consideration of it as a film.

Both *Woodstock* and *Gimme Shelter* are unique in another way; they were made for, and primarily attended by young people. In some way, perhaps, they commercially exploited the affluent youth culture; for instance, the initial ticket prices for *Woodstock* were almost twice the price of tickets for other first run films. In other ways, they are solid documents of the emergence of the color-

ful youth movement of the late 1960's. The size and influence of the
so-called counter culture cannot be denied, anymore than its art, its
artifacts, its costumes, its humor, and its honesty can be disregarded.
Like the training films in World War II, or the British social
documentaries in the 1930's, these films were made under unique
circumstances for clearly-defined audiences; this is not to say that
those audiences were restricted or limited to young people, but that
they were sufficiently well-defined as to suggest to the film makers a
certain composite profile. Repeated observations of New York audiences indicated that many young people sat through several con-
secutive showings of *Woodstock,* but that many of them left after
one showing of *Gimme Shelter* with a look of pain, not joy, on their
faces. Rock was their music, and film was their art; here was a film
that fused the two in a new, disturbing way, and it was all the more
disturbing because it recorded a reality, not a romp.

Gimme Shelter is not totally focused on the affair at Altamont,
for at least half of the film shows the Rolling Stones in other places:
at their concerts in Madison Square Garden, at a recording session
in Muscle Shoals, Alabama, and finally at Altamont. By concentrat-
ing at least half of the film on activities away from California, the
Maysles seem to be showing that the Stones did not necessarily cause
riots wherever they appeared. When the film is over, the cautious
and uninitiated viewer is led to believe that Altamont was a bizarre
phenomenon in the history of the Rolling Stones concerts. But the
other half of the film presents contradictory evidence which suggests
that the Stones are not even aware, let alone responsible, for the
hysterical reactions they cause in their audiences. Jagger is seen as
almost totally out of touch with his fans, strikingly and intensely
involved with his body, his movements, and his music. He seems
just like the devil of his songs—dancing, camping, inciting, but
never exercising the judgment which might have stopped the fracas
which led to death at Altamont. His few attempts to quiet the
crowds are pathetic, ironic failures in contrast to his power to excite
them. While one can argue—and argue convincingly, as the Maysles
seem to—that the violence of California, the bone-dry land, and
the Angels were all there before the Stones arrived, one can also see
the Stones, in the film, unaware of or unconcerned about these

factors. Their reaction to the mass hysteria and fatal stabbing is one of injured innocence, and it is unexplainable. They cannot have failed to know the power of their music; for them to disregard the effect they would have, performing free with the Hell's Angels to protect them against violence, is to credit them with a detachment and a naïveté that is unjustifiable. Jagger's final disbelief, as he watches film rushes of Altamont—a film within a film—is not believable. But, then, this critical reaction reintroduces the central question of art versus reality, a question that, within the context of the nonfiction film, is not easily answered.

Gimme Shelter is a brilliant film, composed of clear, exciting images which capture the Stones in almost every phase of their backstage and onstage activity. The cameras are hand held, and very much there in the rooms, in the audience, and on the stage. As the lawyer called in to assist the Stones in obtaining the Speedway facilities, Melvin Belli is an amusing part of the film—as one reviewer put it, "shunning publicity wherever he could find it." *Gimme Shelter* is also a gripping social document (it was used in court as evidence in the trial of the acquitted Hell's Angels member); it records the fist fighting and subsequent stabbing of a black man by a member of the motorcycle gang, and in two slow-motion repeats, it emphasizes not only the explosiveness of the whole Altamont scene, but also the relationship of the Stones' performance to the violence which it accompanied, if not induced.

Gimme Shelter raises questions, not only because it is entertainment and witness to a crime, but also because it seemingly strives too hard for an objectivity which the facts do not support. For this reason, it can be criticized for not drawing a conclusion; anyone who has attended a concert by Mick Jagger and the Rolling Stones knows that the atmosphere is charged with the kind of electricity that can lead to violence. On the other hand, the film should be praised as an unrivaled piece of detached reporting.

* * *

Between 1960 and 1971, film audiences were exposed to consistently high standards of nonfiction reporting in television docu-

Gimme Shelter: Almost totally out of touch with his audience, Mick Jagger prances through one of his songs, preserving on film the electric vitality of his performance. Photograph courtesy Maysles Films, Inc.

mentaries and news specials and grew increasingly more sophisticated in their expectations. At the same time, they became more
aware of film history and technique, so that as they learned more
about film in general, they were more receptive to the particular
power of the nonfiction film in capturing the real world around
them. The box-office success of such films as *Woodstock, Gimme
Shelter,* and Peter Gimbel's *Blue Water, White Death* encourages
producers and distributors to provide more support for nonfiction
film projects. It would, perhaps, be premature to talk about a "new
wave" for the nonfiction film, but all indications are that its future
will increase and enrich the imaginative possibilities of this remarkably versatile film form.

NOTES

1 The above paragraphs cover a variety of subjects, and the following sources
will be helpful to those interested in pursuing further information on some of
them: (1) Emile de Antonio, "Point of View in *Point of Order!" Film Comment,* 2, No. 1 (Winter 1964), pp. 35–36; and David T. Bazelon, "Background to
Point of Order!" Film Comment, 2, No. 1 (Winter 1964), pp. 33–35; (2) Derek
Hill, "The Short Film Situation," *Sight and Sound,* 31, No. 3 (Summer 1962),
pp. 108–12; (3) Daniel Klughurz, "Documentary—Where's the Wonder," *Television Quarterly,* 6, No. 3 (Summer 1967), p. 38; (4) William D. Routt, "The
Documentary Film Group of Chicago," *Vision,* 1 (Spring 1962), pp. 30–31; (5)
W. Johnson, "Shooting at Wars: Three Views," *Film Quarterly,* 21, No. 2 (Win-
ter 1967–68), pp. 27–36; (6) "Peter Watkins Discusses His Suppressed Nuclear
Film," *Film Comment,* 3, No. 4 (Fall 1965), pp. 14–19; (7) William C. Jersey,
"Some Thoughts on Film Technique," *Film Comment,* 2, No. 1 (Winter 1964),
pp. 15–16; (8) Gordon Hitchens, "An Interview with George Stevens, Jr.," *Film
Comment,* 1, No. 3 (n.d.), p. 2; (9) Richard D. MacCann, "Film and Foreign
Policy: The USIA, 1962–67," *Cinema Journal,* 9, No. 1 (Fall 1969), pp. 23–42;
(10) "Propaganda Films About the War in Vietnam," *Film Comment,* 4, No. 1
(Fall 1966), pp. 4–22.
2 To further complicate the question of definition and origin, it is argued
that Jean Rouch, not Edgar Morin, coined the *cinéma vérité* label.
3 *Documentary in American Television* (New York, Hastings House, 1965),
p. 123.
4 David Maysles quoted in Jonas Mekas, "Movie Journal," *Village Voice*

(March 3, 1966), p. 21. See also, Stewart Wilenski, "The New Documentary Goal: The Revealed Situation," *Vision*, 1, No. 2 (Summer 1962), pp. 63–66. A seminal article is James Blue, "Direct Cinema," *Film Comment*, 4, Nos. 2–3 (Fall–Winter 1967), pp. 80–81.

5 See James Blue, "Interview with Richard Leacock," *Film Comment*, 3, No. 2 (Spring 1965), pp. 15–22; and E. Callenbach, "Going Out to the Subject," *Film Quarterly*, 14, No. 3 (Spring 1961), pp. 38–40.

6 Although it is available for rental, it is a regrettable fact that this film has not been released theatrically or shown on television.

7 Bluem, p. 194.

8 The quality of the sound in these rock films depends heavily on the quality of the speaker systems in the auditoriums in which they are shown.

9 *Allan King*, an interview with Bruce Martin, ed. by Alison Reid (Ottawa, Canadian Film Institute, 1970), p. 19. This pamphlet contains a complete filmography to date.

10 Two examples of such divergent criticism are (1) Jan Dawson, "*Warrendale*," *Sight and Sound*, 37, No. 1 (Winter 1967–68), pp. 44–46; and (2) Parker Tyler, "The Tyranny of Warrendale," *Evergreen* (Aug. 1969), pp. 31–33ff.

11 Alan Rosenthal, *The New Documentary in Action: A Casebook in Film Making* (Berkeley, California, University of California Press, 1971), p. 69.

12 Beatrice Berg, "I Was Fed Up With Hollywood Fantasies" [interview-article on Wiseman], *New York Times* (February 1, 1970), pp. 25–26.

13 John Graham, " 'There Are No Simple Solutions': Frederick Wiseman on Viewing Film," *The Film Journal* (Spring 1971), pp. 44–47.

14 Rosenthal, p. 70.

15 "Cinéma Vérité and Film Truth," *Saturday Review* (Sept. 9, 1967), p. 44.

16 For an account of their equipment and shooting methods, see Charles Reynolds, "Focus on Al Maysles," *Popular Photography* (May 1964), pp. 128–31.

17 Rosenthal, p. 88.

18 The transcript of the film, including stills, production notes by Howard Junker, and an introduction by Harold Clurman is contained in *Salesman* (New York, Signet Books, 1969).

19 *Salesman*, p. 105.

APPENDIX A: PRODUCTION FACTS ON MAJOR FILMS

The following list includes all films *discussed* in this study, but not necessarily all films to which reference is made. All works chosen reflect my own opinion of their quality, significance, and value. Basic information given includes film title, date of release, country in which produced, running time (varies with existing prints), U.S. 16mm distributor, and (when known) major production credits. It is not always possible to obtain complete information for some entries, and there may be errors on my part in recording details; however, every effort has been made to make this listing as complete and accurate as possible. The distributors for the U.S. are indicated by the following key:

A-B   Audio-Brandon
34 MacQuesten Parkway
Mount Vernon, N.Y. 10550

AKA   Allan King Associates
11 Hazelton Ave.
Toronto, Canada

BFI   British Film Institute
81 Dean St.
London W1V, 6AA
Note: BFI prints are usually on 35mm film and are generally not available for U.S. distribution. Those interested, however, should contact the BFI directly.

C   Cinema-5
595 Madison Ave.
New York, N.Y. 10022

CF   Contemporary/McGraw-Hill
Princeton Road
Hightstown, N.J. 08520

FB   Film Bureau
267 W. 25th St.
New York, N.Y. 10001

GP   Grove Press Films
85 Bleecker St.
New York, N.Y. 10012

LP   Leacock-Pennebaker, Inc.
56 W. 45th St.
New York, N.Y. 10036

MB   Maysles Films, Inc.
1697 Broadway
New York, N.Y. 10019

MOMA   Museum of Modern Art
Film Circulating Department
11 W. 53rd St.
New York, N.Y. 10019

MOMA*   MOMA prints designated by an asterisk (*) are archive study prints which do not circulate; they are listed here for reference purposes.

NAVC   National Audio-Visual Center
Washington, D.C. 20409

NTS   National Talent Service
115 E. 62nd St.
New York, N.Y. 10021

NYU   New York University
Film Library
Washington Square
New York, N.Y. 10012

TL   Time-Life Films, Inc.
43 W. 16th St.
New York, N.Y. 10011

UC   University of California
Extension Media Services
2223 Fulton St.
Berkeley, Calif. 94720

WB   Warner Brothers
        16mm Distributing Division
        4000 Warner Blvd.
        Burbank, Calif. 91505

WRS   Walter Reade 16mm Division
        241 E. 34th St.
        New York, N.Y. 10016

ZIP   Zipporah Films
        58 Lewis Wharf
        Boston, Mass. 02110

ALL MY BABIES (1952, USA, 55 min., NYU)
Producer, Director, Script: George Stoney for Georgia State Department of Public Health; *Photography:* Peaslee Bond; *Editor:* Sylvia Bettz.

AUTOBIOGRAPHY OF A JEEP, THE (1943, USA, 10 min., MOMA)
Producer: Joseph Krumgold for USIS; *Director:* Irving Lerner; *Screenplay:* Joseph Krumgold; *Photography:* Roger Barlow; *Editor:* Gene Fowler, Jr.; *Narrator:* Robert Sloan.

BASIC TRAINING (1971, USA, 90 min., ZIP)
Producer, Director, Script: Frederick Wiseman; *Photography:* William Brayne.

BATTLE OF BRITAIN, THE (1943, USA, 54 min., MOMA)
Producer: Frank Capra for "Why We Fight" series; *Director, Script:* Capt. Anthony Veiller; *Narrator* (in part) : Walter Huston.

BATTLE OF CHINA, THE (1944, USA, 64 min., MOMA)
Producer: Frank Capra for "Why We Fight" series; *Directors:* Frank Capra, Anatole Litvak; *Script:* Anthony Veiller, Robert Heller; *Editor:* William Hornbeck; *Narrators:* Walter Huston, Anthony Veiller; *Music:* Dmitri Tiomkin.

BATTLE OF MIDWAY, THE (1942, USA, color, 18 min.)
Producer: U.S. Navy; *Director:* John Ford.

BATTLE OF RUSSIA, THE (1943, USA, 84 min., MOMA)
Producer: Frank Capra for "Why We Fight" series; *Director:* Anatole Litvak; *Script:* Anthony Veiller, Robert Heller; *Editor:* William C. Hornbeck, William A. Lyon; *Music:* Dmitri Tiomkin.

BATTLE OF SAN PIETRO, THE (1945, USA, 30 min., MOMA)
Producer: Army Pictorial Service; *Director:* John Huston; *Photography:* Jules Buck, Signal Corps Cameramen; *Narrator:* John Huston; *Music:* Army Air Force Orchestra, Mormon Tabernacle Choir, St. Brendan's Boys' Choir.

B.B.C.: THE VOICE OF BRITAIN (1935, GB, 60 min.)
Producers: John Grierson and Alberto Cavalcanti, GPO Film Unit; *Director, Script:* Stuart Legg; *Photography:* George Noble, J. D. Davidson, W. Shenton.

BENJY (1951, USA, 30 min., MOMA)
Director: Fred Zinnemann; *Script:* Stewart Stern; *Narrator:* Henry Fonda.

BERLIN: THE SYMPHONY OF A GREAT CITY (1927, Germany, 53 min., MOMA)
Producer: Karl Freund; *Director:* Walther Ruttmann; *Script:* Freund, Ruttmann, from an idea by Carl Meyer; *Photography:* Reimar Kuntze, Robert Baberske, Laszlo Schaffer; *Music:* Edmund Meisel.

BORINAGE (1933, Belgium, 32 min., MOMA*)
Producer: E.P.I., Club de L'Écran, Brussels; *Directors, Script, Photography, Editing:* Joris Ivens, Henri Storck; *Editing of Russian Version:* Helen Van Dongen; *Music:* Hans Hauska.

BRIDGE, THE (1928, Netherlands, 15 min., silent, MOMA)
Director, Script, Photography, Editor: Joris Ivens.

BRIDGE, THE (1942, USA, 30 min., MOMA)
Producer: Foreign Policy Association; *Directors:* Willard Van Dyke, Ben Maddow.

CAMERAMEN AT WAR (1944, GB, 14 min., MOMA)
Producer: Realist Film Unit for the British Ministry of Information; *Compilation:* Len Lye; *Commentary:* Raymond Glendenning.

CHAIR, THE (1962, USA, 60 min., TL)
Producer: Robert Drew Associates for Time-Life, Inc.; *Filmakers:* Gregory Shuker, Richard Leacock, D. A. Pennebaker; *Narrator:* James Lipscomb.

CHANG (1927, USA, 68 min., silent)
Producers, Directors, Script: Merian C. Cooper, Ernest B. Schoedsack; *Titles:* Achmed Abdullah.

CHILDREN AT SCHOOL (1937, GB, 25 min., MOMA)
Producer: John Grierson for British Commercial Gas Association; *Director:* Basil Wright; *Commentary:* H. Wilson Harris; *Photography:* A. E. Jeakins, Erik Wilbur.

CHILDREN MUST LEARN, THE (1940, USA, 30 min., NYU)
Director, Script: Willard Van Dyke; *Photography:* Van Dyke, Bob Churchill; *Music Arrangement:* Fred Stewart; *Narration:* Myron McCormick.

CITY, THE (1939, USA, 55 min., MOMA)
Producer: American Documentary Films, Inc., for American Institute of Planners. *Directors:* Willard Van Dyke, Ralph Steiner; *Script:* Henwar Rodakiewicz, Lewis Mumford, from an outline by Pare Lorentz; *Photography:* Van Dyke, Steiner; *Editors:* Theodor Lawrence, Henwar Rodakiewicz; *Narrator:* Morris Carnovsky; *Music:* Aaron Copland.

CITY OF GOLD (1957, Canada, 30 min., CF)
Producer: NFB of Canada; *Directors, Location Photography:* Colin Low, Wolf Koenig; *Producer, Editor:* Tom Daly; *Narrator:* Pierre Berton.

CITY SPEAKS, A (1947, GB, 68 min., BFI)
Producer: Ministry of Information; *Director:* Paul Rotha; *Script:* Walter

Greenwood, Ara Calder-Marshall, Paul Rotha; *Photography:* Harold Young, Cyril Arapoff; *Music:* William Alwyn.

COAL FACE (1936, GB, 12 min., BFI)
Producer: John Grierson; *Director, Script:* Alberto Cavalcanti; *Editing:* William Coldstream; *Music:* Benjamin Britten; *Verse:* W. H. Auden.

COASTAL COMMAND (1942, GB, 73 min., BFI)
Producer: Ian Dalrymple for Crown Film Unit; *Director, Script:* J. B. Holmes; *Photography:* Jonah Jones, F. Gamage; *Design:* Edward Carrick; *Editor:* Michael Gordon; *Music:* Vaughan Williams.

CONQUEST OF EVEREST, THE (1953, GB, 78 min., color, BFI)
Producer: Countrymen Films for Group Three; A Film by Thomas Stobart and George Lowe; *Commentary:* Louis Macneice.

CUMBERLAND STORY, THE (1947, GB, 35 min., BFI)
Producer: Alexander Shaw, Crown Film Unit; *Director:* Humphrey Jennings; *Photography:* Chick Fowls; *Editor:* Jocelyn Jackson; *Music:* Arthur Benjamin.

CUMMINGTON STORY, THE (1945, USA, 20 min., MOMA)
Producer: Sidney Meyers for USIS; *Directors:* Helen Grayson, Larry Madison; *Editor, Narrator:* Sidney Meyers; *Music:* Aaron Copland.

DAVID (1951, GB, 38 min.)
Producer: James Carr for British Film Institute for Welsh Committee of the Festival of Britain; *Director, Script:* Paul Dickson.

DAVID (1961, USA, 54 min., TL)
Producer: Robert Drew Associates for Time-Life, Inc.; *Filmakers:* D. A. Pennebaker, Gregory Shuker, Bill Ray; *Narrator:* Joseph Julian.

DAWN OF IRAN (1938, GB, 60 min., BFI)
Producer: Arthur Elton, Strand Films, for Anglo-Iranian Oil Company; *Director, Photography, Editor:* John Taylor; *Music:* Walter Leigh.

DAYBREAK IN UDI (1949, GB, 39 min., BFI)
Producer: Max Anderson, Crown Film Unit, for Colonial Office; *Director:* Terry Bishop.

DESERT VICTORY (1943, GB, 62 min., MOMA)
Producer: RAF Film Unit, Army Film and Photographic Unit; *Director:* David MacDonald; *Commentary:* J. L. Hudson; *Music:* William Alwyn.

DIARY FOR TIMOTHY, A (1946, GB, 39 min., BFI)
Producer: Basil Wright, Crown Film Unit; *Director, Script:* Humphrey Jennings; *Photography:* F. Gamage; *Commentary:* E. M. Forster; *Editors:* Alan Osbiston, Jenny Hutt; *Music:* Richard Addinsell.

DIVIDE AND CONQUER (1942, USA, 58 min., MOMA)
Producers: Frank Capra, Anatole Litvak, for "Why We Fight" series; *Director:* Lewis Seiler; *Script:* Anthony Veiller, Robert Heller; *Narration:* Walter Huston, Anthony Veiller; *Editor:* William C. Hornbeck; *Music:* Dmitri Tiomkin.

DONT LOOK BACK (1966, USA, 95 min., LP)
Producer: Leacock-Pennebaker, Inc., *Director:* D. A. Pennebaker.

DRIFTERS (1929, GB, 40 min., BFI)

Producer: E.M.B. Film Unit; *Director, Script, Editing:* John Grierson; *Photography:* Basil Emmott.

EARTH (1930, USSR, 54 min., A-B)

Director, Script: Alexander Dovzhenko; *Photography:* Danylo Demutsky; *Design:* Vasili Krichevsky; *Music:* L. Revutsky.

EASTER ISLAND (1934, Belgium, 25 min., MOMA)

Producer: Henri Storck, Cinéma Éditions; *Director:* John Ferno; *Photography:* John Ferno; *Editor:* Henri Storck; *Commentary:* Henry Lavachery; *Music:* Maurice Jaubert.

EASTERN VALLEY (1937, GB, 19 min., MOMA)

Producers: Paul Rotha, Stuart Legg, Strand Films for Subsistence Production Scheme; *Director:* Donald Alexander; *Photography:* A. Jeakins, S. Onions.

EDDIE (1960, USA, 60 min., T-L)

Producer: Robert Drew Associates for Time-Life; *Filmakers:* D. A. Pennebaker, Richard Leacock, Abbot Mills, Bill Ray, Al Maysles; *Narrator:* Joseph Julian.

ENOUGH TO EAT? (1936, GB, 23 min., MOMA)

Producer: Realist Film Unit for Gas, Light, and Coke Co., London; *Director:* Edgar Anstey; *Photography:* Walter Blakeley, Arthur Fisher; *Commentary:* Julian Huxley.

EVERY DAY EXCEPT CHRISTMAS (1957, GB, 40 min., CF)

Producer: Karel Reisz, Leon Clore, for Ford of Britain; *Director:* Lindsay Anderson; *Photography:* Walter Lassally; *Music:* Daniel Paris; *Commentary:* Alun Owen.

FACE OF BRITAIN, THE (1935, GB, 19 min., BFI)

Producer: G. B. Instructional, Ltd.; *Director, Script, Editor:* Paul Rotha; *Photography:* George Pocknall, Frank Bundy.

FELLOW AMERICANS (1942, USA, 11 min., MOMA)

Producer: OEM Film Unit; *Director:* Garson Kanin; *Script:* Wallace Russell; *Narrator:* James Stewart; *Music:* Oscar Levant.

FIGHT FOR LIFE, THE (1941, USA, 70 min., NAVC)

Producer: U.S. Film Service; *Director:* Pare Lorentz; *Script:* Lorentz from a book by Paul de Kruif; *Photography:* Floyd Crosby; *Music:* Louis Gruenberg.

FIGHTING LADY, THE (1945, USA, 63 min., MOMA)

Producer, Director: Edward Steichen; *Commentary:* John S. Martin; *Editor:* Robert Fritch; *Narrator:* Robert Taylor; *Music:* David Buttolph.

FIRES WERE STARTED (1943, GB, 60 min., CF)

Producer: Ian Dalrymple, Crown Film Unit; *Director, Script:* Humphrey Jennings; *Photography:* Cyril Pennington-Richards; *Design:* Edward Carrick; *Editor:* Stewart McAllister; *Music:* William Alwyn.

FORWARD A CENTURY (1951, GB, 12 min., BFI)

Producer: Stuart Legg, Basic Films, for Petroleum Films Bureau; *Director:*

J. B. Napier-Bell; *Photography:* Larry Pizer, Victor Proctor, Walter Lassally; *Editor:* Derek York; *Music:* Edward Williams.

FOUR HUNDRED MILLION, THE (1939, USA, 56 min., MOMA*)
Producers: Joris Ivens, John Ferno, for History Today, Inc.; *Director:* Joris Ivens; *Commentary:* Dudley Nichols; *Photography:* Ivens, Ferno; *Editor:* Helen Van Dongen; *Narrator:* Frederic March; *Music:* Hanns Eisler.

GAMLA STAN (1931, Sweden, 19 min., MOMA)
Producer: Svensk Filmindustri; *Directors:* Stig Almqvist, Erik Asklund, Eyvind Johnson, Arthur Lundqvist; *Photography:* Elner Akeson; *Music:* Eric Bengston.

GIMME SHELTER (1970, USA, 90 min., color, C)
Producers, Directors: Albert Maysles, David Maysles, Charlotte Zwerin.

GRANTON TRAWLER (1934, GB, 11 min., MOMA)
Producer: John Grierson for E.M.B. Film Unit; *Director:* Edgar H. Anstey; *Photography:* Grierson; *Editor:* Anstey.

GRASS (1925, USA, 64 min., UC)
Producer: Famous Players; *Directors, Script, Photography:* Meriam C. Cooper, Ernest B. Schoedsack; *Editors and Titles:* Terry Ramsaye, Richard P. Carver.

HAPPY MOTHER'S DAY (1963, USA, 30 min., L-P)
Producer: Leacock-Pennebaker, Inc., for Curtis Publications; "A Film by Richard Leacock and Joyce Chopra"; *Narrator:* Ed McCurdy.

HARVEST SHALL COME, THE (1942, GB, 35 min., BFI)
Producer: Basil Wright, Realist Film Unit, for Imperial Chemical Industries, Ltd.; *Director, Editor:* Max Anderson; *Script:* H. W. Freeman; *Photography:* A. E. Jeakins; *Music:* William Alwyn; *Narration:* Edmund Willard, Bruce Belfrage.

HIGH SCHOOL (1968, USA, 75 min., ZIP)
Producer, Director, Editor: Frederick Wiseman; *Photography:* Richard Leiterman.

HIROSHIMA-NAGASAKI: AUGUST, 1945 (1970, USA, 16 min., MOMA)
Producer: Erik Barnouw for Columbia University Press; *Script, Editor:* Paul Ronder; *Narrators:* Paul Ronder, Kazuko Oshima.

HISTOIRE DU SOLDAT INCONNU, L' (1931, Belgium, 15 min., MOMA)
Director: Henri Storck.

HOSPITAL (1969, USA, 60 min., ZIP)
Producer, Director, Editor: Frederick Wiseman; *Photography:* William Brayne.

HOUSING PROBLEMS (1935, GB, 15 min., MOMA)
Producer: Realist Film Unit for British Commonwealth Gas; *Directors:* Arthur Elton, Edgar Anstey; *Photography:* John Taylor.

INDUSTRIAL BRITAIN (1933, GB, 22 min., MOMA)
Producers: John Grierson, Robert Flaherty, for E.M.B. Film Unit; *Director:* Robert Flaherty; *Photography:* Flaherty; *Editor:* Grierson.

ISLANDERS, THE (1939, GB, 17 min., MOMA)
Producer: J. B. Holmes, G.P.O. Film Unit; *Director:* M. Harvey; *Photography:* H. Rignold, J. Jones; *Commentary:* Jack Livesey; *Music:* Darius Milhaud.

JANE (1962, USA, 54 min., TL)
Producer: Time-Life, Inc.; *Filmakers:* D. A. Pennebaker, Richard Leacock, Abbot Mills, Al Wirthimer.

KNOW YOUR ALLY, BRITAIN (1944, USA, 43 min., MOMA)
Producer: U.S. War Department and Signal Corps; *Music:* Army Air Force Orchestra.

LAND, THE (1941, USA, 42 min., MOMA)
Producer: Agricultural Adjustment Agency, U.S. Department of Agriculture; *Director:* Robert Flaherty; *Commentary:* Russell Lord; *Photography:* Irving Lerner, Douglas Baker, Floyd Crosby, Charles Herbert; *Editor:* Helen Van Dongen; *Narrator:* Flaherty; *Music:* Richard Arnell.

LAND OF PROMISE (1945, USA, 68 min., BFI)
Producer, Director: Paul Rotha; *Script:* Ara Calder-Marshall, Miles Tomalin, Miles Malleson, Wolfgang Wilhelm; *Photography:* Harold Young, Peter Hennessy, Reg Wyer, Cyril Arapoff.

LAND WITHOUT BREAD [LAS HURDES] (1932, Spain, 28 min., MOMA)
Producer, Director: Luis Buñuel, *Photography:* Eli Lotar, Pierre Unik, Sanchez Ventura.

LAW AND ORDER (1969, USA, 81 min., ZIP)
Producer, Director, Editor: Frederick Wiseman; *Photography:* William Brayne.

LET THERE BE LIGHT (1946, USA, 59 min.)
Producer: U.S. War Department; *Director, Narrator:* John Huston; *Photography:* Stanley Cortez.

LINE TO THE TSCHIERVA HUT (1937, GB, 10 min., MOMA)
Producers: John Grierson, Harry Watt, G.P.O. Film Unit with Pro Telephon-Zürich; *Director:* Alberto Cavalcanti; *Music:* Benjamin Britten.

LISTEN TO BRITAIN (1942, GB, 21 min., MOMA)
Producer: Ian Dalrymple, Crown Film Unit; *Directors:* Humphrey Jennings, Stewart McAllister; *Photography:* H. E. Fowle.

LONDON CAN TAKE IT (1940, GB, 30 min., BFI)
Producer: Crown Film Unit; *Directors:* Harry Watt, Humphrey Jennings; *Photography:* Jonah Jones, H. E. Fowle; *Narration:* Quentin Reynolds.

LONDONERS, THE (1938, GB, 37 min., MOMA)
Producer: John Grierson, Realist Film Unit; *Director, Editor, Script:* John Taylor; *Verse:* W. H. Auden; *Photography:* A. E. Jeakins.

LOUISIANA STORY (1948, USA, 80 min., MOMA)
Producer: Robert Flaherty for Standard Oil Co., New Jersey; *Director:* Robert Flaherty; *Script:* Robert and Frances Hubbard Flaherty; *Photog-

raphy: Richard Leacock; *Editor:* Helen Van Dongen; *Music:* Virgil Thomson.

MAISONS DE LA MISÈRE, LES (1936, Belgium, 20 min., MOMA*)
Producer: Cinéma Édition for La Société Nationale d'Habitation à Bon Marché; *Director:* Henri Storck; *Photography:* Eli Lotar, John Ferno; *Music:* Maurice Jaubert.

MAN OF ARAN (1934, GB, 76 min., CF)
Producer: Gainsborough Pictures, Ltd., for Gaumont-British Corporation, Ltd.; *Director, Script:* Robert Flaherty in association with Frances Hubbard Flaherty; *Photography:* Robert Flaherty, David Flaherty, John Taylor; *Editor:* John Goldman; *Music:* John Greenwood.

MAN WITH THE MOVIE CAMERA, THE (1929, USSR, 67 min., silent, A-B)
Producer: Vufku, Ukraine; *Director, Script, Editor:* Dziga Vertov; *Photography:* Mikhail Kaufman; *Assistant Editor:* Yelizaveta Svilova.

MARRIED COUPLE, A (1969, Canada, 112 min., color, AKA)
Producer: Allan King Associates for Aquarius Films, Ltd.; *Director:* Allan King; *Photography:* Richard Leiterman; *Sound:* Christian Wangler; *Editor:* Arla Saare; *Music:* Zal Yanofsky.

MEN OF THE LIGHTSHIP (1940, GB, 18 min., MOMA)
Producer: Alberto Cavalcanti, Crown Film Unit; *Director:* David MacDonald; *Script:* Hugh Gray, dialogue by David Evans; *Photography:* Jonah Jones; *Editor:* A. McAllister; *Music:* Richard Addinsell; *Art Direction:* Edward Carrick; *Foreword:* Robert E. Sherwood.

MOANA (1926, USA, 85 min., MOMA)
Producer: Robert Flaherty for Famous Players; *Director:* Robert Flaherty in association with Frances Hubbard Flaherty; *Script:* Flaherty; *Photography:* Flaherty, Bob Roberts; *Editor, Titler:* Julian Johnson.

MONTEREY POP (1968, USA, 82 min., color, LP)
Producer: Leacock-Pennebaker, Inc., for ABC; *Director:* D. A. Pennebaker; *Photography:* Richard Leacock, D. A. Pennebaker, Al Maysles, Roger Murphey, Jim Desmond, Barry Finstein; *Editors:* Pennebaker, Nina Shulman; *Sound:* Wally Heider.

NANOOK OF THE NORTH (1922, USA, 60 min., silent, MOMA)
Producer: Revillon Frères; *Director, Script, Photography, Editor:* Robert Flaherty.

NATIVE LAND (1942, USA, 90 min., MOMA*)
Producer: Frontier Films; *Directors:* Paul Strand, Leo Hurwitz; *Script:* David Wolff, Leo Hurwitz; *Commentary:* David Wolff; *Photography:* Paul Strand; *Editor:* Leo Hurwitz; *Narrator:* Paul Robeson; *Music:* Marc Blitzstein.

NAZIS STRIKE, THE (1943, USA, 42 min., MOMA)
Producer: Frank Capra for the "Why We Fight" series; *Directors:* Capra, Anatole Litvak; *Script:* Eric Knight, Anthony Veiller.

NEGRO SOLDIER, THE (1944, USA, 41 min., MOMA)
Producer: U.S. War Department, Special Services Division.

NEW EARTH (1934, Holland, 30 min., MOMA)
   Producer: Capi, Holland; *Director:* Joris Ivens; *Photography:* Ivens, Joop Huisken; *Editor:* Helen Van Dongen; *Music:* Hanns Eisler.

NEW TOWNS FOR OLD (1942, GB, 8 min., BFI)
   Producer: Strand Films for Ministry of Information; *Director:* John Eldridge; *Script:* Dylan Thomas.

NEW WORLDS FOR OLD (1938, GB, 30 min., MOMA)
   Producer: Paul Rotha, Realist Film Unit, for British Commercial Gas Ass'n; *Director:* Paul Rotha; *Script:* Alistair Cooke; *Photography:* Harry Rignold, S. Onions, A. E. Jeakins; *Music:* William Alwyn.

NIGHT MAIL (1936, GB, 24 min., MOMA)
   Producers: Basil Wright, Harry Watt for G.P.O. Film Unit; *Directors, Script:* Basil Wright, Harry Watt; *Verse:* W. H. Auden; *Photography:* H. E. Fowle, Jonah Jones; *Editor:* R. Q. McNaughton; *Music:* Benjamin Britten; *Sound:* Alberto Cavalcanti.

NINETY DEGREES SOUTH (1912–1933, GB, 75 min., MOMA)
   Producer, Director, Photography, Narrator: Herbert G. Ponting; *Music:* Walter Davies.

NORTH SEA (1938, GB, 22 min., MOMA)
   Producer: Alberto Cavalcanti; *Director:* Harry Watt; *Photography:* H. Fowle, Jonah Jones; *Editor:* R. Q. McNaughton; *Music:* Ernst Meyer.

NORTHWEST U.S.A. (1945, USA, 20 min., MOMA)
   Producer: OWI; *Director:* Willard Van Dyke; *Commentary:* Ben Maddow; *Script:* Van Dyke, Philip Dunne, Sidney Meyers; *Photography:* Larry Madison, Benjamin Doniger; *Editor:* Sidney Meyers; *Narrator:* Walter Huston; *Music:* Norman Lloyd.

OLYMPIA (1938, Germany; Pt. I, 100 min., Pt. II, 105 min., MOMA)
   Director, Editor: Leni Riefenstahl; *Photography:* Hans Ertl, Walter Frentz, Guzzi Lantschner, Kurt Neubert, Hans Scheib, Willy Zielke; *Music:* Herbert Windt.

ON THE BOWERY (1956, USA, 65 min., GP)
   Producer, Director: Lionel Rogosin; *Editor:* Carl Lerner; *Music:* Charles Mills; *Photography:* Richard Bagley; *Script:* Mark Sufrin.

OUR COUNTRY (1944, GB, 45 min., BFI)
   Producer: Alexander Shaw for Ministry of Information; *Director:* John Eldridge; *Script:* Dylan Thomas; *Narrator of Introduction:* Burgess Meredith.

PALE HORSEMAN, THE (1945, USA, 22 min., MOMA)
   Producer: USIS; *Director, Script:* Irving Jacoby; *Editor:* Peter Elgar; *Music:* Henry Brant.

PEACE OF BRITAIN (1936, GB, 4 min., MOMA)
   Producer: Strand Films; *Director:* Paul Rotha.

PLOW THAT BROKE THE PLAINS, THE (1936, USA, 21 min., MOMA)
   Producer: Resettlement Administration, U.S. Government; *Director, Script:*

Pare Lorentz; *Photography:* Ralph Steiner, Paul Strand, Leo Hurwitz; *Editor:* Leo Zochling; *Music:* Virgil Thomson.

POWER AMONG MEN (1958, GB, 90 min., color & b/w, FB)
  Producer: UNESCO; *Director:* Thorold Dickinson; *Narrator:* Laurence Harvey.

POWER AND THE LAND (1940, USA, 35 min., MOMA)
  Producer: U.S. Film Service for U.S. Rural Electrification Administration and Department of Agriculture; *Director:* Joris Ivens; *Script:* Edwin Locke; *Commentary:* Stephen Vincent Benét; *Photography:* Floyd Crosby, Arthur Ornitz; *Editor:* Helen Van Dongen; *Narrator:* William D. Adams; *Music:* Douglas Moore.

PRELUDE TO WAR (1943, USA, 53 min., MOMA)
  Producer: Frank Capra for "Why We Fight" series; *Director:* Frank Capra; *Script:* Eric Knight, Anthony Veiller; *Editor:* William Hornbeck; *Narrator:* Walter Huston; *Music:* Dmitri Tiomkin.

PRIMARY (1960, USA, 60 min., TL)
  Filmakers: Richard Leacock, D. A. Pennebaker, Al Maysles, Robert Drew, Terry Filgate.

QUEEN IS CROWNED, A (1953, GB, 90 min., color, WRS)
  Producer: J. A. Rank Organization; *Director:* Castleton Knight; *Commentary:* Christopher Fry; *Narrator:* Laurence Olivier.

QUIET ONE, THE (1949, USA, 65 min., A-B)
  Producer: Janice Loeb for Film Documents, Inc.; *Direction, Script, Editing:* Sidney Meyers, Janice Loeb, Helen Levitt; *Commentary and Dialogue:* James Agee; *Photography:* Richard Bagley, Helen Levitt; *Narrator:* Gary Merrill; *Music:* Ulysses Kay.

RAMPARTS WE WATCH, THE (1940, USA, 100 min., MOMA)
  Producer: Louis de Rochemont for "March of Time"; *Director:* Louis de Rochemont; *Script:* Robert L. Richards, Cedric R. Worth; *Editor:* Lothar Wolff, *Photography:* Charles E. Gilson, John A. Geisel; *Music:* Louis de Francesco, Jacques Dallin, Peter Brunelli.

REPORT FROM THE ALEUTIANS (1943, USA, 45 min., color, MOMA)
  Producer: U.S. Army Signal Corps; *Director, Narrator:* John Huston.

RETOUR, LE (1946, USA, 34 min., MOMA)
  Producer: USIS; *Director:* Henri Cartier-Bresson; *Commentary:* Claude Roy; *Photography:* Cartier-Bresson, Andre Bac, and the cameramen of the U.S. Signal Corps and Air Force; *Editors:* Cartier-Bresson, Richard Banks; *Music:* Robert Lannoy.

RIEN QUE LES HEURES (1926, France, 45 min., silent, MOMA)
  Producer: Néofilm; *Director:* Alberto Cavalcanti; *Photography:* Jimmy Rogers; *Art Direction:* M. Mirovitch.

RING OF STEEL (1942, USA, 9 min., MOMA)
  Producer: Philip Martin, Jr., for Office of Emergency Management Film

Unit; *Director:* Garson Kanin; *Photography:* Carl Pryer, Ray Foster, Louis Tumola; *Narrator:* Spencer Tracy; *Music:* Morton Gould.

RIVER, THE (1937, USA, 32 min., MOMA)

Producer: Farm Security Administration, U.S. Government; *Director, Script:* Pare Lorentz; *Photography:* Floyd Crosby, Stacy Woodward, Willard Van Dyke; *Music:* Virgil Thomson.

SALESMAN (1969, USA, 90 min., NTS)

"A Film by Albert Maysles, David Maysles, Charlotte Zwerin."

SAN FRANCISCO—1945 (1945, USA, 17 min., MOMA)

Producer: Willard Van Dyke for U.S. Information Office; *Director:* Van Dyke; *Script:* Waldo Salt; *Photography:* Lawrence Madison, Benjamin Doniger; *Editor:* Sidney Meyers; *Music:* Morton Gould.

SAVING OF BILL BLEWITT, THE (1936, GB, 23 min., BFI)

Producer: John Grierson; *Director, Script:* Harry Watt; *Photography:* S. Onions, Jonah Jones; *Music:* Benjamin Britten.

SHOWMAN (1963, USA, 53 min., MB)

"A film by The Maysles Brothers"; *Narration:* Norman Rosten.

SILENT VILLAGE, THE (1943, GB, 33 min., MOMA)

Producer: Crown Film Unit for Ministry of Information; *Director:* Humphrey Jennings; *Photography:* H. E. Fowle; *Editor:* Stewart McAllister.

SMOKE MENACE, THE (1937, GB, 15 min., MOMA)

Producer: John Grierson, Realist Film Unit, for Gas Industry of Great Britain; *Director:* John Taylor; *Photography:* A. E. Jeakins; *Narrator:* Peter Hine.

SONG OF CEYLON, THE (1934, GB, 40 min., MOMA)

Producer: John Grierson for Ceylon Tea Propaganda Bureau; *Director, Script, Photography:* Basil Wright, assisted by John Taylor; *Narrator:* Lionel Wendt; *Music:* Walter Leigh.

SPANISH EARTH, THE (1937, USA, 53 min., A-B)

Producer: Contemporary Historians, Inc.; *Director:* Joris Ivens; *Commentary:* Ernest Hemingway; *Photography:* John Ferno; *Editor:* Helen Van Dongen; *Music:* Marc Blitzstein, arranged by Virgil Thomson.

SPARE TIME (1939, GB, 16 min., MOMA)

Producer: Alberto Cavalcanti; *Director:* Humphrey Jennings; *Commentary:* Laurie Lee; *Photography:* H. Fowle.

SPRING OFFENSIVE (1940, GB, 20 min., MOMA)

Producer: Alberto Cavalcanti; *Director:* Humphrey Jennings; *Script:* Hugh Gray; *Commentary:* A. G. Street; *Photography:* Eric Gross, H. Fowle, *Editor:* Geoff Foot.

SQUADRON 992 (1939, GB, 24 min., MOMA)

Producer: Alberto Cavalcanti for G.P.O. Film Unit; *Director:* Harry Watt; *Photography:* Jonah Jones; *Music:* Walter Leigh.

STRAVINSKY PORTRAIT, A (1964, USA, 53 min., LP)
Producer: Rolf Liebermann for Norddeutscher Rundfunk; *A film by* Richard Leacock and Rolf Liebermann"; *Photography, Editor:* Leacock.

TARGET FOR TONIGHT (1941, GB, 60 min., CF)
Producer: Ian Dalrymple, Crown Film Unit; *Director, Script:* Harry Watt; *Photography:* Jonah Jones; Edward Catford; *Design:* Edward Carrick; *Editor:* Stewart McAllister; *Music:* Leighton Lucas.

TEN DAYS THAT SHOOK THE WORLD [OCTOBER] (1928, USSR, 161 min., silent, MOMA)
Producer: Sovkino; *Directors, Script, Editors:* S. M. Eisenstein, G. V. Alexandrov; *Photography:* Eduard Tissé.

THEY ALSO SERVE (1940, GB, 8 min., MOMA)
Producer: Realist Film Unit for Ministry of Information; *Director:* R. I. Grierson; *Photography:* A. E. Jeakins.

THURSDAY'S CHILDREN (1953, GB, 20 min., CF)
Producer: World Wide Pictures; *Directors, Script:* Guy Brenton, Lindsay Anderson; *Photography:* Walter Lassally; *Narrator:* Richard Burton; *Music:* Geoffrey Wright.

TITICUT FOLLIES, THE (1967, USA, 87 min., ZIP)
Producer, Director, Editor: Frederick Wiseman.

TO THE SHORES OF IWO JIMA (1945, USA, 20 min., color, MOMA)
Producer: OWI, Warner Brothers; photographed in combat areas by cameramen of the U.S. Navy, Marine Corps, and Coast Guard; *Narrator:* Harry Jackson.

TOBY AND THE TALL CORN (1954, USA, 20 min.)
Producer: Ford Foundation TV-Radio Workshop for *Omnibus; Director, Photography:* Richard Leacock; *Writer, Narrator:* Russell Lynes.

TODAY WE LIVE (1937, GB, 25 min., MOMA)
Producer: Paul Rotha, Strand Film Co., Ltd., for National Council of Social Service, London; *Directors:* Ruby Grierson, Ralph Bond; *Script:* Stuart Legg; *Photography:* S. Onions, Paul Burnford; *Narrator:* Howard Marshall.

TOSCANINI: THE HYMN OF NATIONS (1944, USA, 31 min., MOMA)
Producer: Irving Lerner for OWI; *Director:* Alexander Hammid; *Script:* May Sarton; *Photography:* Peter Glushanok, Boris Kaufman; *Editor:* Irving Lerner; *Narrator:* Burgess Meredith.

TOWN, THE (1944, USA, 12 min., MOMA)
Producer: Joseph Krumgold for OWI; *Director:* Josef von Sternberg; *Script:* George Milburn; *Photography:* Larry Madison; *Editor:* Alan Antik; *Narrator:* Myron McCormick.

TRANSFER OF POWER [LEVER-AGE] (1939, GB, 22 min., MOMA)
Producer: Stuart Legg for Shell Film Unit; *Director, Script, Editor:* Geoffrey Bell; *Photography:* Sidney Beadle.

TRANSPORT (1950, GB, 20 min., BFI)
Producer: Peter Baylis, Film Centre, for "Wealth of the World" series; *Director:* Peter Bradford.

TRIUMPH OF THE WILL, THE (1936, Germany, 120 min., MOMA)
Producer: NSDAP; *Director:* Leni Riefenstahl; *Photography:* Sepp Allgeier, Karl Attenberger, Werner Bohne; *Editor:* Riefenstahl; *Music:* Herbert Windt.

TRUE GLORY, THE (1945, USA–GB, 85 min., MOMA)
Producer: OWI, USA, and Ministry of Information, GB; *Directors, Editors:* Carol Reed and Garson Kanin; *Photography:* combat cameramen of Allied armies.

TURKSIB (1928, USSR, 90 min., A-B)
Producer: Vostok Film; *Director, Script:* Victor Turin, with scenic assistance by Alexander Macheret and Victor Shklovsky; *Photography:* Yevgeni Slavinski, Boris Frantzisson; *English Version Editor and Titler:* John Grierson.

VALLEY OF THE TENNESSEE (1944, USA, 30 min., MOMA)
Producer: OWI; *Director:* Alexander Hammid; *Script:* May Sarton; *Photography:* Peter Glushanok; *Narrator:* Frederic March; *Music:* Norman Lloyd.

VALLEY TOWN (1940, USA, 25 min., MOMA)
Producer: Documentary Film Productions, Inc., for Educational Film Institute of New York University; *Director:* Willard Van Dyke; *Script:* Spencer Pollard, Van Dyke; *Photography:* Roger Barlow, Bob Churchill; *Editor:* Irving Lerner; *Music:* Marc Blitzstein.

VOCATION (1936, France, 30 min., MOMA)
Producer: Bertrand Glauzel; *Director:* Jean-Yves de la Cour; *Photography:* Jean Bachelet, George Clerc; *Editing:* de la Cour, S. Damm.

WAR COMES TO AMERICA (1945, USA, 70 min., MOMA)
Producer: Frank Capra for the "Why We Fight" Series; *Director:* Anatole Litvak; *Script:* Anthony Veiller.

WARRENDALE (1966, Canada, 100 min., GP)
Producer: Allan King Associates for the Canadian Broadcasting Corporation; *Director:* Allan King; *Photography:* William Brayne; *Editor:* Peter Moseley; *Sound:* Russel Heise, Michael Billings.

WATERS OF TIME (1951, GB, 38 min., BFI)
Producer: Basil Wright, International Realist, Ltd., for the Port of London Authority; *Directors, Script, Editors:* Basil Wright, Bill Launder; *Photography:* Reg Hughes, Cyril Moorhead; *Music:* Alan Rawsthorne.

WAVERLY STEPS (1949, GB, 30 min., BFI)
Producer: John Fletcher; *Director:* John Eldridge.

WE CONQUER THE SOIL [WIR EROBERN LAND] (1936, Germany, 15 min., MOMA)
Producer: UFA Kulturfilm; *Director, Script:* Dr. Martin Rikli; *Photography:* Kurt Stanke; *Music:* Hans Ebert.

WE LIVE IN TWO WORLDS (1937, GB, 14 min., BFI)
Producer: John Grierson, G.P.O. Film Unit; *Director:* Alberto Cavalcanti; *Photography:* John Taylor; *Editor:* R. Q. McNaughton; *Narration:* J. B. Priestley; *Music:* Maurice Jaubert.

WEATHER FORECAST (1934, GB, 18 min., BFI)
Producer: John Grierson, G.P.O. Film Unit; *Director, Script:* Evelyn Spice; *Photography:* George Noble; *Sound:* Alberto Cavalcanti.

WESTERN APPROACHES (1944, GB, 85 min., color, BFI)
Producer: Ian Dalrymple, Crown Film Unit; *Director:* Pat Jackson; *Script:* Pat Jackson, Gerry Bryant; *Photography:* Jack Cardiff; *Design:* Edward Carrick; *Music:* Clifton Parker.

WHAT'S HAPPENING! THE BEATLES IN THE U.S.A. (1964, USA, 52 min., MB)
"A film by The Maysles Brothers."

WHEN WE BUILD AGAIN (1945, GB, 30 min., MOMA)
Producer: Donald Taylor, Strand Films, for Cadbury Bros., Ltd.; *Director:* Ralph Bond; *Script:* Reg Groves; *Commentary:* Dylan Thomas; *Photography:* Charles Marleborough; *Narrators:* Dylan Thomas, James McKechnie; *Music:* V. Hely Hutchinson.

WITH LOVE FROM TRUMAN: A VISIT WITH TRUMAN CAPOTE (1966, USA, 29 min., MB)
"A Film By Albert Maysles, David Maysles, Charlotte Zwerin."

WOODSTOCK (1970, USA, 183 min., color, WB)
Producer: Bob Maurice; *Director:* Michael Wadleigh; *Photography:* Wadleigh, David Myers, Richard Pearce, Donald Lenzer, Al Wertheimer; *Editors:* Martin Scorsese, Stan Warnow, Jere Huggins, Yeu-Bun Yee; *Sound and Music Editor:* Larry Johnson.

WORLD IS RICH, THE (1947, GB, 47 min., BFI)
Producer: Paul Rotha, Films of Fact, for Central Office of Information; *Director, Editor:* Paul Rotha; *Script:* Arthur Calder-Marshall; *Photography:* James Ritchie; *Music:* Clifton Parker.

WORLD OF PLENTY (1943, GB, 45 min., MOMA)
Producer: Paul Rotha for Ministry of Information; *Director, Editor:* Paul Rotha; *Script:* Eric Knight, Paul Rotha; *Photography:* Peter Hennessy, Wolfgang Suschitzky; *Narration:* Eric Knight, E. V. H. Emmett, Robert St. John, Thomas Chalmers, Henry Hallatt; *Music:* William Alwyn.

WORLD WITHOUT END (1953, GB, 60 min., MOMA)
Producer: Basil Wright for UNESCO; *Directors:* Basil Wright, Paul Rotha; *Script:* Rex Warner; *Photography:* José Carlos Carbajal (Mexico) and Adrian Jeakins (Thailand) ; *Narrator:* Michael Gaugh.

APPENDIX B: MAJOR NONFICTION AND DOCUMENTARY AWARDS

The information in the following listings comes from several sources, including the award-giving organizations themselves. Often there are discrepancies between the year of production, the year of release, and the year of award. When known, the director's name is given; otherwise, the producer's name is indicated. When both a foreign title and a translated title are used, they are both given, if known; otherwise, the most familiar title to U.S. viewers is indicated. More complete listings for the sporadic nonfiction awards of the major international festivals (Venice, Berlin, Cannes) as well as other listings of major awards are provided in P. J. McInerney and J. L. Anderson's "Prize Winners: Selected Listings of Awards Given at Three Major Film Festivals and by Five American Motion Picture Organizations," *The Journal of the University Film Association*, 22, No. 3 (1970).

National Board of Review of Motion Pictures

When a nonfiction film was listed as one of the "Ten Best" films chosen by this organization, it is included here.

1930
  Earth (Alexander Dovzhenko, USSR)
  Storm over Asia (V. I. Pudovkin, USSR)
1934
  Man of Aran (Robert Flaherty, GB)
1936
  New Earth (Joris Ivens, Netherlands)
1937
  The Spanish Earth (Joris Ivens, USA)
1939
  Crisis (Herbert Kline, Hans Burger, Alexander Hammid, France)
1940
  The Fight for Life (Pare Lorentz, USA)
1941
  Target for Tonight (Harry Watt, GB)

1942
  Moscow Strikes Back (Slavko Vorkapich, USSR)
1943
  Desert Victory (David MacDonald, GB)
  The Battle of Russia; Prelude to War (both "Why We Fight" films, Frank
    Capra, USA)
  Saludos Amigos (Walt Disney, USA)
  The Silent Village (Humphrey Jennings, GB)
1944
  The Memphis Belle (William Wyler, USA)
  Attack! [The Battle for New Britain] (U.S. Army, USA)
  With the Marines at Tarawa (U.S. Navy, USA)
  Battle for the Marianas (U.S. Marine Corps, USA)
  Tunisian Victory (Frank Capra-Hugh Steward, USA–GB)
1945
  The True Glory (Carol Reed-Garson Kanin, USA-GB)
  The Fighting Lady (Edward Steichen, USA)
1948
  Louisiana Story (Robert Flaherty, USA)
1950
  The Titan (Curt Oertel, Switzerland)
1951
  Kon-Tiki (Thor Heyerdahl, Norway)
1953
  Conquest of Everest (Thomas Stobart and George W. Lowe, GB)
1954
  The Vanishing Prairie (Walt Disney, USA)
1955
  The Great Adventure (Arne Sucksdorff, Sweden)
1956
  The Silent World (Jacques-Yves Cousteau and Louis Malle, France)
1964
  World Without Sun (Jacques-Yves Cousteau, France)
1966
  John F. Kennedy: Years of Lightning, Day of Drums (Bruce Herschensohn,
    USA)
[Since 1966—no nonfiction awards]

Academy of Motion Picture Arts and Sciences Awards for Best Documentary Film

1941
  Churchill's Island (Canadian Film Board)

1942
   Battle of Midway (John Ford, U.S. Navy, USA)
1943
   December 7th (U.S. Navy, USA)
   Desert Victory (David MacDonald, GB)
1944
   With the Marines at Tarawa (U.S. Marines, USA)
   The Fighting Lady (U.S. Navy, USA)
1945
   Hitler Lives? (Warner Bros., USA)
   The True Glory (Carol Reed-Garson Kanin, USA-GB)
1946
   Seeds of Destiny (U.S. War Department, USA)
1947
   First Steps (United Nations)
   Design for Death (Theron Warth and Richard O. Fleischer, USA)
1948
   Toward Independence (U.S. Army, USA)
   The Secret Land (O. O. Dull, USA)
1949
   A Chance to Live (Richard de Rochemont, "March of Time," USA)
   So Much for So Little (Edward Selzer, USA)
   Daybreak in Udi (Terry Bishop, GB)
1950
   Why Korea? (Edmund Reek, USA)
   The Titan: Story of Michelangelo (Curt Oertel, Switzerland)
1951
   Benjy (Fred Zinnemann, USA)
   Kon-Tiki (Thor Heyerdahl, Norway)
1952
   Neighbours (Norman McLaren, Canada)
   The Sea Around Us (Irwin Allen, USA)
1953
   The Alaskan Eskimo (Walt Disney, USA)
   The Living Desert (Walt Disney, USA)
1954
   Thursday's Children (Lindsay Anderson and Guy Brenton, GB)
   The Vanishing Prairie (Walt Disney, USA)
1955
   Men Against the Arctic (Walt Disney, USA)
   Helen Keller in Her Story (Nancy Hamilton, USA)
1956
   The True Story of the Civil War (Louis Clyde Stoumen, USA)
   The Silent World (Jacques-Yves Cousteau and Louis Malle, France)

1957
   Albert Schweitzer (Jerome Hill, USA)
1958
   Ama Girls (Walt Disney, USA)
   White Wilderness (Ben Sharpsteen and Walt Disney, USA)
1959
   Glass (Bert Haanstra, Netherlands)
   Serengeti Shall Not Die (Bernhard Grzimek, Germany)
1960
   Giuseppina (James Hill, GB)
   The Horse with the Flying Tail (Larry Lansburgh, USA)
1961
   Project Hope (Frank P. Bibas, USA)
   The Sky Above—The Mud Below (Pierre-Dominique Gasseau, France)
1962
   Dylan Thomas (Jack Howells, GB)
   The Black Fox (Louis Clyde Stoumen, USA)
1963
   Chagall (Simon Schiffrin, USA)
   Robert Frost: A Lover's Quarrel with the World (Robert Hughes, USA)
1964
   Nine from Little Rock (Charles Guggenheim, USA)
   World Without Sun (Jacques-Yves Cousteau, France)
1965
   To Be Alive! (Francis Thompson, USA)
   The Eleanor Roosevelt Story (Richard Kaplan, USA)
1966
   A Year Toward Tomorrow (Edmond A. Levy, USA)
   The War Game (Peter Watkins, GB)
1967
   The Redwoods (Mark Harris and Trevor Greenwood, USA)
   The Anderson Platoon (Pierre Schoendorffer, France)
1968
   Why Man Creates (Saul Bass, USA)
   Journey into Self (Bill McGaw, USA)
1969
   Czechoslovakia 1968 (Denis Sanders and Robert M. Fresco, USA)
   Artur Rubinstein—The Love of Life (Bernard Chevry, USA)
1970
   Woodstock (Michael Wadleigh, USA)
   Interviews with My Lai Veterans (Joseph Strick, USA)

BIBLIOGRAPHY

Agee, James. *Agee on Film*. Boston: Beacon Press, 1958.
——. "Seeing Terrible Records of War." *The Nation*, 160 (March 24, 1945), 342.
Allan King. An Interview with Bruce Martin, ed. Alison Reid. Ottawa: Canadian Film Institute, 1970.
Anderson, Lindsay. "Angles of Approach." *Sequence*, 2 (Winter 1947), 5–8.
——. "Only Connect: Some Aspects of the Work of Humphrey Jennings." *Sight and Sound*, 23, No. 4 (April–June 1954), 181–86.
Bazelon, Donald T. "Backgrounds to *Point of Order!*" *Film Comment*, 2, No. 1 (Winter 1964), 33–35.
Benjamin, Burton. "The Documentary Heritage." *Television Quarterly*, 1, No. 1 (February 1962), 29–34.
Berg, Beatrice. "I Was Fed Up with Hollywood Fantasies." *New York Times* (February 1, 1970), 25–26.
Berger, John, "Clouzot as Delilah." *Sight and Sound*, 27, No. 4 (Spring 1958), 196–97.
Blue, James. "Direct Cinema." *Film Comment*, 4, Nos. 2–3 (Fall–Winter 1967), 80–81.
——. "One Man's Truth: Interview with Richard Leacock." *Film Comment*, 3, No. 2 (Spring 1965), 15–22.
Bluem, A. William. *Documentary in American Television*. New York: Hastings House, 1965.
Calder-Marshall, Arthur. *The Innocent Eye: The Life of Robert Flaherty*. London: W. H. Allen, 1963.
Callenbach, E. "Going Out to the Subject." *Film Quarterly*, 14, No. 3 (Spring 1961), 38–40.
Capra, Frank. *The Name Above the Title*. New York: The Macmillan Company, 1971.

Cavalcanti, Alberto. "Advice to Young Film Makers." *Film Quarterly*, 9 (Summer 1955) , 354–55.

Corliss, Richard. "Leni Riefenstahl: A Bibliography." *Film Heritage*, 5, No. 1 (Fall 1969) , 27–36.

Dawson, Jan. *"Warrendale." Sight and Sound*, 37, No. 1 (Winter 1967–68) , 44–46.

De Antonio, Emile. "The Point of View in *Point of Order!" Film Comment*, 2, No. 1 (Winter 1964) , 35–36.

Delahaye, Michel. "Leni Riefenstahl," in *Interviews with Film Directors*, ed. Andrew Sarris. Indianapolis, Indiana: The Bobbs-Merrill Company, Inc. 1967.

Devine, J. "British Wartime Shorts." *Public Opinion Quarterly*, 5 (June 1941) , 306–07.

Dunne, Philip. "The Documentary and Hollywood." *Hollywood Quarterly*, 1, No. 2 (January 1946) , 166–72.

Eisenstein, Sergei. *Film Essays and a Lecture*, ed. Jay Leyda. New York: Praeger Publishers, 1970.

Elson, Robert T. *Time Inc.: The Intimate History of a Publishing Enterprise, 1923–1941*. New York: Atheneum, 1968.

Engle, Harrison. "Thirty Years of Social Inquiry: An Interview with Willard Van Dyke." *Film Comment*, 3, No. 2 (Spring 1965) , 24–37.

The Factual Film (An Arts Enquiry Report) . London: Oxford University Press, 1947.

Gallez, D. W. "Patterns in Wartime Documentaries." *Film Quarterly*, 10 (Winter 1955) , 125–35.

Goodman, Ezra. "Fact Films to the Front." *American Cinematographer*, 25, No. 2 (February 1945) , 46–47ff.

Graham, John. " 'There Are No Simple Solutions': Frederick Wiseman on Viewing Film." *The Film Journal* (Spring 1947) , 44–47.

Gray, Hugh. "Robert Flaherty and the Naturalistic Documentary." *Hollywood Quarterly*, 5 (1950–51,) , 41–48.

Greenberg, Alex, and Wald, Malvin. "Report to the Stockholders." *Hollywood Quarterly*, 1, No. 4 (July 1946) , 410–15.

Grenier, Cynthia. "Joris Ivens: Social Realist and Lyric Poet." *Sight and Sound*, 27, No. 4 (Spring 1958) , 204–07.

Grierson, John. "E.M.B. Film Unit." *Cinema Quarterly*, 1, No. 4 (Summer 1933) , 203–08.

———. *Grierson on Documentary*, ed. Forsyth Hardy. New York: Harcourt, Brace and Company, 1947.

———. *Grierson on Documentary*, ed. Forsyth Hardy. London: Faber and Faber, Ltd., 1966.

———. "Production Unit Planned: Mass Media to Be Used for Peace." *UNESCO Courier* (February 1948) , 3.

———. "Prospect for Documentary: What Is Wrong and Why." *Sight and Sound*, 17, No. 66 (Summer 1948) , 55–59.

———. "Review of *Moana*." *New York Sun* (February 8, 1926) .

————. "Robert Flaherty." [n.d., n.p., copy in files of Film Study Center, The Museum of Modern Art, New York]

Griffith, Richard. *Films of the World's Fair: 1939.* New York: American Film Center, 1940.

————. "Post-War American Documentaries." *Penguin Film Review,* 8 (1949), 92–102.

————. "The Use of Films by the U.S. Armed Forces," in Paul Rotha, *Documentary Film.* New York: Hastings House, 1952.

Gunston, D. "Leni Riefenstahl." *Film Quarterly,* 14, No. 1 (Fall 1960), 4–19.

Harcourt, Peter. "The Innocent Eye." *Sight and Sound,* 34, No. 1 (Winter 1964–65), 19–23.

Hemingway, Ernest. *The Spanish Earth.* Cleveland, Ohio: The J. B. Savage Company, 1938.

Hill, Derek. "The Short Film Situation." *Sight and Sound,* 31, No. 3 (Summer 1962), 108–12.

Hitchens, Gordon. "An Interview with George Stevens, Jr." *Film Comment,* 1, No. 3 (n.d.), 2.

————. "An Interview with a Legend." *Film Comment,* 3, No. 1 (Winter 1965), 4–10.

Holmes, Winifred. "What's Wrong with Documentary?" *Sight and Sound,* 17, No. 65 (Spring 1948), 44–45.

Huaco, George. *The Sociology of Film Art.* New York: Basic Books, 1965.

Hull, David Stewart. *Film in the Third Reich.* Berkeley, California: University of California Press, 1971.

Ivens, Joris. *The Camera and I.* New York: International Publishers, 1969.

Jacobs, Lewis, ed. *The Documentary Tradition: From Nanook to Woodstock.* New York: Hopkinson and Blake, 1971.

Jersey, William C., Jr. "Some Thoughts on Film Technique." *Film Comment,* 2, No. 1 (Winter 1964), 15–16.

Johnson, W. "Shooting at Wars . . . Three Views." *Film Quarterly,* 21, No. 2 (Winter 1967–68), 27–36.

Joseph, R. "Cinema: Films for Nazi Prisoners." *Arts and Architecture,* 62 (May 1945), 16ff.

————. "Film Program for Germany." *Arts and Architecture,* 62 (July 1945), 16.

————. "Germans See Their Concentration Camps." *Arts and Architecture,* 63 (September 1946), 14.

Junker, Howard. "The National Film Board of Canada: After a Quarter Century." *Film Quarterly,* 28, No. 2 (Winter 1964–65), 22–29.

Klugherz, Daniel. "Documentary: Where's the Wonder?" *Television Quarterly,* 6, No. 3 (Summer 1967), 38.

Knight, Arthur. "Cinéma Vérité and Film Truth." *Saturday Review* (September 9, 1967), 44.

Kolaja, J., and Foster, A. W. "Berlin: The Symphony of a City as a Theme of Visual Rhythm." *Journal of Aesthetics and Art Criticism,* 23, No. 3 (Spring 1965), 353–58.

Kracauer, Siegfried. *From Caligari to Hitler.* Princeton, New Jersey: Princeton University Press, 1947.

Lawson, John Howard. *Film: The Creative Process.* New York: Hill and Wang, 1964.

Lebedev, Nikolai. *History of the Soviet Silent Cinema.* Moscow: Iskusstvo, 1965.

Legg, Stuart. "Shell Film Unit: Twenty One Years." *Sight and Sound,* 23, No. 4 (April–June 1954), 209–11.

Levin, G. Roy. *Documentary Explorations: 15 Interviews with Film-Makers.* New York: Doubleday & Company, 1971.

Leyda, Jay. *Films Beget Films.* New York: Hill and Wang. 1964.

——. *Kino: A History of the Russian and Soviet Film.* London: Allen and Unwin, 1960.

Lightman, Sgt. Herb A. "Shooting Production Under Fire." *American Cinematographer,* 26, No. 9 (September 1945), 296–97ff.

Lorentz, Pare. *The River.* New York: Stackpole Sons, 1938.

——. "Documentary Film and Democratic Government: An Administrative History from Pare Lorentz to John Huston." Unpublished Ph.D. Dissertation, Harvard University, 1951.

MacCann, Richard Dyer. "Documentary Film and Democratic Government: An Administrative History from Pare Lorentz to John Huston." Unpublished Ph.D. dissertation, Harvard University, 1951.

——. "Film and Foreign Policy: The USIA, 1962–67." *Cinema Journal,* 9, No. 1 (Fall 1969), 23–42.

Mast, Gerald. *A Short History of the Movies.* New York: Pegasus, 1971.

McDonald, J. "Film and War Propaganda." *Public Opinion Quarterly,* 4 (September 1940), 519–22; 5 (March 1941), 127–29.

Mekas, Jonas. "Movie Journal." *Village Voice* (March 3, 1966), 21.

Michelson, Annette. *"The Man with the Movie Camera:* From Magician to Epistemologist." *Artforum,* 10, No. 7 (March 1972), 60–82.

Monegal, Rodriguez. "Alberto Cavalcanti: His Career." *The Quarterly of Film, Radio, and Television,* 9, No. 4 (Summer 1955), 341–54.

Movie Lot to Beachhead. Ed. by Editors of *Look.* New York: Doubleday and Company, 1945.

Mullen, Pat. *Man of Aran.* Cambridge, Massachusetts: MIT Press, 1970.

"Peter Watkins Discusses His Suppressed Nuclear Film, *The War Game,* with James Blue and Michael Gill." *Film Comment,* 3, No. 4 (Fall 1965), 14–19.

The Plow That Broke the Plains. Washington, D.C.: United States Film Service, 1938.

Presenting NFB of Canada. Ottawa: National Film Board, 1949.

"Prize Winners: Selected Listings of Awards Given at Three Major European Film Festivals and by Five American Motion Picture Organizations," compiled by P. J. McInerney and J. L. Anderson, *The Journal of the University Film Association,* 22, No. 3 (1970), 59–94.

"Propaganda Films About the War in Vietnam." *Film Comment,* 4, No. 1 (Fall 1966), 4–22.

Read, John. "The Film on Art as Documentary." *Film Culture*, 3, No. 3, 6–7.

Renan, Sheldon. *An Introduction to the American Underground Film*. New York: E. P. Dutton & Company, 1967.

Reynolds, Charles. "Focus on Al Maysles." *Popular Photography* (May 1964), 128–31.

Riefenstahl, Leni. *Schönheit im Olympischen Kampf*. Berlin: Im Deutschen Verlag, 1937.

Rosenthal, Alan. *The New Documentary in Action: A Casebook in Film Making*. Berkeley, California: University of California Press, 1971.

Rotha, Paul. *Documentary Film*. New York: Hastings House, 1952.

———. "Television and the Future of Documentary." *Film Quarterly*, 9 (Summer 1955), 366–73.

Routt, William D. 'The Documentary Film Group of Chicago." *Vision*, 1 (Spring 1962), 30–31.

Salesman, intro. Harold Clurman; notes, Howard Junker. New York: Signet Books, 1969.

Snyder, Robert L. *Pare Lorentz and the Documentary Film*. Norman, Oklahoma: Oklahoma University Press, 1968.

Stebbins, R., and Leyda, J. "Joris Ivens: Artist in Documentary." *Magazine of Art*, 31 (July 1938), 392–99ff.

Strand, Paul. "Realism: A Personal View." *Sight and Sound*, 19 (January 1950), 23–26.

Sussex, Elizabeth. *Lindsay Anderson*. London: Studio Vista, Ltd., 1969.

Tallents, Sir Stephen. "The Documentary Film." *Journal of the Royal Society of Arts* (December 20, 1946), 68–85.

———. *The Projection of England*. London: Faber and Faber, Ltd., 1932.

Tyler, Parker. "The Tyranny of *Warrendale*." *Evergreen* (August 1969), 31–33ff.

Van Dongen, Helen. "Robert J. Flaherty: 1884–1951." *Film Quarterly*, 17, No. 4 (Summer 1965), 2–14.

Van Dyke, Willard. "Letters from *The River*." *Film Comment*, 3, No. 2 (Spring 1965), 38–60.

———. "The Interpretive Camera in Documentary Films." *Hollywood Quarterly*, 1, No. 4 (July 1946), 405–09.

"Vertov, Dziga." *Film Comment*, 8, No. 1 (Spring 1972), 38–51.

Waley, H. D. "British Documentaries and the War Effort." *Public Opinion Quarterly*, 6, No. 4 (December 1942), 604–09.

Welles, Orson. "But Where Are We Going?" *Look*, 34, No. 22 (November 3, 1970), 34–36.

White, William L. "Pare Lorentz." *Scribner's*, 105, No. 1 (January 1939), 7–11ff.

Wilenski, Stewart. "The New Documentary Goal: The Revealed Situation." *Vision*, 1, No. 2 (Summer 1962), 63–66.

Wright, Basil. "Documentary: Flesh, Fowl, or . . .?" *Sight and Sound*, 19, No. 1 (March 1950), 43–48.

———. "Documentary Today." *Penguin Film Review*, 2 (January 1947), 37–44.

———. "On the Bowery." *Sight and Sound*, 26, No. 2 (Autumn 1956), 98.

INDEX

Material from the Appendixes not included in this Index.
Page numbers in boldface denote illustrations.

326 | Index

Gimme Shelter, 252, 263, 266, 281, 287, 288, 290–2, 293, 294
Gitlin, Irving, 244
Goebbels, Paul Joseph, 165
Goldman, John, 145
Golightly, J. P. R., 58
Goretta, Claude, 234; Nice Time, 234
G.P.O. Film Unit (General Post Office), 37, 40, 49, 50, 51, 54, 58, 61, 63, 64, 70, 71, 79, 167, 206, 207, 222, 226
Grain That Built a Hemisphere, The, 217
Granton Trawler, 42, 51, 168
Grapes of Wrath, The, 121n, 149
Grass, 11, 19
Great Britain, nonfiction film in, 26, 30, 37–80, 142, 206–15, 216, 225, 229–36, 238, 252, 291; sponsorship of: commercial, 55, 61, 70, 74, 79, 208, 212, 213; government, 39, 41, 54, 61, 79, 207, 214; see also war films, British
Grierson, John, 1, 2, 7–9, 10, 17, 26, 35, 37–59 6on, 70, 71, 74, 80, 83, 88, 98, 100, 106, 107, 109, 119, 124, 138, 139, 142, 147, 157, 163, 207, 208, 214, 216, 222–3, 224n, 231, 232, 235, 243, 246, 248, 252, 269, 272; Drifters, 17, 42, 43, 45, 57, 119n, 168
Grierson, Marion, 78; For All Eternity, 78
Grierson, Ruby, 78, 168; They Also Serve, 163, 168, 192, 210; Today We Live, 72, 76, 78
Griffith, Richard, 216
Gruenberg, Louis, 109
Guam: I Saw It Happen, 196

Hammid, Alexander (Hackenschmied), 35, 216, 217, 218; Better Tomorrow, A, 218; Library of Congress, 218; Toscanini: The Hymn of Nations, 218–19; Valley of the Tennessee, 217
Hans Westmar, Einer von Vielen, 85, 166
Happy Mother's Day, A (Quint City, U.S.A.), 251, 254–5, 272
Harvest of Shame, The, 248

Harvest Shall Come, The, 208, 210, 212
health, 107–8, 239, 240, 272, 277
Heart of Spain, 94, 111
Hellman, Lillian, 122n
Hemingway, Ernest, 92
Henningsen, Poul, 82; Film of Denmark, The, 82
Heyerdahl, Thor, 20; Kon Tiki, 20, 231
High School, 272, 275–7, 288
Hiroshima-Nagasaki: August, 1945, 203
Histoire du Soldat Inconnu, L', 82
Hitler, Adolf, 85, 162, 166, 182, 186, 188, 191
Holland, nonfiction film in, 24–5, 27, 29, 32, 88–98, 119
Holmes, J. B., 170; Coastal Command, 168, 170, 171
Hospital, 272, 274, 277–8
Houseman, John, 218; Tuesday in November, 218
housing, 72, 83–4, 211, 213
Housing Problems, 54, 72, 73, 74, 76, 83, 84, 89, 100, 146, 212
How Good is a Gun?, 192
hunger, 84, 89, 149, 212; see also nutrition
Hunting Big Game in Africa, 19
Hurdes, Las, see Land Without Bread
Hurwitz, Leo, 111, 112, 122n, 149, 216; Native Land, 111, 112–13
Huston, John, 3, 126, 161, 193, 194, 198–200, 226, 238; Battle of San Pietro, The, 163, 178, 194, 195, 196, 200; Let There Be Light, 3, 164, 165, 196, 198–200, 226; Report from the Aleutians, 164, 178, 193–4, 200
Huxley, Julian, 78; Private Life of the Gannets, 78

IBM, 13
Idlers That Work, 232
Idylle à la Plage, 35
Images d'Ostende, 35
I'm Going to Ask You to Get Up Out of Your Seat, 241
Imperial Chemical Industries, 208, 210
incentive films, 163, 192, 209
India, nonfiction film in, 204n

India Marches, 204n
Industrial Britain, 44, 46–7, 48, 57, 79, 141, 142
Industrial Symphony, see Philips-Radio
International Tea Bureau, 213
Interviews With My Lai Veterans, 248
In the Street, 224n
Iron Horse, The, 18
Islanders, The, 68, 69
Ivan, 26
Ivan the Terrible, 23
Ivens, Joris, 3, 6, 29, 32, 34–5, 74, 81, 83, 84, 87–98, 100, 109, 111, 113, 119, 122n, 141, 209, 210, 283; Borinage, 74, 83, 84, 88–9, 90, 91, 94; Breakers, The, 88; Bridge, The, 32, 34, 88, 91; 400 Million, The, 88, 94, 96, 111; New Earth, 91, 94, 100; Philips-Radio (Industrial Symphony), 88; Pile Driving, 88; Power and the Land, 88, 94, 95, 96, 97, 98, 99, 109, 115, 121, 209, 210; Rain, 34–5, 88; Song of Heroes, 88; Spanish Earth, 3, 88, 92, 93, 94, 111, 115

Jacoby, Irving, 216, 219–20; Pale Horseman, The, 212, 219–20; Photographer, The, 219
Jackson, Pat, 170; Western Approaches, 168, 170
Jane, 251, 262, 263, 265, 266
Jeakins, A. E., 50; Cable Ship, 50, 54
Jennings, Humphrey, 65–6 68, 79, 168, 172, 210, 213, 231, 232, 235, 237; Cumberland Story, The, 213, 214; Defeated People, 174; Diary for Timothy, A, 176, 177; Fires Were Started, 170, 172, 173, 174, 213, 237; Listen to Britain, 164, 172, 174, 180, 182, 210; London Can Take It, 79, 167, 172, 174; Silent Village, 174, 175, 176; Spare Time, 66, 172; Spring Offensive, 58, 168, 210; True Story of Lili Marlene, 174
Jersey, William C., 245, 252
JFK: Years of Lightning, Day of Drums, 248
Johnson, Eyvind, 82; Gamla Stan, 28, 82, 214

travel films, 10, 11–12, 14,
19, 78, 83, 213, 238
Triumph of the Will, The,
85, **86**, 87, 165, 166
True Glory, The, 198, 200,
202
True Story of Lili Marlene,
174
Tuesday in November, 218
Tunisian Victory, 178
Turin, Victor, 21, 26;
Turksib, 26, 39
Turksib, 26, 39
"Twentieth Century, The,"
245, 247
Twenty-Four Dollar Island,
141, 158n
Two Down, One to Go, 183

Ullman, Frederic, Jr., 110
Undefeated, The, 226
Under the City, 50, 54
UNESCO, 13, 224, 224n, 229
United Action, 111
United Nations, 119, 229,
231; Film Services, 231
United States: Agricultural
Adjustment Administration,
90, 99; Department of
Agriculture, 94; Depart-
ment of State, 219; Film
Service, 98, 99, 107, 121n;
Information Agency, 220,
248, 249; Office of War Information (OWI), 118,
216–20
United States, nonfiction film
in, 2, 7, 21, 27, 35, 81, 85,
96, 98–119, 206, 207, 214,
215–22, 223–4, 237–42,
252–66, 271–92; concerns
of, 98, 114, 216–17, 219,
223; romantic tradition,
18–20, 27, 41, 81; sponsorship, 107, 216, 219, 239;
war films, 82, 92, 94,
163–5, 180–202
Upstream, 44

Valley of the Tennessee, 217
Valley Town, 116, 118
van Dongen, Helen, *see* Dongen, Helen van
Van Dyke, Willard, 2, 10,
28, 81, 104, 107, 113–19,
122n, 161, 207, 210, 212,
216, 217, 218, 219, 237;
Bridge, The, 219; *Children
Must Learn, The,* 113, 116,
118; *City, The,* 28, 107,
113, 114–16, **117**, 210,
211, 212, 213; *Journey into*

Medicine, 219; *Northwest
U.S.A.,* 217; *Oswego,* 118;
Pacific Northwest, 118;
Photographer, The, 219;
San Francisco, 218; *Sarah
Lawrence,* 116; *Steeltown,*
118; *Tall Tales,* 116; *To
Hear Your Banjo Play,* 116;
Valley Town, 116, 118
Venice Film Festival, 106,
110, 146, 147
Vertov, Dziga, 17, 21, 23–5,
26, 219, 256; *Anniversary
of the October Revolution,
The,* 23; *Man With the
Movie Camera, The,* 24,
26; *Sixth of the World,
The,* 25; *Stride, Soviet,* 25
"Victory at Sea" series, 245
Victory in the West, 166
Vigo, Jean, 267
Vocation, 84
Voice of the World, 44

Wadleigh, Michael, 288–90;
*No Vietnamese Ever Called
Me Nigger,* 248, 290;
Woodstock, 3, 252, 263,
266, 287, 288–91, 294
Wakefield Express, 232
War Comes to America, 172,
181, 184, 188–90, 191,
210
War Department Report, The,
193
war film, 66, 70, 160–205,
209; American, 82, 92, 94,
163–5, 180–202; Austra-
lian, 204n; British, 66, 70,
71, 82, 162, 163–5, 167–
80, 181, 183; Canadian,
167, 204n; French, 167;
Indian, 204n; Nazi, 165–6,
181, 183; Russian, 167;
patterns in, 163; production
units, 161; *see also* combat films, incentive films,
training films
War Game, The, 176, 248
Warrendale, 233, 242, 252,
267–9, 270, 275
War Town, 192
Water: Friend or Enemy, 217
Waters of Time, 226–7
Watkins, Peter, 176; *War
Game, The,* 176, 248
Watt, Harry, 44, 51, 64, 66,
70, 79, 170, 209; *London
Can Take It,* 79, 167, 172,
174; *Night Mail,* 42, 50,
51, **52**, 53, 57, 58, 68, 98,
100, 109, 115, 125, 142,

146, 172, 174; *North Sea,*
43, 53, 54, 70, 168, 172,
Saving of Bill Blewitt, The,
53, 54, 64, **65**, 209;
*Squadron 992 (Floating
Elephants),* 66, 67, 167,
209; *Target for Tonight,* 5,
169, 170
Watt, R. H., 50; *Droitwich,*
50; *Six-Thirty Collection,*
50, 54
Wave, The (Pescados), 111
Wavell's 30,000, 178
Waverly Steps, 214
Way Ahead, The, 176, 209
"Wealth of the World" series,
215, 226; *Transport,* 215
We Are the Lambeth Boys,
234
Weather Forecast, 50, 54
*We Conquer the Soil (Wir
Erobern Land),* 85, 166
We Live in Two Worlds, 53,
54, 64, 66
Western Approaches, 168,
170
Weston, Edward, 113, 219
*What's Happening! The
Beatles in the U.S.A.,* 281
282
When We Build Again, 72,
74, 208, 210, 212, 213
White Flood, The, 111
"White Paper, The" series,
244
"Why We Fight" series
(Frank Capra), 92, 94, 164,
167, 170, 180, 181, 182,
183–91, 193, 198; *Battle of
Britain, The,* 184, 186,
188; *Battle of China, The,*
94, 184, 186, 188; *Battle
of Russia, The,* 94, 167,
184, 186, 188–9, **190**; *Divide and Conquer,* 184,
186, **187**; *Nazi Strike, The,*
184, 186; *Prelude to War,*
184, **185**; *War Comes to
America,* 172, 181, 184,
188–9, 191, 210
Wild Beauty, 19
Windmill in Barbados, 44
Window Cleaner, The, 218
Wings of Youth, 204n
*Wir Erobern Land, see We
Conquer the Soil*
Wiseman, Frederick, 252,
267, 271–80; *Basic Training,* 272, 278, **279**, 280,
288; *High School,* 272,
275–7, 288; *Hospital,* 272,
274, 277–8; *Law and*